The THIRSTY THURSDAY SAILORS

500 or so small, medium, and large sailboats
race together weekly during the summer in
local Newport Harbor. . .the outgrowth of a
friendly dockside challenge by a favorite
old sailing friend, Dick Schumacher.

Suppose you were taking a large powerboat down
the harbor during the race. . .

SAILING ILLUSTRATED

The Sailor's Bible since 1956

written and illustrated by
Patrick M. Royce

Published by
Western Marine Enterprises, Inc.
Box Q
Ventura, CA 93002
U S A

Hampton

Laser

Turnabout

OK Dink

Shore Bird

Bird

Thunderbird

Raven

National

Lido 14

Highlander

Fireball

Sailfish

FJ
Flying Junior

Sunfish

Rhodes 1?

Sprite

Mercury

Dyer Dhow

Interlake

6

6 Meter

12

12 Meter

Other books by Patrick M. Royce:
Trailerboating Illustrated
Sailing Illustrated Workbook

©1956, 1957, 1958, 1960, 1963, 1965, 1968, 1969, 1971, 1972, 1974, 1979 by Patrick M. Royce.

Researched, written and illustrated by Patrick M. Royce. Printed in USA by Delta Lithograph Co., Van Nuys, Calif. 91411.

Library of Congress Cataloging in Publication Data

Royce, Patrick M.
    Sailing illustrated.

1. Sailing — Handbooks, manuals, etc. I. Title.
GV811.R6 1979   797.1´24   79-17909
ISBN 0-930030-14-1

Published by
Western Marine Enterprises, Inc.
Publishers of the *Pacific Boating Almanac*
and other marine books. Catalog on request.
Box Q, Ventura, California 93002

Flying Fifteen

Celebrity

Yngling

Albacore

Pelican

Sailing Illustrated is dedicated to my patient first mate Hilda, to our crew Richard and Tina, and to the memory of a lovely daughter.

Wayfarer

Inland Cat

Maverick

Force 5

Tornado

Pioneer

Westsail 32

GP 14

Explorer

Mercury (cb)

Zephyr

Excalibur

Beetle Cat

Samuri

Ensign

Ariel

Seminole

A 35
Alberg 35

Manui Kai
20' cat

E22
Etchells 22

Amphibicon

NA-3
Naval Academy

Morgan 33

Catalina 22

Windrose series

Tanzier 22

V
Venture

CCC
Cape Cod Cat

Matilda

N̄16
Newport 16

B☼23
Balboa 23

↙ This page includes portable cabin sailboat insignias. ↱

E☼20
Ensenada 20

B☼21
Balboa 21

B☼26
Balboa 26

WW Potter

San Juan 21

⑤22
South Coast 22

Ⓜ
Mariner

㉒
O'Day 22

Santana 21

R̄23
Ranger 23

M
Montgomery 17

②1
Cal 21

24' Yankee Seahorse

Irwin

Columbia 23

Helsen 22

212
Newport 21'

Midship 25

American 25

M13
Guppy 13

Some dinghy letters represent yacht clubs.

MYC
Miami Yacht Club

SYC
Seawanhaka Yacht Club

EYC
Edgartown Yacht Club

DYC
Darien Yacht Club

Naples
Sabot, pg. 23   Penguin, pg. 24   Int'l 14, pg. 26   Finn, pg. 29

Down East 38   Grampian   Seafarer   Westsail 32

Lightning,   Flying   Tech Dinghy,
pg. 35   Dutchman, pg. 39   Tempest   Snipe, pg. 33

Int'l 110,   5.5 meter   Soling,   Pacific Cat
pg. 41   pg. 47

M-20   Columbia   Newporter,   CSK Cats,
Scow, pg. 45   Challenger, pg. 63   pg. 75   pg. 79

Hobie Cat   Thistle, pg. 32   Star, pg. 43   Comet

name   Rieper
address   19 Dodge Rd
Coronado 15   phone   Marblehead, MA.

Flattie,
Geary 18

Windmill   Aqua Cat   Kite   El Toro

Welcome —

HI!

This book is the product of an artist from Wyoming who bought his first sailboat in New York on Staten Island. It proved a catastrophe...there had to be a better answer.

We tried to develop an illustrated book, so a newcomer could study the sailing world pictorially, making it easier for our readers to understand the complex specialized sailing language, methods, and a variety of sailboats.

Our first 1956 edition started with accepted standards, promptly falling apart in practice with our sailing lessons. And the changes still take place as a result of our sailing lessons offered when time permits.

Then we have a continuous updating of boats and equipmen as sailing is a constantly changing, ENDLESS lifetime sport for all ages.

We want to thank owners of boats detailed for their help to insure accuracy of information for your use. The language battle continues as we try to hang onto time proven terms adopting new ones only after they have proven themselves

When you find errors, please report them to us. Our first edition sheet bend made to our instructions promptly fell apart. And in one printing the port and starboard tacks closehauled were reversed in an illustration.

When you have experiences contrary to ours, let us know. Heavy weather research was prompted by a reader after a serious capsize. We tested the standards of the time in a five hour April storm ending in a force 9, to find a sloop sails best under jib only, see page 133, a new idea.

Our book sells worldwide with orders from North and South Poles a day apart. Sailing is good medicine for doctors, leading in direct sales. A letter from a lawyer requesting a copy added a hurriedly scribbled note —
"P. S., Please send your book soon as possible before I drown myself!"

The EVER CHANGING world of sailing has proved most interesting through the years. Our First Edition in 1956 covered the basics of wooden boats, and canvas sails.

1960 began a change of materials to Dacron sails, and the fiberglass hulls began to grow longer, yet most of the information still required was basic.

1963 introduced the Tempest, wiping out all IYRU competition, yet little was accomplished as a class.

The real Tempest contribution was to prove the need for better, more specialized hardware, permitting each class to develop more of its specialized personality. This sent us back to the drawing board and typewriter to revise our book from stem to stern, detailing many popular class boats, and new sail draft standards, which followed the stabilizing of Dacron cloth, and the new controlled flexing of aluminum masts.

The next period was that of the big boat with the best of racing hardware and hull design, yet these boats were more like big dinghy ocean racers . . . followed by a luke-warm interest in cruising boats after builders found in a survey less than 10% of cabin sailboats actively raced.

Around 1970 a new world mushroomed, the trailerable cabin sailboat. The sailor was no longer restricted to that of the large slip berthed keel sailboat with 4 months operation a year in many parts of the U.S., the rest of the time sitting lifeless in a boatyard.

A major emphasis shifted to the large cruising boats coming in all sizes, shapes, and designs with so many to choose from, it now became a difficult decision. At present the major thrust seems to be in all sizes and kinds of sailboats, not just certain areas.

Mans oldest form of water transportation under sail has undergone tremendous changes since 1956. Your guess is as good as ours where it will be ten years from now.

Happy Sailing, Patrick M. Royce
Newport Beach, California

There are a wide variety of racing classes and handicapping (formula) methods to be analyzed.

- ONE-DESIGN sailboats are made to same design spec's with owners joining class association for racing and comradeship. STRICT*one-design classes (Laser) allow no modification of sail, rigging, hull shape. OPEN**one-design classes provide self improvement standards varying class to class.

- DEVELOPMENT CLASSES***similar to one-design classes with wider rule latitude. Flying Dutchman has elastic deck and equipment rules, strict hull, mast spec's. Int'l 14 is closer to meter rules as hull design changes may also be involved.

- OLYMPIC CLASSES for 1984 are Flying Dutchman, Star, Finn, Tornado Cat, 470, and Soling. These are the classes chosen for the next International Olympic use by the International Yacht Racing Union (IYRU) presiding over international sailboat racing. Letters on sail numbers will refer to owners country such as US–United States, MX–Mexico, K–United Kingdom. It is wonderful to see a 1911 design back in the Olympics . . . the Star.

- METER craft have various sizes (ratings pg. 64) designed to a mathematical formula, juggled within the rules to try to make each new meter boat a better performer.

- HANDICAP RATING (pgs. 258-9) is a theoretical mathematical rated length/seconds per mile of given rating, to help provide a method for various kinds, sizes, and lengths of sailboats to compete on an equal basis.

- OOAK SERIES refer to YACHTING "One-of-a-Kind-Races" so one-design and other classes are able to compete against each other every three years in five divisions.

- PORTSMOUTH HANDICAP (pg. 258) is a yardstick used for competition between one-design classes, parallel to OOAK one-design handicapping methods.

- LEVEL RATING (pgs. 64-5) cover various "tonner" ratings similar to meter formula thinking with length, beam, bulk, and sail area are major factors involved.

*minimum evolution **controlled evolution ***control flexibility

square sail
pgs. 282-9

lateener
pgs. 275-9

lugger
pgs. 280-1

sprit
pg. 271

quadrilateral
or gaff rig
pgs. 4, 5, and
elsewhere
sliding gunther
pg. 271
older version
with short gaff
called shoulder-
of-mutton

triangular
marconi
jib-headed
bermudian

early version
was called
leg-of-mutton

topping lift

lazy jacks

QUADRILATERAL or GAFF RIG

The gaff rig was the first advancement over the lugger, the lateener and square rigs. It became the standard fore and aft rig up to the marconi rig.

A gaff rig was ideal for coastal trading and fishing when the wind was on the oceans surface and often abeam. Under these conditions the shorter masts requiring a minimum of staying.

peak too low

A large catboat has been shown that was very popular around the turn of the century. Its primary advantage was for fishing with the large cockpit area ideal for handling nets and lines.

The large cat often has much to be desired in todays sailing. It may carry a lot of weather helm, while the long boom, round bottom, and huge rudder, are combination that make downwind sailing tricky.

peak o. k.

With improved engineering and better metals, many of the gaff rigged boats have changed to the higher marconi rig eliminating gaffs, lazy jacks, and one of the halyards. An advantage of the gaff in a sudden blow, is that the sail may be "scandalized" pg. 148, to reduce excess wind pressure.

peak too high

Traditional gaff sails were usually laced to gaff and boom, secured to mast with wooden hoops. Those desiring more information read "Gaff Rig" by John Leather, Int. Marine Pub. Co., Camden, Maine 04843, 272 pages.

4

Sailing Illustrated

Gaff Rig

gaff rigged schooner

Dutch coastal sailing vessel

short gaff with bend loosefooted mainsail

bowsprit

double gaff for rapid scandalizing

reef cringle

clew

topping lift (slacked)

mainsheet

barndoor rudder

traveler

running backstay

peak

peak halyard

gaff

telltale

Sail is laced to boom and gaff.

vertical cut sail without a roach

head

leach

jackstay

third reef

throat halyard

gaff jaws

second reef

reef points

throat

jackstrut

luff

first reef

*lazyjacks

mast hoops

mast

foot

boom

tack

boom jaws

mainsheet

mast hoops

shroud

*Lazyjacks contain sails for easy handling while they are being raised or lowered.

Traditional gaff rig is detailed on typical New England catboat, in the early 1900's.

centerboard

ROYCE

5

The popular sailing rig with a triangular mainsail most commonly seen today is called the BERMUDIAN RIG by the British, the MARCONI RIG by most U. S. sailors, and JIB-HEADED RIG by others. As early examples of this type of craft were overstayed, the nickname resulted when they often resembled early marconi wireless towers.

The marconi rig is of major importance to both the racing and cruising sailor as the marconi rig will point higher than the gaff rig when sailing closehauled .. which averages more than half of your sailing time.

Most of our sailing is for short tacks with frequent tack changes by coming about or jibing. The marconi or jib-headed rig is adaptable for this kind of use with its simplicity of operation, eliminating the peak halyard and running backstays used by the gaff rig. Running backstays are still used on larger meter boats, and older sailing craft.

The taller mast of the marconi rig is an important factor to those sailing in inland areas where the wind isn't always on the water's surface. While the gaff rig with the shorter mast may operate successfully in the ocean side of Long Island, the taller marconi rig is preferred on the Long Island Sound where the useful wind may be a considerable distance above the waters surface in the daytime.

This phenomenon is due to HEAT THERMAL UPDRAFTS caused by daytime heating of the land's surface, plus heat emissions from autos and manufacturing plants. After dark as land temperature and other heat making methods are reduced, the wind drops lower to the surface of the Long Island Sound, and other inland sailing areas.

An early version of the Lightning class is shown at right. It is an excellent basic sailboat to study if you want to analyze the reasons behind the specialized racing hardware found on "Sea Fever", pages 34 through 37.

Marconi Rig

running backstay

gaff mainsail

traditional sloop rig

bowsprit

3/4 jib rig (fractional)

standard sloop rig

* roach

masthead sloop rig

outhaul

ttle rudder
pport fits
o gudgeon
transom,
e pgs. 22-23.

rudder

main halyard

headboard

head

batten in pocket

class insignia

permanent backstay

mast

spreader

leach

class number

mainsail

reef points

shrouds

boom

clew

foot

plastic window

tack

mainsheet

vang

clew

seat

jib fairlead

tiller

cb trunk

It is also known as the BERMUDIAN RIG and the JIB-HEADED RIG.

jumper stays

jumper strut

jib halyard

head

leach

jib stay

luff

jib snaps

jib

JIB halyard is carried on PORT side of mast; MAIN halyard, on STARBOARD side of mast.

downhaul

foot

tack

jib sheet

splashboard

luff

Royce

Lightning shown above is an older generalized version. Later racing version of this class is detailed on pgs. 34-37.

*After edge of sail which must be supported by battens to avoid its curling, is called the roach.

centerboard

7

Endless varieties of sail combinations are used for different sailing areas and interests. Common types are shown at right with page references for additional information.

Readers are provided with a foundation in operational variables of both the MONOHULL (one hull) and the MULTIHULL (catamaran and trimaran) to help provide exposure to both sides of the sailing world.

A sailboat with one sail regardless of size is generally called a catboat. The catamaran has two hulls and any variety of sail combinations, including if desired, the catboat rig.

Sloops, originally called knockabouts if they didn't have a bowsprit, are the most common type seen in the U.S., having a mainsail and jib. Jibstay or headstay goes to the top of the mast on a MASTHEAD rig, while it doesn't go to top of the mast on a STANDARD or FRACTIONAL sloop rig. A CUTTER basically has two headsails or jibs, with mast stepped further aft than on a sloop.

Two masted fore and aft rigged sailboats are generally recognized from distance by relationship of sails.... and when closer, by location of tiller and rudder post.

Yawl generally has small sail aft of tiller, while a ketch has masts of similar size, with the forward mast being taller, the tiller located aft of both masts. A schooner has both masts the same height, or after one taller.

Sail ASPECT RATIO. At right we show three sail craft with identical hulls and same total sail area. First boat has a short mast with long boom called LOW aspect ratio mainsail. Third boat has a HIGH aspect ratio with tall mast and short boom, increasing upwind drive area of mainsail shown by shaded area. The higher aspect ratio main has longer drive area with steadier wind currents aloft, minimizing wind disturbance on waters surface.

8   Sailing Illustrated

1 pgs. 4-5

catboat

2 (highest mast)

standard sloop
jibstay part way
up the mast

If 2, 3, 4, have
identical hulls
and same total
sail area ....

3 pgs. 6-7,
260-1

masthead sloop
jibstay goes to
top of the mast

4 (shortest mast)

pgs. 262-3

cutter with
two jibs

5, 6, 7, have
identical hulls
and same total
sail area ...

5 pgs. 264-5

yawl

tiller between masts

6 pgs. 266-7

ketch

tiller aft of both masts,
with forward mast taller

7 pgs. 268-9

schooner

both masts same height,
or after mast is taller

8

standard schooner rig

9

staysail schooner

10 pgs. 282-7

traditional types

If hulls 11, 12, 13 are identical
with same total sail area ....

longest drive area

11

low
aspect
ratio

12

medium
aspect
ratio

13

high
aspect
ratio

9

draft → | draft ↗ | ← draft
new canvas sail | sail 'broken in' | sail blown out

Draft was originally built into forward third of cotton and canvas sails. After a few hours use, draft would move aft somewhat to position shown, being classed as 'broken in'. After much use, or draft destroyed due to absence of topping lift pg. 97, the draft moved further aft with useful upwind life of mainsail coming to an abrupt end.

The jib seemed the main factor with upwind drive force in our 3rd Edition. The mainsail shortly received a lot more attention especially with draft control, pg. 117, improving the wind flow funnel between the main and jib.

Your sails may look good to you ... yet check your sails from another boat, or take photos underway checking trim, cut, wrinkles, etc., which may prove an eye opener.

New dacron sail cloth has been a great boon to sailmakers and sailors, having a lighter, stronger and more adaptable surface. Due to present stability of material, draft is now built into sail eliminating the 'break-in' period. Panels started with 18" widths, increasing until 36" panels are now standard. This cloth stability has also eliminated the need for the miter cut jib, pg. 13, for normal use.

In the last couple of years the miter cut jib and main have made a tremendous comeback in racing craft as they can be trimmed flatter than crosscut or miterless main and jib, yet sailmakers say lifespan is reduced. For information on battens see page 91.

Mainsails should be cut to fit your local wind conditions. Identical boats in our Southern California Newport Harbor will have a full draft due to light winds. Similar craft in San Francisco normally expecting much stronger winds, will have a flatter cut or flatter draft mainsail.

It has been fascinating to watch the change from canvas to Dacron and nylon sail cloth around 1960, followed by a continuous series of improvements in cloth and sailmaking techniques not available at any price twenty years ago.

Sail cloth may be made of a tight weave without a filler, or if it has a very smooth surface a filler has been added after the cloth comes off the loom.

the Mainsail

Junks have used full length battens for hundreds of years. For use on larger boats read Yachting, pg. 49, May '68 issue.

diagonal or miter cut main

full length battens

roach

rigid headboard

head

head band

tabling

upper girthline measurement

strongest direction of cloth

Vertical cut mainsail without a roach

battens arent required.

Full batten mainsail with large roach

batten in pocket

Roach area of mainsail must be supported by battens, see page 91.

second reef

leach sets better cut batten to batten

rope stability needed on bias at foot & luff

luff rope

leach

mid girthline measurement

FD class has three sets of hoist limits

luff hoist limits for racing

Early crosscut main without a roach

leach

first reef

lower girthline measurement

luff

slides

Anti-trip reef points prevent boom from digging into waves in storm conditions on reach to run.

leach line, pg.13

clew

Foot reef for draft control.

foot

tack

tack band

clew band

Crosscut mainsail with average roach

ROYCE

11

Forward sail on a sloop is usually called a jib. A 100% working jib has area 1/2 I x J, see shaded area. 150% genoa is 50% larger, clew well aft of mast. Gennie and working jib are used for closehauled or beating. Reaching jib provides softer wind funnel for reaching.

#1 gennie usually has soft cloth, full draft for light winds. A same size #1 may be heavier with flatter cut for stronger wind. #2 gennie with reefed main, is smaller with higher clew permitting wave breaking aboard to drain under its foot. #3 gennie has a shorter luff with full length wire pennant, cut very flat for strong winds.

The working jib is often used for relaxing afternoon sailing, or for cruising especially if short handed. It is also called a lapper as it slightly overlaps the mast.

genoas and lapper

We've taught on many Lido 14's, with no two jibs cut identical. If leach broke first, move jib fairlead forward. If foot broke first, move fairlead aft till foot and leach break at same time as a boat heads into the wind.

leach flutter

move fairlead forward

move fairlead aft

foot flutter

1. correct trim   2. sail higher   3. pinching

Sew yarn telltales to jib luff, see location facing page, to analyze sail trim by air flowing past its surfaces.

1. Correct controlled flow. 2. Vertical leeward flow, stalled, sail higher, or harden jib sheet. 3. Pointing too high, found on narrow beam boats or ones with narrow sheeting base.

12   Sailing   Illustrated

Jib CLEWBOARD is used to eliminate wrinkles at clew.

the full cut reacher or reaching jib

luff yarn telltale

high clew   high cut foot

sheeted to boom

For upwind sailing the jib is usually trimmed first and the mainsail, second.

leach lines also control leach flutter, see pgs. 117-121

funnel

wind direction

wind funnel or slot between jib and main

funnel

the flat cut genoa or 'gennie'

miterless or mitreless cut genoa jib

leach line adjusts

lower clew   low cut foot

sheeted to deck

wind direction

For boat with single jib, foot adjust can bag jib for reaching or running.

upper swivel

jib furling is excellent for small cats, see pg. 47.

pull furl line to furl jib

pull sheet to open

reel or drum

Care must be taken in stormy weather to see it cannot open partially at your slip, on a mooring, or under power as the flapping exerts considerable wear on the jib and rigging.

pull trim line to furl

furling gear trim line or lanyard

Luff wire secured to jib only at head of sail.

Cloth luff 'tunnel' slides up and down luff wire, see page 34.

adjustable luff jib

jib luff wire inside

jib tack downhaul or jib tack variluff

miter cut jib

scotch or angular cut jib

vertical cut jib

ROYCE

13

For several years we puzzled over the best way to show the variety of cloth weights, and increasing kinds of sails available to the sailing public.

The folder at right produced by sailmaker Don McKibbin may provide many of the answers you are seeking.

Don feels the combination of sails and cloth weight will apply to sloops in the 24 to 30 foot range. Cloth weight listed under sail types will average out for that used on a 30' sloop. With such a foundation you may adjust the numbers up or down to fit the size of your boat, local weather conditions, and whether your major interest is racing, cruising, or a combination of both.

We thank Don for letting us use a reproduction of his chart on the facing page. As reduction is considerable write for a copy of his chart in its full 18" by 22" size. Also ask for his booklet discussing modern sail materials, uses, trim, and maintenance.

Send your request to McKibbin Sails, 1821 Reynolds Ave., Irvine Industrial Complex, Irvine, CA 92714.

●

Then we come to sails found on older boats, seldom seen today, though they may show up tomorrow as the latest breakthrough. A sample is the "spitfire", a heavy weather English jib, a name which has also been applied to drifters, reachers, etc., but doesn't stick for very long.

One of the humorous names of sails checked into, developed during a discussion many years ago with the manager of the Ratsey Sail Loft who made the first "mule". With a wry smile he said the term "mule" was the kindest term he could find for that sail.

George Mixter wanted a circus tent size sail for his "Teregram" he accidentally called a "gollywobbler", pg. 269, which now goes only to the foremast of most schooners.

the "mule"

forestys1
or 'jumbo'

George Mixter's
original
"gollywobbler"

14

After you have the basic mainsail, working jib, a 150% gennie jib, and an all-purpose chute, what is the next kind of sail to choose for your boat... and how heavy the cloth.

wind
propulsion

turn of
bilge

wine-glass shaped hull
with carvel planking

keel
weight
counterbalance

round

V bottom

clinker

Sailors have depended on weight stability in the form of cargo and movable ballast, since before the days of the Phoenicians. In todays sailing for pleasure, most weight is carried outside hull as part of keel.

Keel weight stability provides resistance to upset. Further a boat heels, the more effect the keel weight will provide to resist or counteract additional heel angle. Weight stability of narrow beam, wine-glass shaped hull, is often puzzling to the newcomer climbing aboard this kind of keel boat at the dock, seeming to have very little stability in the upright position.

Smooth hull with rounded or wine-glass section is usually preferred on larger boats for ocean use, as it will pound less than a keel boat with a hard chine. Small day racers with this type hull often have rolling tendencies, noted in downwind sailing. Many of todays open one-design having keels used on larger lakes and coastal waters, prefer the arc or V bottom with less rolling tendencies for downwind sailing.

The clinker-built hull was popular for a few years, but is seldom seen in boats being built today. Resistance of the overlapping planks not only proved unnecessarily noisy, but they also increased the hull drag..which reduced its speed. When leaks developed between planks of this type hull and caulking is used, the opening may enlarge as the caulking swells.

Abbreviations commonly used throughout our book to conserve space are...cb-centerboard, db-daggerboard, **16** hlyd-halyard, fwd-forward, stbd-starboard, sp-spinnaker.

flat bottom

chine

Monohulls are shown above, multihulls, below.

dory   arc   V bottom

Hull provides heel resistance called initial stability.

Monohulls using cb and db leverage to resist leeway for upwind sailing, pages 18-19, usually require hull to also have initial stability for heel resistance. Many of these open one-designs as a result have flat bottoms, arc bottoms, and V bottoms. This hull shape also provides upset resistance in an upright condition... especially important when climbing aboard from the dock, pg. 88.

After 45° to 50° heel angle has been exceeded, a neutral point is reached. Add a few more degrees of heel, and the cb and db craft finds itself more stable in the upset position. Best advice is to use an inclinometer with heel limitations of your craft clearly marked, pages 134, 144.

Multihulls also use leverage stability to resist capsize or upset. The wide beam to length ratio of cats and tris, produces tremendous initial stability, also permitting them to keep weight to a minimum.

The high initial stability of a good cat, permits it to use the wind more efficiently on all courses than a monohull. The high initial stability of a good trimaran, is of some help on an upwind course, and especially advantageous when romping downwind such as in the Multihull Transpac to Hawaii.

Same length monohull sailing downwind under similar conditions, can't maintain same speed due to rolling motion, additional drag, additional frontal area, and its limiting waterline-length speed factor, page 141.

outrigger   catamaran   trimaran

Daggerboard

Daggerboard leverage stability is used on monohull dinghies, catamarans, and trimarans of varied sizes. Early Snipes had choice of daggerboard or centerboard. Daggerboard version pointed higher and footed faster than Snipe with centerboard, due to better aspect ratio. Cats improved this by carrying straight edge on fwd side.

Less cockpit space is required for db well, sailing upwind. It also decreases drag or turbulence of longer cb slot. Disadvantage becomes apparent sailing downwind, with board removed, becoming a wet, clumsy object to trip over. In larger multihulls, boards are raised out of the way in their own compartments. If rapidly moving craft using db hits solid object such as stump or rock, damage may result to daggerboard or well structure.

Leeboard

Leeboards pivot on sides of sailing vessel. They originated in Europe to minimize leeway for upwind sailing, and for flat bottom craft having to settle on marsh or mud flats without damage due to great tidal ranges common in the Netherlands.

Though still found on English Thames Sailing Barges and cargo vessels in Holland, the leeboard seems restricted to small dinghies such as the Sabot in the U.S.

Int'l 14 board goes forward of vertical

cb up — 'Finisterre'

cb well

cb down

pivoting board

fore and aft helm adjust

high aspect ratio

The centerboard started as a pivoted board for sailboats 20' or smaller, mainly used for shallow water or "dry sailing", stored on trailers when not in use. Purpose was to provide leverage against the water to reduce leeway when sailing upwind. If board hit a rock, stump, or sand, it would swing up without damage. It was raised up into centerboard well out of way for downwind sailing.

Designers started to add centerboards to keel boats to reduce weight and draft, also to reduce upwind weather helm, pg. 135. The board is all way down when beating in light breeze. As wind increases, board is raised sufficient amount to trim rudder for neutral helm, pages 132-3.

The Int'l 14 is a proving ground for many ideas in center-board usage. Newer boats have long slim boards for high aspect ratio leverage with minimum drag.

The 45' "Salty Tiger", a combination centerboard/keel boat, was designed by Bob Derecktor to race as a yawl or as a sloop. The centerboard pivot point was able to move fore and aft about six feet in down position, to balance the helm when changing from sloop to yawl rig, and to balance out minor weather helm variables. Int'l 14 has used a saddle to also permit fore and aft trim without raising its centerboard, see illus. above and page 26.

Double rudders and double bilgeboards of cb or db designs are used on most wide beam, flat bottom sailing scows, see page 49, to always have one rudder and board in the water while sailing at their normal excessive heel angle. A note of caution to all centerboard boat owners large and small... occasionally check pivot pin for wear.   19

Tahiti Ketch

keel mounted rudder

spade rudder/fin keel

skeg rudder/fin keel

stern mounted dinghy rudder

fin keel,   cb, or db

DIRECTIONAL STABILITY–
Tahiti Ketch has long keel
to hold course for long periods
with little effort, yet difficult
to change tack.

The other hulls are easier
to change tack in narrow
channels & turning at a dock.

Spade and dinghy rudders
are excellent for racing by
those 'sailing on their ear'
to reduce heeling weather
helm, pgs. 133-4. Disadvantage,
damage in grounding, being
bent by whales, etc., pg. 74.

Keel mounted rudder is
excellent for shallow water
and cruising, as keel usually
protects rudder if going
aground. Fin keel/skeg rudder
design combines the best
of both extremes for larger cruising boats IF the skeg
affords rudder protection during accidental grounding.

max. deadrise

heavy
disp.

DISPLACEMENT means weight...a ratio of
tonnage to waterline length. Beam is a minor
factor, though wider beam boats provide more
heeling leverage resistance, not always requiring
as deep nor as heavy a keel.

min. deadrise

light
disp.

Up to 1960 the narrow beam, heavy ballasted
HEAVY displacement craft, meter boat thinking
was in its prime, replaced by LIGHT displacement
wide beam hulls with more usable space.

ULTRA LIGHT DISPLACEMENT racing dinghies
to 75' may have fin keel, cb or db, minimum deadrise,
aft dinghy rudder such as
Windward Passage.

Tempest   bulb keel   Star

ADVANTAGES. If your sailing area has enough deep water, you don't intend to do much trailering and hoists are available, the keel boat may be preferred. Major advantage is resistance to upset in strong wind.

Keel is standard for larger sailboats. Some wooden boats such as "Finisterre" use combination centerboard and keel for which all other factors equal, require more bracing as not all ribs are continuous in large centerboard hulls.

DISADVANTAGES. Keel boat may sink if swamped, so check flotation methods. Avoid shallow water on ebb tide, as keel boat may be left high and dry on its side. During winter in boatyard, have boat on adequate cradle stored well above hurricane high water limit, pg. 166.

skeg bilge keel →

SINGLE vs TWIN KEEL. Around '64 the English developed twin keel sailboats for their tidal "mud flats" sailing. They required less water, had less rolling tendencies downwind, were easier to trailer. If caught aground they had a better chance to remain upright without support than single keel.

Then we come to the fleets of portable cabin sailboats without fixed keels starting a battle of semantics. Most dinghy centerboards are light providing leverage, while

most centerboards used in cabin sailboats provide leverage AND weight in down position.

The most difficult part of sailing whether to learn to sail or to read sea stories, is the foreign sailing LANGUAGE. Because of this we follow the policy an illustration is more useful and communicative than a thousand words. We hope our emphasis on visual terms and theory will make your sailing easier to understand and put to practice.

•

The U.S. has many popular dinghy classes. The Naples Sabot detailed is the Southern California leader, while similar El Toro (Sec'y, Box 487, San Leandro, CA 94577) with daggerboard and decked over bow, has a parallel growth in Northern California.

•

The Laser is an excellent car top dinghy which proved an overnight success, a strict one-design class "sailing saucer". If all boats are equal, difference in racing ability goes back to the skipper...not the boat. The Penguin has been an east coast dinghy leader for many years which is very popular in the Chesapeake Bay area.

•

International 14 is a custom built boat of development or open design going back 80 years. The 'Daring' detailed placed 1-1-1-1-1 in Yachting's 1966 OOAK series.

Saddle is used to trim out weather helm by moving center-board fore or aft, without raising centerboard. Sockets are provided for removable 16" hiking posts, one shown.

Turnbuckles are eliminated with shroud tension adjusted using jack under mast. Tackle is used to increase forward jumper tension sailing downwind. Mainsail draft is flattened with foot and luff zippers. Considerable roach requires use of vang even when sailing closehauled.

•

Finn detailed was sailed by Henry Sprague III for 2nd in 1970 Finn Worlds, still representative of the competitive "one man torture rack" class. Facing it is a Kite, one of our favorites, a lovely, lively, self rescuing sailing dink.

CLASS SECRETARIES change often in some classes. If you have a problem locating one, contact the USYRU, Box 209, Newport, RI 02840, or phone (401) 849-5200.

Naples Sabot

sleeve of Naples Sabot

wooden mast
pivots with sail

fixed gooseneck

cheekblock

outhaul

pram bow

mast partner

mast sleeve

strap bolted to sleeve

head

luff

6199

Sec'y Peggy Lenhart
690 Senate Street
Costa Mesa, CA 92627

clew

foot

tack

leach

batten

block hanger

downhaul

outhaul

wire or rod traveler

lee board

boom

bullet blocks

two purchase vang

traveler adjust

thwart

becket

three purchase mainsheet

main sheet 'Sea lock'

outhaul

tube or V-jam cleats

outhaul

hiking stick

downhaul

shock cord raises hiking strap

tiller

3/16" or 1/4" braided may be used for all lines

vang adjust on either side

rudder lock

Naples Sabot shown has basic racing rig adaptable to many other pram sailing dinghies.

LOA 7' 10" beam 3' 10"
38 sq. ft. of sail area
min. weight 95 lbs.

shock cord minimizes droopy boom

outhaul

pintle

gudgeon

skeg

rudder

TILT

Majority of todays Southern California well known Congressional, One Design, Olympic, Transpac leaders, enjoyed their first taste of sail in the Naples Sabot as yacht club juniors . . . . and to the North, in the El Toro.

It is an excellent first boat for juniors sailing protected areas as it is sensitive with LOW performance, easy to upset. Juniors must work continually to keep the dinghy racing over short course which improves their ability much more rapidly . . . making them a much better sailor when ready for their next boat preferably a sensitive, high performance craft. A larger first dinghy is recommended for adults.

23

the Penguin

gooseneck
headstay
mast
shroud
mast partner
self rotating mast

tack downhaul
downhaul
mast partner
lanyard
shroud adjust
shroud adjust

vang
mast step
cb trim line
cb cleat
centerboard trunk

shroud is
sometimes
called a
sidestay

designed
waterline

chine

centerboard,
centreboard (Br.)

outhaul adjust
traveler
adjust
halyard

batten in pocket
4 part mainsheet
gunwale
oarlock holes for rowing

storage
thwart
mainsheet
cam cleat

hiking straps

LOA 11'5"
LWL 11'2"
beam 4'8"
board down 4'0"
sq.ft. sail 72

loose footed mainsail
boom

tiller
hiking stick

Sec'y William Holmes
198 Little East Neck Rd. So.
Babylon, NY 11702

transom

gudgeon
skeg
rudder
pintle

clew
outhaul

24

Laser

When reefing, reduce sail area by wrapping sail around mast.

two piece mast

foil shaped daggerboard

wind pennant

19091

window

Cunningham downhaul

jibing vang

compass (optional)

Daggerboard safety lanyard is optional . . . may be very useful in an upset.

non-jibing daggerboard

hiking strap, adjustable

hiking stick

self bailing cockpit drain

LOA	13'10 1/2"
DWL	12' 6"
beam	4' 6"
sail area	76 sq.ft.

positive flotation of 350 lbs. is built in

for quick release of sail.

2 to 1 outhaul purchase

clew retaining line

overboard upset 'grab rail'

rudder securing line cleat

flexible traveler

tiller retaining pin

tilt-up rudder

Performance Sail-craft Corp.
33 Duffy Place
San Rafael, CA 94901
USA

Performance Sail-craft Inc.
91 Hymus Blvd.
Pointe-Claire,
Quebec, Canada

25

'Daring' is one of the most complex and most interesting 14' sailboats. i

Int'l 14 uses a center-board which angles or points to windward, called a 'jibing board'.

LOA 14'
beam 5'6"
sq.ft.sail 165-170
spinnaker can be
unlimited size.

leeward high pressure side

cb well

fwd

aft

windward low pressure side

spinnaker

sp guy/sheet

Cunningham hole

tack downhaul

sp guy/sheet

mast wedges

outhaul lever

vang (kicking strap-English)

cb track & saddle

outhaul

6 part main

jib sheet

sp guy/sheet

sp/guy sheet

vertical jib sheet track

air tank inside

tiller

hiking stick

gunwale

thwart

continuous cb trim line

cb trunk

centerboard saddle

control wire

saddle winch

removable hiking post

mast step

mast jacked up, eliminates turnb'kle

jib sheet

jumper tension off upwind

saddle control wire

cbd saddle fwd position

cbd saddle aft position

high aspect ratio centerboard with razor sharp after edge

mast tip aft

14 US 800

luff zipper

reef points are seldom used

foot zipper

cb is angled

Saddle permits fore and aft adjustment of centerboard to compensate for helm, without raising centerboard

S.S.A.

26

International 14

The Int'l 14 is a development or open design class raced worldwide, with a history of over 70 years.

Jumper tension off upwind, and on downwind. Tension increases as wind eases.

high aspect ratio rudder(vs. catboat barn-door rudder, see page 5)

Lee shroud has semi-automatic release lever used for sailing off the wind.

Jumper tension method was later changed to Hyfield Lever on forward side of mast.

ROYCE

27

the Kite

mast is flexible, swiveling, unstayed

halyard

mast chafe reduced by Teflon ring

luff tension adjust

fixed boom

outhaul adjust

splashboard

mast thwart

mast keeper

bow eye

halyard lock pg. 29

headboard

halyard

mast telltale

head

luff

luff telltale

tack

1040

batten in pocket

foot

clew

leach

roach

adjustable daggerboard

vang

5 part sheet for juniors, 3 part sheet for adults

hiking strap

mainsheet swivel cam cleat

tube cleat

traveler

hiking stick

ROYCE

cam cleat for running

nonskid surfaces

LOA 11'7"
beam 5'0"
78 sq.ft. of sail
mast length 19'6"
board down-3' draft
205 lbs. wt. rigged

Double bottom Kite and Coronado 15 are SELF RESCUING... they can be swamped, then righted without lowering sails and continue to race competitively while many dinghies such as Sabot, Penguin, etc., must have sails dropped, boat righted, and often bailed on shore before racing or sailing again.

clew band

double bottom section view

* full length air tank may be foam filled

tiller length is adjustable

transom

High performance Kite, a self rescuing catboat with positive flotation, is excellent second step boat for juniors as it is an active, sensitive, easily moving dinghy.

*Full length air tank may be filled with foam to make easily rowed or sailing, nonsink lifeboat

pintle

gudgeon

rudder lock

cockpit drains p & s

air tank drain.. don't forget the plug!

rudder

PORT

TACK

The Lido 14 appeared in 1958. It had a good name plus one of the first quality fiberglass hulls. It is the standard of simplicity as rigging and controls are well designed, helping to make the Lido 14 a happy boat to sail as it is delicate to the helm and sensitive to weight placement. When the wind comes up you have a very spirited boat, ideal for the first boat owner . . . and for high school and college sailing instruction and racing competition. I've taught on over 40 of this class, on one Lido three times as owners sold the boat to newcomers, when they bought larger sailboats, see facing page.

●

The Sandy Douglass designed Thistle appeared in 1945. Growth has been slow but steady, with Thistle sailors enjoying a comradery many classes dream about . . . yet few seem to realize. About 6000 registered Thistles were in existence at time of printing, see page 32.

Thistle is an open 17' dinghy with air tanks to keep it afloat during upset. She planes easily and seems ready to take on her share of newcomers. . . indicated by "The Green Thing" (#2744) first overall in the 1969 Yachting's OOAK races. A discussion whether Thistle could beat Lightning gave impetus to first 1949 OOAK.

●

The Snipe, designed 1931 by William F. Crosby, was the largest one-design classic to the late sixties, withstanding the test of time due to continuous class self improvement. We've had a Snipe in every edition of our book starting with a basic one. The next two, belonged to Earl Elms who dominated the Snipe Worlds for over a decade.

When we asked its secretary for todays best representative Snipe, he recommended one of a dozen identical boats being built for the 1979 Pan-American competition. The builder recommended #24001 for the sail. Yet for several reasons we decided it best to omit the sail number.

Collect as many boat supply catalogs as possible, but also obtain the yearly SPYGLASS Guide, 2415 Mariner Square Drive, Alameda, CA 94501. It strives to have the latest hardware information, new products, and manufacturers.

Lido 14

main halyard to stbd,
jib halyard to port
side of tabernacle

tabernacle

downhaul

vang adjust to port

outhaul adjust

jib fairlead

quick release main
sheet cam cleat

jib sheet with
quick release cam cleat

cb trim to stbd

traveler adjust

hiking strap has
tension adjust

hiking stick

tilt up rudder

L14 80

4500 Lido 14's sail worldwide

A popular, good quality, all-round sailboat, excellent for a
new boat owner, being responsive, yet with few adjustments.
It is popular for college instruction, and inter-college racing.

The author spent many wonderful afternoons sailing #80 with
Mel Keim, now deceased. He was the first officer in WW I to
be assigned to those new-fangled aeroplanes. Though he could
have bought any boat in the bay . . . this was his favorite.

LOA 14'0"
beam 6'0"
111 sq. ft. sail
310 lbs. weight

Sec'y— box 1252
Newport Beach, CA
92663

31

Thistle

pole lift

air tank

running guy

shock cord
downhaul

main halyard

jib halyard

all halyards internal

outhaul adjust
drum under

handle or tubing

shroud

vang

topping lift

shroud
lever

cb cleat   fore guy

running guy downpull

slotted boom

jib sheet

jib sheet

running guy

sp sheet

cb trunk

main sheet

running guy

air tank

hiking
straps

air tank

LOA & LWL 17'0"
beam 6'0"
hull draft 9"
board down 4'6"
sq. ft. sail 175

tiller

hiking stick

running guy

3 part main

sp sheet

traveler

Sec'y Mrs. Marlin Abramson
1811 Cavell Ave.
Highland Park, IL 60035

Typical late model Thistle
has been illustrated.

the Snipe

shock cord return

jib luff downhaul

flexing to leeward

pivot point

jib luff downhaul

Magic Box (6 to 1 purchase) halyard tensioner

mast bends aft
and to leeward

shroud adjuster below deck

swept back spreaders

slot between main & jib
opens as wind increases
reducing weather helm

main luff
downhaul

reaching hook

builder - - -
Pheonix Boat Co.
1556 W. 11th Street
Long Beach, CA 90813

main sheet cam cleat

daggerboard has
rounded fwd edge

3 to 1 vang purchase

jib sheet cam cleat

jib fairlead

puller/pushers
eliminate mast wedges

splashboard

self bailer

Sec'y-Lowry Lamb
Privateer Road
Hixson, Tenn. 37343

main traveler adjust P & S

mainsheet bridle

athwartship mast
puller/pusher P & S

sharp atter edge

cb safety line

mast puller

mast pusher

LOA 15'6"
LWL 13'6"
beam 5'0"
draft 8"
board down 3'6"
116 sq. ft. sail

bridle adjust
under deck

maximum area
drain ports

rudder lock

flexible aluminum mast in 10-15 knot wind

33

Barber Hauler slack

full draft

minimum slot between sails

jib sheet

Closehauled or reaching
in a light wind.

also see
pages 118-119

A controlled laminar air flow between main and jib is important to win races, the lack of such a funnel or slot eliminates catboats from sloop competition.

San Diego sailors, identical Barber twins Manning and Merritt, took their idea to Carl Eichenlaub who built their Lightning. The new hauler proved an instant success in heavy competition the following Saturday.

The air flow can be squeezed when sailing in light and/or disturbed air at the start, with jib sheet tension direct to jib fairlead as shown above.

As wind increases when reaching or closehauled, the slot is opened by hardening on the Barber hauler for a better laminar air flow without backing mainsail.

Jib wire and jib cloth adjusts are eased to squeeze the slot in light wind, and backstay eased to increase mainsail draft. Jib wire and jib cloth are hardened enough to remove luff wrinkles to open slot as wind increases.

The flexible aluminum mast is also important to slot control. As wind increases, so should the amount of rake or bend to flatten mainsail. This helps open the slot, reducing heel, changing most wind pressure into forward drive. In a very strong wind, excessive mast bend lets upper part of mainsail feather aft, which would otherwise overpower the boat, reducing excess heel and weather helm.

slot open

jib sheet

flat draft

Closehauled or reaching
in a strong wind.

Barber Hauler taut

Sailing
Illustrated

Lightning

(yellow)
all halyards and topping lift are internal
cloth luff hanks
jib cloth adjust
jib luff wire
cunningham

Spinnaker halyard/guy/sheet assembly can be pulled from one side to the other around the bow from the cockpit.

jumpers aren't required with aluminum mast

cloth jib luff hanks

Tom Allen aluminum mast

16191

SEA FLYER

internal outhaul, adjust to port

fixed gooseneck at lower limit

Barber hauler

single sided cam cleat adjusts guy/sp pole

jib fairlead

jib cloth adjust
jib luff wire adjust
centerboard adjust

backstay adjust

main sheet cam cleat

hiking stick

cunningham adjust port and starboard
splashboard

an International Racing Class

spinnaker halyard
port barber hauler under console
Nashmarine TRIGGER cleat

sp sheet/guy (red)

sp sheet/guy (green)

stbd barber hauler under console

Mrs. Helen Limbaugh
808 High Street
Worthington, Ohio 43085

LOA 19'0"
LWL 15'3"
beam 6'6"
draft 6"
board down 4'11"
177 sq. ft. sail
min. disp. 700 lbs.

6 to 1 backstay adjuster, drum use is prohibited

Class boats have to be self-rescuing after 1/1/69.

jib cloth adjust
jib luff wire adjust
spinnaker pole lift adjust

The most widely known and best-loved centerboarder worldwide is the Lightning, granted the status of an International Racing Class in 1962. The association has existed since 1939 now with over 460 chartered fleets worldwide. It was designed by Sparkman and Stephens.

Lightning sailors are highly competitive, yet their boat is also comfortable for family afternoon sailing... while many other racing machines not as comfortable seldom leave the dock except to race.

This is the 3rd Lightning we've detailed. The first was in 1966, the "Glass Magic", the most perfect boat I can remember sailing. The second in 1971 was boat builder Carl Eichenlaub's "AJC", the first of the class we were told with built-in flotation for self rescuing.

A method peculiar to the Lightning Class is the spinnaker halyard/sheet/guy assembly rigged together as shown, then pulled out of the way, supported at bow with a tang. Helmsman or crew can pull the assembly from one side of the boat to the other without leaving the cockpit.

Most races are on a triangular course leaving marks to port, so the chute halyard/sheet/guy are secured to chute in bag or basket to port. Pole is raised just before mark, with halyard raised the moment mark is turned. Chute is raised, pulled to the pole by the running guy, and sheet is set. Jib is dropped and secured as shown.

The mast has changed from wood to aluminum eliminating the jumpers. The new flexibility of controls allows same crew weight to be used more effectively in a much wider variety of wind and water conditions.

Many factors are involved to keep a large worldwide class expanding, starting with its hard-working secretary of many years Helen Limbaugh, who provided a list of local boats to choose for detailing. The owner chosen summarized, "The boat is ideal for lake sailing and racing. Owners love their boats staying with the association for a long time". This boat is Mike Boswell's 3rd Lightning.

36   Sailing Illustrated.

Lightning

reduce chance of jib falling into water, acting as a sea anchor.

wire pole lift

jib secured under shock cord with chute up

running guy end of chute

chute free end

tweaker

shock cord downhaul

lead goes to vang detailed upper left

Barber hauler

tweaker prevents pole from lifting

spinnaker sheet adjust

vang adjust

single side cam cleat

spinnaker guy adjust

three separate hiking straps

mainsheet snubber

vang off

vang on

Shock cord pulls vang wire out of way when not in use.

Vang wire tube guide

Differential drum provides leverage power for boom vang.

drum purchase 8:1

13/9'

wire pole lift

spinnaker halyard (yellow)

running guy

spinnaker container to port

vang adjust

spinnaker sheet (red)

spinnaker guy (green)

Typical Lightning spinnaker rig, ready to raise at mark.

Rigging details were installed by owner Mike Boswell.

Boat, sails, and mast made by— Allen Boat Co., 655 Fuhrman Blvd., Buffalo, NY 14203

sp sheet/guy

cb trunk

thwart

sp sheet/guy

rough texture for foothold traction with crew out on trapeze

double traveler adj

traveler rod

rollerslide

jib sheet

jib fairlead

jib furl

vang

lower cb

compass or stopwatch location

raise cb

pole lift

sp halyard

aft strut

main cam cleat

spring loaded pin downhaul adjust

outhaul tension lever

on

off

vang

Sec'y Peter Wells
Box 152
Rindge, NH 03461

Single-bottom FD version belonged to Terry Dahleheite of Guadalajara, Mexican National champ at time of detailing.

6 part main

round section for comfortable hiking

fwd strut

inspection port

aft strut

cb fore/aft saddle adjust

suction bailer

transom flap drain

sp sheet/guy under

air tank inside

trim lines raise/lower rudder

sp halyard

Spinnaker ready to be raised.

rolled sides for sitting

jib fairlead

trapeze ring

shroud lever

jib snubbing winch

shock cord

38

cb down

cb up

thwart

jib cam cleat

Royce

Flying Dutchman is a two man centerboard Olympic Class.

Tremendous equipment and deck arrangement variables may be found between FD boats, even made the same year by the same builder.

Two trim lines are required to control centerboard. Saddle used on some Fds can pull cb forward in light wind, and aft, in strong wind without raising, to reduce weather helm. Saddle details for an Int'l 14 are shown page 26.

Flying Dutchman

clew

jib furled

Furled jib is opened by pull on jib sheet.

shock cord

light retriever cord

pole lift

downhaul

furling reel (below decks)

well

jib furling line

tack

running guy

halyard

opening

sp sheet

thwart

cb raised

raise cb
halyard
pole lift

mast step

FD

MX 55

running guy

guy inside

limited swing spreaders

SPINNAKER STOWAGE/RAISING

Before race, and after use in race, halyard, sheet, and guy are slacked at same time, so spinnaker can be pulled down into tunnel from cockpit for stowage, with retriever line.

Chute can be raised rapidly with sp halyard by helmsman, while crew snaps pole to running guy, then trimming sheet and guy.

Launching tube was developed by Bill Roberts & Bernie Kerr.

guy

sheet

tunnel

red corner

sp halyard

retriever

sp sheet/guy

tunnel opening fwd of headstay

chute in launching tube

green corner

LOA 19' 10"
beam 5' 7"
draft 3' 8"
sq.ft. sail 200
sq.ft. spinnaker 190
minimum sailing weight 374 lbs.

retriever

Spinnaker launching tube method is shown. Retriever is secured to foot or third of way up chute.

Water drains into cockpit and out through bailers.

39

The Flying Dutchman was selected after extensive testing as the two man centerboarder for Olympic competition starting in 1960. Its designer, U. van Essen of Holland.

Former Class Secretary Alford classed it a highly complex machine with rigid hull and mast spec's, yet considerable flexibility in layout and equipment to stimulate the thinker and gadgeteer.

He called it a research class, which due to sensitivity to tuning and equipment variables isn't conducive to make it a large, popular class. He told us to stress the idea that to race an FD it requires two EQUAL skippers ... the helmsman for the feel, and crew for the mechanics.

The present class secretary takes a different approach feeling at least 90% of FD sailing at the weekend fleet level is by quite average sailors.

"Most would not be competitive at the Olympic level but have a great time sailing just as in any other class ... many are husband and wife combinations.

"The FD is a very easy boat to sail—but very difficult to sail well! Therein lies the challenge—and the attraction".

A few changes have taken place since the Plastrend shown was detailed. The air tanks have been replaced by a double bottom forward, the thwart has been removed, and the spinnaker tube comes back into the cockpit. Minimum weight has been increased by 21 pounds to 374 pounds.

●

The 110 is an outstanding performer regardless how you compare it except for popularity ... as it looks different. Our one day race series on the 110 detailed found it was pointing much higher than other classes, and due to the long waterline and minimum turbulence it passed all the other one-design classes racing.

The beautiful, bilious international orange 110 detailed was a museum display model, totalled by a dump truck on the freeway a day after its illustration was completed.

the 110

bow line

built-in spinnaker well

splashboard

110
434

300 lb. fin keel

Designer: C. Raymond Hunt, 1939
LOA & LWL 24'0"
beam 4'2"
draft 2'9"
sq. ft. sail 170

main luff downhaul

outhaul adjust

bicycle handle

vang hardened

pedestal

jib fairlead

Name 110 refers to original sail area before spinnaker was added.

socket for boom crutch

single traveler adjust method

double traveler adjust used

built-in stern line

Sec'y: Albert Peloquin, 505 S. Birney, Bay City, Michigan 48708

41

William Sweisguth designed the Star in 1911 as a poor man's boat. A late fully-equipped racing Star now starts at $10,000. Its high peaked gaff main was changed to a low headed marconi rig in 1921. As the version was too tame, the first flexible lofty rig was introduced in 1929 with a wooden mast, replaced by the super "wet noodle" aluminum mast, the best controlled of all flexible rigs.

We decided to include the Star only because it is involved in the 1984 Olympics, not the choice for a new boat owner. It gives equal trophies to crew and skipper even in local races, and owners say they have an excellent organizatio behind them. Our problem was to find and detail a late Star which would be most representative of its class.

Harrison Hine stepped forward offering his YAWAES, a year or so old, with 130 blocks, its rigging fortunately in the middle, not to either extreme. He is a marine hardware manufacturer*who has taken considerable time and effort to record all blocks by catalog number, plus length, color, and diameter of ropes in his 16 different installations.

Harrison feels the Star a pleasure to sail upwind, and very exciting to sail downwind. It is extremely responsive to delicate tuning with everything adjustable. The Stars are so equally matched they normally race in a pack with any one of five leaders ready to take over the lead in an unexpected situation, or a slight wind shift.

Harrison has a clean deck layout for skipper and crew with dual controls port and starboard, except for outhaul and jibstay mast puller. Jib slot control is interesting as jib fairlead car adjusts fore and aft, inboard to outboard, acting as a barber hauler in outboard position.

Below deck rigging we've always shown on previous class sailboats has been eliminated as it was so complex many more detail pages would have been required. Anyone wanting the latest information in hardware for this 68 year young and other competitive one-design classes, ask for *Seaway Supply Catalog, 4201 Redwood Ave., Los Angeles, CA 90066.

the Star

6161

LOA 22'8 1/2"
LWL 15'6"
beam 5' 8"
draft 3' 4"
281 sq. ft. of sail
min. weight — 1480 lbs.

Designer:
Wm. Sweisguth, 1911

upper backstay 6:1

lower backstay 3:1

jumpers have been eliminated

Ease upper backstay, mast lever forward, harden jibstay mast puller, for whole mast to go forward when running.

an International Racing Class and a 1984 Olympic Racing Class

lower shroud

jib cloth downhaul

numbers at partner show mast rake

shock cord return for backstay track

mast bender lever

compasses P & S

boom vang track 16:1

lower backstay

hand pump

boom vang

hiking strap

barney post

backstay track adjuster

mainsheet

to mainsheet fine tune

Deck sweeper boom is trimmed close to deck.

mainsheet fine tune

skipper hiking strap adjust

Traveler setting is very critical in the Star class.

Sec'y: 1545 Waukegan Road, Glenview, Ill. 60025, USA

chine suction bailer P & S

Leeward backstay moves all way forward when running.

jibstay mast puller

stuffer is eased as wind increases

inspection port to check/repair cables

jib slot control traveler adjusts fore and aft, also inboard and outboard. It becomes a barber hauler hauled all the way outboard.

jib traveler pivot point

flotation compartments in bow and stern

mast lever up (fwd)

mast lever down (aft)

mainsheet traveler 3:1

cunningham

outhaul

stuffer

window to check if seaweed is on the keel

jibstay mast puller

dual midship controls port and starboard

light weather jib cleat

jib car

jib slot control

jib cloth downhaul

crew hiking strap adjust

YANKEE'S

43

monkey bar

twin bilgeboards

The pulse quickens when inland sailors hear the magic word 'scow', which has thrilled them for many years. The scow has a wide beam, shallow draft, and a square bow. It is a light, lively and extremely tender 'souped-up' machine for smooth water sailing.

While minimum heel angle is stressed in most classes, scows with twin centerboards or daggerboards ....are often designed to sail their best at a 20° heel angle. On many scow classes, the crew may be using the bilge-boards as a foot rest, while hanging onto the 'monkey bars' shown above to keep the scow on its lines.

Majority of scow classes have been standardized classics proving their merit continually during competition in the past years. One of the few new scow designs to appear in recent years, is the M-20 scow detailed.

The M-20 is the brainchild of Bud Melges with his #1, winning its division in the 1963 OOAK(page 2), with his crew the well known boating writer, Bill Bentsen.

Bud and Bill as a team have collected hardware in a wide variety of classes, so they had a practical understanding of layout, hardware, and performance requirements.

We detailed the "Splash", a stock M-20 used in the '66 OOAK Race, while en route to its owner. It won second in its division, against rugged competition such as the Flying Dutchman, 505, and others. At first glance the M-20 may look considerably different to the one-design sailor. A closer examination will prove the hardware and other arrangements quite similar to many one-designs, and easy to adapt to on short notice.

Other classes are the 20' cat-rigged Class C scow. The Class D scow is 20' long and sloop-rigged. The Class E scow is 28' and sloop rigged. The Class A scow is 38' long and has been officially clocked at 28 knots.

the Scow

jibstay or headstay
(Boston, forestay)

pole lift

jib variluff

sp pole

running guy

downhaul

spinnaker well

splash rail

adjust for
internal hlyds

jib fairlead

mast
swivels

halyards inside mast

vang

bilge board adjusts

snubbing winch

jib variluff cleat

traveler adjust
at either end

jib sheet

shroud tube
adjusters

bow entry

tunnel

splash rail

10° bilge board angle

LOA 20'0"
LWL 16'0"
beam 5'8"
hull draft 6"
boards down 2'6"
sq. ft. sail 167

sp sheet

5 part main

main sheet

Royce

guy cam cleat

SPLASH

hiking stick for
twin tillers/rudders

twin rudders

Sec'y Dick Penticoff
Melges Boat Works
Zenda, WI 53125

M
201
728

45

Multihull day sailing is a specialized world of its own. The dream . . . fly a hull clear of the water for long periods with wind and spray singing through your rigging. Everything is on the ragged edge. Will a sudden puff flip you, will the lee bow stub its toe causing a cartwheel, followed by boneyarding . . . is not for the weak of heart.

Cats have come and cats have gone, both the happy, quality, solid-wing Pacific Cat which has withstood the test of time, now has a younger brother which should be showing its rudder blades to other multihull classes for the next decade.

We feel the first successful small cat was the Carter Pyle Pacific Cat produced in '62. It was so well built that as far as we know, even Pacific Cat #1 is still competitive.

After a few years in hibernation, P Cat production was taken over by a neighbor, Owen Minney. His racing background includes almost all west coast long distant races, plus being a continual contender in various one-design classes chasing around the buoys. His favorite of all class boats for a long time has been the P Cat.

After much heavy competition testing, his new P Cat 2/18 emerged in a 1978 New Year's Day Regatta against 138 boats, posting first on overall corrected time, first in its class, fastest elapsed time around the course, and first to finish on elapsed time. Since then the P Cat 2/18 has won numerous open class sailing events.

Owen has reduced overall hull weight structure by 100 pounds by changing from tilt-up boards to daggerboards, reducing well length, and using lighter, stronger strengthening members. If you want a quality solid wing fun-loving 2nd generation multihull, check the P Cat 2/18 details.

The boat is equipped with a continuous mainsheet & traveler adjust. Outhaul and cunningham adjustments are made under tension. Jib slot control is excellent. The cat has jib-furling, kick-up rudders, and lots of dry storage space for sweaters, purses, small stowaways, lunch, refreshments, etc., not found in other cats.

46   Sailing   Illustrated

Pacific Cat

jib furling reel

strut

jib furler

halyard lock hook

pull jib sheet to unfurl jib

jib draft indicators

furling jib

R18

all halyards are internal

luff downhaul

Cunningham downhaul

jib luff tension adjust

fixed gooseneck

swiveling mast

jib sheet cleated to windward

high aspect sail rig

full batten main

daggerboard tiedown

daggerboard canted 5° fwd of vertical

Solid wing construction is used between symmetrical hulls.

jib clew board

boom vang is eliminated

Westport Pacific Boats, Inc.
447 North Newport Blvd.
Newport Beach, CA 92663

internal outhaul

outhaul adjust can be made under tension

mast turn adjust

barber hauler

jib traveler adjust

main jam cleat

rudder tiedown

storage compartment

the P 2/18--
LOA 18'9"
beam 7'11"
hull draft 7"
boards down 2'11"
270 sq.ft. sail
450 lbs. weight rigged

6 part main sheet

continuous mainsheet and traveler

main traveler adjust

jib traveler

3 1/2" cockpit venturi drain

rudders tilt up

The sweetest of hot boats, built for efficient sail handling

47

Then we come to those not satisfied with ordinary sailing.

1. SANDBAGGERS were centered in the New York Harbor from 1870 to 1900, using hulls from 20-30' long. A boat having hull length of 20' often measured 70' from boomkin to jib tack, carrying up to 1600 square feet of sail. All ballast was inside ... with 600-700 pounds required to keep it from capsizing at anchor. Canvas ballast bags containing 50-60 pounds of gravel each, were piled on the weather side by large & active crews while racing. The combination shallow draft centerboard hull with barndoor rudder made the sandbagger quite tender.

2. 14' BERMUDA RACING DINGHIES have three different rig arrangements to be used according to the weather. The largest includes spinnaker totaling 700 square feet of sail. As races are beats or runs, the spinnaker, pole & lines are sometimes thrown overboard rounding the last mark in a race. As this racing machine uses live ballast that is expendable... the questions, 'Can you swim?', or 'Would you like to bend on the jib?'(the bowsprit sticks 9 1/2' past the bow), bear serious consideration.

3. The New Zealander 18 FOOTER is a sportsmans dream. With no limit to sail area, a jib and main may have up to 400 square feet of sail. If a spinnaker is added, the total may go up to 1,400 square feet. Some of these boats also have RINGTAILS (note extension to leach of mainsail) formerly used as extension to the spankers on square riggers in order to increase the sail area.

The Malibu Outrigger, right page, was the first craft capable of sailing off Southern California ocean beaches, out thru the breakers, and return. It enjoyed a good fifteen year span, to be replaced by the Hobie 14 and 16 with standardization and better sailing performance. We have 48 many fond memories of the Malibu "Lot" Club sailors.

Malibu Outrigger

tapered mast

stubby mast

modified lateen rig

677

"ama" or outrigger float

LOA 18'10"
float length 17'10"
beam 11'8"
hull draft 5"
board down 4'5"
weight rigged 400 lbs.
sq. ft. sail 192

"iako" or arm

foreward arm

stubby mast

collar

tapered mast

Malibu designer Warren Seaman's
Mai Tai' is detailed.

Daggerboard can be canted fore
and aft to compensate for helm.

stiffner

waterproof
hatches

dagger board

ROYCE

aft arm

hiking boards

hiking bar

kick up rudder
blade for beaching

write Malibu Yacht Club
box 1161
Malibu, Calif. 90265

outhaul

49

The practical, trailerable cabin sailboat popularity began around 1970, then expanded at a faster rate than anyone anticipated. Many went to inland areas such as Oklahoma and Arkansas where the sailing bug was just beginning to bite, and to shallow water areas such as the Puget Sound and New England. Others went to Arizona, New Mexico, the Great Lakes, and other areas where the portability/vacation factors, along with the backyard home port storage became main advantages.

Three representative portable cabin sailboats are shown, the Catalina 22 now over 9000 strong, and the Balboa 21 and 23, formerly called Aquarius 21 and 23.

A wide variety of trailerable cabin sailboats from 20' to 28' are available. If you desire this kind of sailboat try to find the practical overnighter which can be towed behind the family auto or camper. Also consider the kind of sailing areas you expect to use, plus the kind of launching ramps or hoists you will be using.

Try to be as practical as possible and don't be oversold by advertising when it comes to looks vs size as some boats may look quite large in brochures, yet shrink considerably after spending a few days aboard.

Size is confusing. If all other factors are equal, the 24' sailboat is not just 4' longer than a 20' boat, but TWICE the cubic capacity... making it TWICE the size. While the larger sailboat is more comfortable on the water underway, the extra capacity or size must be reckoned with while launching, loading, trailering, and in storage.

Trailerable sailboats are often made much lighter than hefty full keel relatives designed for much more rugged ocean use. When the hull weight is reduced, so is the amount of material in the boat reducing its price. While this makes the portable cabin sailboat easier to launch, recover, and trailer, its use in coastal areas should be restricted to good weather sailing, though it opens new sailing areas not practical for their heftier and larger full keel relatives.

Sailing   Illustrated

Catalina 22

sail area–212 sq.ft.
mast height–25'0"

mast trailering support

mast tabernacle

double lower shrouds

measurement from road to top of mast with boat on trailer 31'6"

storage lockers under bunks

measurement from waterline to top of mast is 29'0"

masthead rig
LOA 21'6" LWL 19'4"
Beam 7'8" Draft 20"
Centerboard down draft 5'0"
Ballast 550 lbs.
Displacement 1850 lbs.

head

galley slides aft out of way when not in use

storage under

dinette changes to double bunk

sliding AND pop up top

long shaft outboard motor 4 to 6 hp 3 blade prop

self-bailing cockpit

stowage for winch handles, etc.

two aft cockpit stowage hatches

removable transom rudder

Catalina 22
production boat
detailed built by
Catalina Yachts,
21200 Victory Blvd.
Woodland Hills,
Calif. 91364

44"

5'6"

7'0"

51

Balboa 21

measurement from waterline to top of mast is 25'8".

mast tabernacle

Measurement with boat on trailer, mast up, from road to top of mast is 28'2".

Storage lockers are located under all bunks shown.

7/8 jib rig
LOA 21'0"   LWL 18'3"
Beam 7'10"   Draft 12"
Draft cb down–47"
1900 lbs. displacement
Centerboard weight 165 lbs.

mainsail–98 sq.ft.
working jib–93 sq.ft.
150% gennie jib–117 sq.ft.
spinmaker–210 sq.ft.

jib fairlead

pop up top

head area

cb crank

swing up table

cb well

long shaft outboard motor to 9 1/2 hp, 3 blade prop, motor is mounted on bracket

electrical switch panel

battery box

stern locker

Centerboard is fully retractable in well

removable transom rudder

Production boat detailed built by Coastal Recreation, Inc.,
1630 S. Sinclair
Anaheim, CA 92806

Sec'y–N.A.S.A.
P.O. Box 3104
Newport Beach,
Calif. 92660

mast trailering support

6'8"   4'11"   3'11"

52

Balboa 23

150% gennie-145 sq. ft.
spinnaker-276 sq. ft.

measurement from road to top of mast with boat on trailer 33'3".

Storage lockers are located under all bunks.

mast tabernacle

7/8 jib rig

LOA 22'8" LWL 21'2"
Beam 7'11" Draft 13"
Centerboard weight 165 lbs.
total ballast 815 lbs.
2280 lbs. displacement

pop up top jib fairlead

enclosed head with sink

cb winch

swing up table

centerboard trunk

galley

Sec'y-N.A.S.A.
P.O. Box 3104
Newport Beach,
Calif. 92660

gennie fairlead

electrical switch panel

Centerboard is fully retractable into well so boat sits low on trailer.

measurement from waterline to top of mast is 30'9".

stbd hatch stowage

battery under

Bracket on port stern carries an outboard motor to 9 1/2 hp. A 3 blade prop is required.

production boat detailed, built by Coastal Recreation

7'7"

5'0"

4'2"

53

Weight is as important and critical to the trailerable cabin sailboat as it is to a light airplane... if either is overloaded or the weight improperly located.

1. Weigh trailer without boat on local public scales.

2. Weigh boat on its trailer as it came from factory, then subtract trailer weight to find boat weight.

3. Weigh loaded boat on trailer with outboard motor, full fuel and water tanks (see weight pg. 144), tool kit, anchors and anchor line, sails, radio, cooking gear, etc. Subtract #2 from #3 for weight of equipment aboard which normally increases the longer you own the boat.

Does weight of boat with full equipment weigh more than maximum weight capacity for trailer? If considering a boat/trailer rig with trailer having a 15% or so safe load factor when boat is empty... the boat fully loaded may exceed listed maximum weight which not only reduces useful lifespan of trailer and tires, but may also become a hazard. A stronger trailer with a larger load weight capacity factor should be considered.

After you know the weight of your boat relatively empty, then when it's loaded, this will help develop a sensitivity to know if your boat is dull and listless on the water if it is overloaded, OR if you have a light crew, to add extra weight below to improve your boat speed. Keep your portable cabin sailboat on a continual diet to perform to its best ability.

54

carpenters level in cockpit

waterline of boat

Sailboat fore and aft balance, is delicate especially on light portable cabin sailboats.If the boat is out of balance it begins to slow down, often dragging the rudder as it is no longer sailing on its lines.

Sail your boat on its lines by installing a simple carpenters level the helsman can easily see when he is steering the boat...by having it parallel to waterline.

Weight DISTRIBUTION is important as a sailboat is a floating teeter totter.Trim your sails,and trim the weight so it sails itself with rudder only used for minor steering corrections (pg. 115) using two light fingers on tiller.

Bow up, stern down. Boat is off its lines, out of balance, reducing speed and pointing ability.

Excessive teeter–totter action, improper balance. Confused boat hesitates, reducing speed.

Sailboat balanced, on its lines.It has rapid recovery with minimum hesitation to meet new wave angle.

As wind increases when flying chute, gennie, or with working jib in storm (pg. 123), pull on mast depresses bow.Move crew weight aft till carpenters level indicates your boat is again sailing on its fore and aft lines.

jibstay

Is jibstay pigtail required?

roller

secure shroud to spreader

jib halyard

gin pole

mast step fulcrum

trailer pole

to jib or trailer winch

5' lift pole helps to start raising mast

Attach backstay and desired shrouds before winching up mast.

gin pole fork

round aft 1/2 of mast bottom

Too many hazards exist when a mast is raised by physical force instead of using simple, easily available pole leverage on a sailboat on its trailer at the launching ramp as concrete isn't the softest landing pad if you trip on the cabin top.

● GIN POLE. The first time we faced this problem was in 1964 on Islander 24 #1. We added a line to the jibstay turnbuckle, then led it forward through a bow block, and back to the jibsheet winch, providing full control while lowering the mast.

Before raising, we noticed an unusual saddle fitting a short way up the mast, and a strange pole lashed to the deck. One end of the pole slid into the saddle, the outer end had a ring. We secured the jibstay turnbuckle to the ring, then tied a line to the ring which led forward to a block on the bow, and back to the jibsheet winch... or it can also go to the trailer winch, making it easy to raise the mast single handed.

● TRAILER POLE. Secure bottom of mast to step or tabernacle, then connect backstay and upper shroud to their deck fittings. Secure bitter end of jib halyard to port/mast cleat, and tie a line to the jibstay snap. Put this line over pole roller, and install pole in trailer frame fitting with V shaped collar resting against bow, then raise mast with trailer winch.

After the mast is vertical, reach jibstay turnbuckle with a boat hook, then lock it to bow tang. Flip line off roller, remove and secure pole to trailer frame for use the next time.

sail cover

Have sailmaker add slugs to mainsail luff and foot, pg. 87. Add sail to boom and secure with gaskets, then add sail cover to keep sail clean.

After mast is up and secured, add boom gooseneck to mast, feed luff slugs into mast slot, then add stop so slugs won't fall out of mast slot.

stop

● When lowering mast using either method, add a line to the jibstay turnbuckle, run it through a bow block, then take it back to jib sheet winch for full control when lowering mast.

main sheet hoist

bridle

boom lever

(adequate) topping lift or main halyard

jib sheet winch control

hinge pin

Attach jibstay and desired shrouds before winching up mast.

round fwd 1/2 of mast bottom

● The Dutch mast raising method is popular for sailboats entering Huntington Harbor in Southern California which unfortunately has a low bridge across its entrance.

We asked Fred Lanting making this installation on our "Pink Cloud" why he preferred a mast to tilt forward.

"When I was a boy in Holland I often worked on my fathers general merchandise floating store. He didn't want to pay endless bridge keepers to raise their bridges as he made his monthly rounds. He could use this method to lower and raise the mast singlehanded from the cockpit using the main sheet as leverage on his 60' boat to go under the bridges".

Our upper shroud has a 3" spacer added with a hinge pin, forming a pivot point in line with the pivot of the mast, (other methods prefer using a lower shroud) with a bridle above to prevent boom from swinging while raising and lowering. Quick disconnect hardware is necessary for both backstay and lower shrouds. A longer mainsheet is required which sometimes gets in the way when teaching sailing. Forward bottom half of mast must be rounded as shown.

● Dockside raising-the gin pole is good for boats to 25', while the Dutch method is efficient for full keel sailboats to 60' to lower and raise a mast to go under a bridge, to replace burned out light bulbs, to check and/or replace mast fittings, and to paint the mast.

● Launching ramp raising - the trailer pole seems to have an edge for the trailerable sailboat since the only time a person has to spend on the cabin top is to secure the base of the deck-stepped mast to its shoe, step, or tabernacle, considerably reducing the chance of a person falling off the cabin top of his boat on its trailer.

Others prefer the gin pole method requiring a little more rigging time on top of the cabin before raising the mast.

The size and cost of a sailboat are secondary factors to how often it is used. Systematically rig your boat with all controls coming to the cockpit so your sailboat will be used a lot more...as it is much more fun to sail.

Endless fleets of trailerable cabin sailboats have been launched since 1970. Many were equipped with minimum hardware to cut cost. It can become a blessing in disguise as we face a new economic world.

Most of these boats are light compared to same size full length keel sailboats. When a fast moving storm moves in they heel considerably. It then becomes a hazard to go forward to drop sails or lower anchor.

Take your time to rerig these sailboats so all controls lead to the cockpit. Take your time to analyze each installation so hardware and leads are simple, practical, and easy to use.

When a storm hits, drop the mainsail, with the main halyard to starboard coming to its pouch so surplus line is out of the way. Shock cord installed along boom is flipped over main so sail is secured out of way, pg. 86, and cannot break open.

Many boats now sail under jib only. If it still has too much sail area, jib halyard can be released to drop jib, requiring jib downhaul so jib stays on deck...otherwise jib might lift and fill periodically causing erratic steering action.

The option is to run before a storm up to broad reach under bare poles, or drop anchor which can be handled from cockpit.

Jam cleats jam under pressure, the reason they have to be replaced with cam cleats for main and jib sheets under pressure, pg. 144. Probably the best cam cleat tested recently is the highly versatile Nashmarine TRIGGER cleat, page 35, 32906 Avenida Descanso, San Juan Capistrano, CA 92675.

All fittings must be able to operate under storm pressures needing wooden or stainless backing plates, page 190, to spread fitting stress on fiberglass over a larger area.

Token cleats are monted on bow of many boats for anchor and dock lines. Replace with bitt, pg. 190, requiring less space, also handling larger diameter lines. Also replace standard chocks with larger Skene chocks, pg. 188, which are able to secure and handle larger diameter lines. If you want to enjoy your sailboat, good cockpit controls should be considered.

luff grommets and slides installed by sailmaker, pg. 86

shock cord sail tiedown, pg. 86

cam cleat releases normally under pressure, pg. 87

jam cleat use is questionable as it may jam under pressure

lock prevents sail slides falling out of mast groove, pg. 87

stern dockline

bitt, pg. 190

skene chock, pg. 188

Port and starboard bow docklines are carried when boat is underway.

jib downhaul

jib downhaul

main luff tension adj

jib halyard pouch either location

main halyard

eye for bitter end

reef hook

jib halyard

stainless Swedish snap hook, pg. 92

halyard bitter end secured to eye

cloth pouch

swivel block

jib downhaul

turn block

snap hook for jib downhaul

Rig your cabin sailboat, especially the trailerable, so all halyards, dock lines, and anchor line, may be handled from the cockpit in a fast moving storm. Expect rigging leads and hardware variables.

Jib downhaul is important in storm to keep jib on deck so it cannot raise and fill in a strong wind and wave action.

open hole cleat, pg. 190

stern dockline

anchor holder

59

Many outboard and outdrive trailerboats with tilt trailers may be launched without submerging trailer wheel hubs. Most portable cabin sailboats require "submarine" boat trailers which have to be submerged, allowing the boat to float off its trailer, proving a hazard if automotive hubs are used which are almost impossible to seal completely.

Automotive hub limitations restricted growth of the portable cabin sailboat till bearing protectors such as the Bearing Buddy®detailed were introduced; Aquappliances, Inc., 135 Sunshine Lane, San Marcos, CA 92069.

The "submarine" hub reversed the traditional thinking of the automotive hub. Bearing Buddy®is installed in the hub as detailed, then the hub completely filled with grease through a grease fitting. This grease is held under a slight pressure by a spring loaded piston. When the hub is submerged, pressure inside hub will be greater than pressure outside hub, keeping water out. If the correct kind of grease is used, the hub can't be overpacked nor overpressurized since the piston moves out beyond the "O" ring to relieve excess grease as shown in the facing illustration.

New ideas introduce new problems. Complaints we've heard with this product usually go back to owners adding Bearing Buddy®to existing axle with faulty hubs. Grease begins to leak out seals onto the brakes, and water may begin to leak into the hub, causing heat and metal failure from corroding, expanding metal surfaces.

If you use the Bearing Buddy®protectors, use their own Spindo®Seals to prevent seal leakage.

Our new revision was ready to go to the printer when we heard of a new product for "submarine" boat trailers. The name of the product is New Departure Hyatt (NDH) Integral Ball Bearing Spindle, the company is NDH Bearings, GMC Division, 2509 Hayes Ave., Sandusky, OH 44870.

The inner bearing races are integral parts of the spindle, while outer bearing races are a part of the hub. They are assembled, plus balls, cages, and retainers, then lubricated and permanently sealed without further lubrication nor adjustment. It has a new kind of bearing seal to keep out water while retaining its factory installed lubricant.

If damage results, a simple wrench can remove the damaged assembly to be replaced with a new one. This new product while new to the boating field, was developed for GMC new car durability 100,000 mile tests.

Contact NDH directly for your specific questions such as axle weights, plus recommended braking systems for tongue surge coupler, or hydraulic disc brakes.

AVOID submerging automotive hub bearings!

Auto Hub

Submersion can damage unprotected wheel bearings.

inner seal

hub

dust cap

spindle

inner bearing

outer bearing

air inside hub

correct amount of grease

Fiber type wheel bearing grease is used in this type of hub.

water flowing past seal

nut
cotter pin

cone

cage

lug bolt

roller

race

water and grease emulsifying

trade terms

CUP–race
CONE–cage, rollers, cone

Protected Hub

the submarine trailer

hub

inner stop

spring loaded piston

dual-lip spring loaded seal
(avoid automotive seals!)

bearings

spindle

grease fitting

stainless steel seal ring

'O-ring seal'

outer stop

less outside water pressure

more internal pressure

piston

too much internal grease pressure

piston

Use regular grease NOT fiber type wheel bearing grease.

piston in sealed position

piston in relief position

61

standard sheer

straight sheer

reverse sheer

(walk over) raised deck

(walk around)

trunk cabin

Curve of deck viewed from the side is called SHEER, with various kinds shown above. Greatest number of sailboats with cabins built today, use either a straight or standard sheer. For boats under 30', the raised deck or walk-over deck provides more space below, topside and in the cockpit, than the other kinds shown which have a trunk cabin walk-around deck.

We chose a 24' raised-deck Challenger for our full day sailing lessons, since it was more comfortable for up to five persons aboard, due to reasons listed above.

Visibility is another prime consideration for instruction with the raised-deck craft providing better visibility. Jib tack was raised 17", and jib fairlead moved sufficient amount aft to improve visibility, see page 232.

Bulkheads, bunks, head and sink, were factory installed. Rest of the work was done to fit our specialized instruction needs, as well as to test and report ideas to readers which may make your boat more comfortable and practical.

Fiberglass hull was chosen with minimum wood trim to require maintenance. Yearly bottom paint is required to retard bottom growth affecting speed and pointing ability.

Our 1964 boat was a challenge then due to newness of this type craft(presently the trailerables)with MINATURIZATIO requiring all installations built to closer tolerances than found on larger boats. Tools required are electric drill, electric saw, sewing machine, curiosity, and a lot of patience.

NOTE: many installations in our boat will be found through-out the book, which may be just as applicable to other sailboats. A considerable amount of references to manufacturers, class secretarys, products, items, etc., are listed as an additional reference service to our readers. It is NOT intended to be paid for ... nor is it implied advertising.

Sailing Illustrated

Pink Cloud

17" jib pennant
14 candlepower running light
roller bitt
whisker pole
downhaul
humidity indicator
compass pg. 243
charts laminated on plywood
midship cleat
rdf, pg. 243
PINK CLOUD
Right-of-Way decals
boom vang & preventer
tiedown gasket
cockpit railing
dock line cam cleats
Shock cord tiller tiedown
boat hook
genoa fairlead
skene chocks
red kerosene night light
rope locker
below
12 volt
100 amp battery
Lewco battery charger
drive motor
course changer
swim, dive platform
vents
outrigger release
telltale
white stern light
outhaul
boom lift
bail
dockside power inlet
barometer
tensor light
fathometer pg. 222, 243
transducer
switch panel
extinguisher
autopilot compass
outboard controls
preserver locker
6 hp. outboard pg. 180

stowage for flopper stoppers, Para-Anchor, etc.
clothing stowage
mast step
head
15 gal. water tank
bunk straps
inclinometer
alcohol stove
sink

Our 'Pink Cloud' is a 24½" raised deck Challenger built by Columbia Yachts, Corp.

ROYCE

63

6 meter "rating"   12 meter "rating"

It is difficult for a new sailor to understand the varied FORMULA kinds of sailboat racing due to a battle of semantics. The rating of a sailboat doesn't mean the boat will have that waterline or overall length, and though a meter is about 39 1/3", 12 meter boats may be from 64' to 70' long. After trying to explain this to students, they are often more confused than before my answer.

Meter boats are built to a flexible formula providing when all factors are finalized, they fall into a certain rating. The boxes above for example have a measured cubic capacity. One can be long and squat, or tall and slim yet still have the same cubic capacity.

Meter and ton boats are designed in a similar manner to be competitive as possible under their formula.

The ton idea began in 1898 when a Paris yacht club developed a trophy for international competition in a "One Ton" open design class. It was later reassigned to the six meter class, lasting till 1962 when European interested waned in this class.

The ton thinking was then applied for a boat to boat rating for offshore racing including minimum accommodations to assure the boats could be used for offshore racing, not limited to afternoon racing around the buoys. The IOR rating was based on RORC(Royal Ocean Racing Club) hull scantlings, CCA rule for sail and other measurements.

TON RACING also called "level racing", or "level class rating'became popular in U.S. around 1970. Builders were able to design and build boats to this formula in which with all racing gear, etc., the boats are able to measure in under IOR (International Ocean Rule) rating.

It is a rating in feet, similar to flexible box idea above, with main elements being length, beam, bulk, and sail area involved. For more details write USYRU Offshore Office, P.O. Box 209, Newport, R.I. 02840.

64   Sailing   Illustrated

- QUARTER TON—19' to 28' loa (approx.) with 18.0 IOR Rating: two berths, lockers, 3-4 crew maximum.

- HALF TON–26' to 31' loa with 21.7 IOR Rating; 3 berths, galley, lockers, hanging locker, 4-5 crew maximum.

- THREE-QUARTER TON–27' to 35' loa, 24.5 IOR Rating; four berths, galley, lockers, head, bulkheads, maximum crew 5 to 6.

- ONE TON–32' to 39' with 27.5 IOR Rating. Same as 3/4 tonner accommodations, maximum crew 6 to 7.

With such size variables it is obvious that the ton boats aren't look-alike boats found in one-design racing.

It might interest readers that first draft of our 'tonner' copy was given to Carl Reinhart, UC Irvine sailing coach, providing a liberal education to the both of us; the final draft changes, thanks to Naval Architect Gary Mull.

We had included the story of Dr. Jerry Milgrams "ugly duckling" 37' cat ketch used in '73 SORC Class E with minimum crew, minimum sails. The hull was similar to a "one tonner" with 22.8 IOR rating instead of 27.5 IOR one ton rating. His "Cascade" might have won first overall if it hadn't missed a turn buoy . . . which launched endless technical and emotional magazine articles.

While Carl felt it should be left out, he said this was just a continuation, as Bill Luders was shooting holes in the CCA rule with "Storm" during the 50's, followed by Bill Lapworth in the 60's with the Cal 40. About all one can be assured of is changes to produce better boats, better hardware, and better sailors, the fascinating story of sailboat racing.

Many tonners have excellent upwind ability due to high aspect main, poor performance downwind. For running, a chute is used plus a loosefooted 1/2 chute or "blooper", the mainsail may be dropped.

Overspecialization is common in many large monohull ocean sailboats with too much emphasis on one purpose especially found in "ton" boats, while sacrificing features which might provide more comfortable cruising.

We recently attended a local on-the-water sailboat show which exhibited a large number of multipurpose boats for cruising, vacationing, and easy racing, boats with a wide variety of personalities. One of the first examples of the multipurpose sailboat was the shallow draft, wide beam "Finisterre" detailed, which was launched in 1954.

"Finisterre" seemed the first real break away from the meter thinking of sleek, narrow beam, deep keel, wet, heavy displacement boats. Traditionalists did an about face when this boat became the first to win the Bermuda Race first overall in three consecutive races.

She was beamy and heavy with 10 tons displacement. Her centerboard provided 7'7" draft when down which was trimmed to reduce weather helm, and 4'0" draft when up for crossing reefs or inshore docking in shallow water.

Endless look alike yawls were spawned in the wake of Carleton Mitchells "Finisterre" which in Spanish means "End of Land". Many basic ideas with variations shown will still be found on many sailboats from 35' to 55'.

Pages 70-73 show the "Iris" built for and owned by John Martucci of Brooklyn. She was featured in many magazine articles during the years when John was alive to 1956, receiving the "Blue Water Cruising Award" in 1939.

When preparing these illustrations in 1952, John asked us to detail his early gaff cruising rig carried for over 20 years, as he felt this kind of information would soon become difficult to find . . such as the "scotchman".

It is most gratifying through the years to have the help of so many outstanding dinghy to large boat sailors who provided endless cooperation in preparing our book, as they wanted to pass on their ideas to help future sailors. The sailing fraternity we have known . . . has no equal.

the Finisterre

jibstay

bow pulpit

green running light

overlapping genoa jib

tack pennant

Dorade type vent

shroud roller

forward lower main shroud

intermediate and upper shrouds

aft lower main shroud

masthead fitting

mainmast

topping lift

geared roller reefing gooseneck

roller reefing mainsail

smoke head

skylight

genoa rail track

Finisterre is sailing closehauled, pg. 135.

There are two kinds of rigging; STANDING rigging which is permanent including shrouds and stays, and RUNNING rigging which raises, trims and controls sails including halyards, sheets, vangs, preventers, haulers, etc.

dodger

companionway

stanchion

double ended main sheet

genoa sheet

sheet winches

lifeline

forward mizzen shroud

jackstay

jackstrut

wheel steering

binnacle

mizzen mast

mizzen or jigger

mizzen spreader

topping lift

stern light

stern pulpit

upper mizzen shroud

lower mizzen shroud

67

mast tangs

upper spreader

upper shroud

cotter key

locking pin

chafe resistant material

swivel shackle

spinnaker halyard

masthead fitting

slot

clamp

running backstay

intermediate shroud

halyard block

forestaysail stay

red top is standard for spinnakers used on the Finisterre

upper spreader, see detail above

260

forestay is secured to port side of mast

running backstay normal position

Temporary running backstay reinforces mast in heavy weather if double rig, jib and forestaysail, is used.

from deck mainmast is 49' 9 1/2"

forestay

working jib- 309 sq.ft.
#2 jib- 161 sq.ft.
storm jib- 58 sq.ft.

260

337 sq.ft.

light gray hull

5660 pound lead keel

LOA 38'8"
LWL 27'6"
beam 11'3"
draft—
board up 3'11"
" down 7'7"
disp. 10 tons
cruising sails-
710 sq. ft.

running backstay

65 sq. ft.

boot top

'527 lb. bronze centerboard

'Finisterre'—home port Annapolis, Md.

68

the finisterre

tang fitting

terminal fitting

(jaw)

(eye)

toggle

cotter key   locking pin

chainplate

tack

fore guy

spinnaker pole lift

jib halyard

jibstay

after guy

shroud

terminal fitting

location for tack of large mizzen staysail

spinnaker pole

Turnbuckle has locking nuts on ends, and screw threads using cotter keys to prevent unwinding.

lower spreader

spreader light

stbd spreader signal halyard

spinnaker staysail (balloon staysail)

preventer

boom vang

running backstay secured out of way

Typical shroud assembly is shown at right. Jibstay assembly is similar, secured to stemhead fitting on bow.

scupper (drain)

self draining cockpit

speed indicator

wind indicator

small mizzen staysail

spinnaker sheet

staysail sheet

afterguy

Finisterre sailing on broad reach with centerboard in up position.

permanent backstay

marker is shown at left.

yellow code flag 'O'

preserver

float

weight

drag

17 pole erboard light

windward mizzen backstay only used while running

staysail sheet is preventer for the mizzen

horseshoe preserver

transom stern

ring preserver

69

WIND PENNANT

HEAD STAY

WEATHER SPREADER

F'ST'YS'L STAY

JIB TOPSAIL

GAFF TOPSAIL (OR YANKEE)

SCOTCHMAN

PEAK HALYARD

TOPS'L SHEET

GAFF

GAFF BRIDLE

RUNNERS } UPPER
PREVENTERS } LOWER
BACKSTAYS }

TACK DOWNHAUL

TOPPING LIFT (QUARTER LIFT)

JACKSTAY

PERMANENT BACKSTAY

RUNNING BACKSTAY

TRAILBOARD

BOOMKIN

BOWSPRIT

DOGHOUSE

BACKSTAY LEVER

CLIPPER BOW

BOBSTAY

BOOMKIN STAY

WHISKER STAYS

TOP VIEW

Older Yawl

BOOM WITHE
WHISKER STAYS
BOWSPRIT
BOBSTAYS
FORE STAYS'L
WINDLASS OR WINCH
JIB BOOM
FORESTAYS'L TRAVELER
UPPER SHROUD
LOWER SHROUD
MIDDLE SHROUD

(ALSO PG. 81)
TACKLE
WINDWARD POSITION
LEEWARD POSITION
LEVER
THE RUNNING BACKSTAY

REEF POINTS
MAST HOOPS
RUNNING LIGHT
GOOSENECK
ROYCE
SCUPPER
LIFE LINES AND STANCHIONS
RUNNER
BOOT TOP

MAIN SAIL
CHARLIE NOBLE
CLEW OUTHAUL
REEFING TACKLE
MAIN SHEET

BATTENS
MIZZEN SAIL OR JIGGER
GOOSENECK
SAMPSON POST
CLEW OUTHAUL
REEFING TACKLE
MIZZEN SHEET
BOOMKIN 'BUMKIN'
LOWER SHROUDS
RING BUOY
UPPER SHROUD
CHAIN PLATE
RUDDER
MAIN TRAVELER

L.O.A.   36'0"
L.W.L.   29'0"
BEAM   10' 3½"
DRAFT   5' 6"

71

WEDGES

STEERING GEAR HATCH

SLIDING HATCH OPENING

PORTHOLE

SLIDING HATCH

COAMING

WHEEL

BOOMKIN STAY

SHELF

CLAMP

MIZZEN CHAIN PLATES

ENGINE

CABIN FLOOR

HORN TIMBER

DEADWOOD

RUDDER TRUNK

KEEL

RUDDER

SKEG

WOOD KEEL

FALSE KEEL

STOP WATER

P.&S. 28 GAL. FUEL TANKS

LODGING KNEES

TIE ROD

KING PLANK

MAIN SHEET TRAVELER

HATCH OPENING

SLIDING HATCH

HAND RAIL

WATER TIGHT SELF BAILING COCKPIT

72

COAMING

SCUPPER

VENT

BRIDGE DECK

CABIN ROOF
COACH ROOF (BR.)   FIFE OR PIN RAIL
BELAYING PIN
WATER TIGHT
VENTILATOR
BITT
CARLINE
BS OR FRAMES
HANGING KNEES
BILGE STRINGER
CUTWATER
STEM
FOREFOOT
MAST STEP
MAST HEEL
TRUNK
CABIN SIDE
RAIL CAP
BULWARK
SHEER
STRAKE
KNEE
CARVEL
PLANKING
HAND RAIL
CARLINE
SHELF
CLAMP
BILGE
STRINGER
FLOOR
GARBOARD STRAKE
LIMBER
HOLES
CARLINE
MAST
PARTNERS
DECK BEAMS
CABIN BEAMS
HATCH
FIFE OR PIN RAIL
VERING BOARD
STAYSAIL TRAVELER
DECK BEAMS
DECKING
Royce
ANCHOR LINE PIPE
WINDLASS
BREAST
HOOK
KING PLANK
WHISKER STAY

73

There are three kinds of sailboats...open boats,week-enders,and boats suitable for extended periods of living aboard and cruising. Cruising boats are difficult to evaluate at first glance, made to a wide variety of compromises.

On one extreme is a lean, wet, racing boat with spartan accommodations, converted to cruising. Its tight living and storage areas soon produce temper clashes.

The other extreme is a heavy, sluggish, undercanvassed gaff rigger, cranky and dull upwind, moving good downwind in a blow...generally doing most sailing "dockside".

Between these extremes a compromise is found permitting considerable storage area with comfortable bunk and living space adding to windage, reducing pointing ability. Galley layout is important so cook is protected with food cooking on stove or in oven, while the crew is coming below or going topside.

Sail handling should be designed for one man operation raising and lowering sails, plus reefing in heavy weather. SEAWORTHINESS of boat is important...so the boat takes care of itself in a storm after its crew has quit.

The active cruising boat may occasionally go aground. Will you be able to refloat it without rudder damage... the reason an exposed spade rudder should be avoided.

"Ack" Ackerman spent three years sailing the South Seas for preparation to build his ideal, the first comfortable and practical cruising sailboat, the Newporter ketch. We have spent much time on Newporters cruising, racing, vacationing, and enjoying its special kind of sailing.

Though we spend considerable time at boat shows, if we wanted to cruise the South Seas with time and bank account permitting, we'd still choose the Newporter except with cutter rig which points higher and is faster upwind. We have been through our share of storms in Newporters, the best big sailboat we've been on in sloppy weather.

74

Newporter

Newporter specs.,
LOA 40'0"
LWL 32'0"
beam 13'0"
working sails—
837 sq. ft.
Disp. 23,000 lbs.

trailboard, pg. 70

the 'Pink Cloud', a ketch rigged Newporter

the 'Raven', a cutter rigged Newporter

running lights
bowsprit
pulpit
jib downhaul
jib pennant
genoa jib
whisker stay
life net
white anchor
bohstay
Royce
winch
ratlines
cap rail
sampson post
roller
continuous handrail
stanchion
lifeline
boot top
mainsail
chafing gear, baggy wrinkle, or monkey fur
boom vang tang
smoke head with water deck iron
scuppers
topping lift
outhaul
boom crutch
inner bulwark
charley noble
doghouse
outer bulwark
traveler
main sheet
taffrail cover
self-bailing cockpit
horn
binnacle
fantail
boom gallows
mizzen
topping lift, pg. 96-7
outhaul
overboard light
mizzen sheet
stern light
davit
fall
Newporter dinghy

For reference read, "The Ocean Sailing Yacht", by Don Street, Jr., W. W. Norton & Co.; and "Cruising Under Sail", and others of his fine series by Eric Hiscock, both experts in ocean cruising sailboats.

75

A new sailing acquaintance asked, "Was the 50 footer I bought last week the right boat for me...and was it worth (1968 prices) $76,000?"

There are several items to consider when buying your first boat in the 30' to 50' length. On one extreme is the ultra light, all-out racing machine, spartan below, with your local jail probably having more comforts. On the other, is a clumsy, under-rigged floating bungalow that seldom leaves the dock. What is the best compromise for you?

Students sometimes ask us to help them choose their first sailboat. We feel the size of a boat is a secondary factor, as the major consideration is how they plan to use their boat underway and dockside for 75% of the time. Then we try to have them find a sailboat that fills these needs with a personality that best fits their personalities.

It is a sad scene when a person buys a large racing sail boat he doesn't intend to race that doesn't fit his personality. And on the other extreme is a high strung, competitive person buying a large, clumsy cruising sailboat. Then add to that an owner without sufficient sailing experience for a large craft, leaving him at the mercy of a dictatorial crew...otherwise the boat wouldn't leave the dock.

We meet several people interested in larger boats with the cost of little concern. After a day on our 24' sail boat, they begin to understand the operational function of a sailboat so they are no longer limited by the whims and slogans of advertising copy.

After discussing the above traps, some instead decide to buy a sailboat around 25' to gain sufficient experience so they will be comfortable later on when they buy their larger sailboat. It will better fit their kind of sailing and sailing area ...and their personality.

The public has never had such a wide variety of sailboats and equipment to choose from as are available today. If the choice is the right one and you are prepared to handle it competently, you might find that sailboat one of the best investments of your lifetime.

leisurely cruising, some racing

Down East 38'

the all-out racing machine

44.42' Swan

If you are competitive, choose a competitive class sailboat common in your area, locally we may recommend the Cal 25. Become involved in yacht club activities and class association to enjoy the company of others with similar interests and personalities.

If you want to buy a large cruising boat for the first one, still consider buying a class sailboat to 25' until you have picked up enough practical experience to become comfortable handling the larger sailboat.

In the meantime develop a file on cruising boats and equipment from magazine articles, cruising books, and advertising folders. Also join a yacht club or sailing association to exchange ideas and learn from others.

Such exposure is important so you will be ready for the cruising boat, and it will be ready for you. Meanwhile you have time to analyze the compromises and tradeoffs involved with comforts and storage space vs sailing ability to make your boat practical to live aboard for long periods at a time.

Try to find ways to charter, cruise, or crew on a few cruising sailboats so you become aware of the variety of boat personalities for one that best fits your personality.

Good sailboats hopefully last for several decades. Consider tradeoffs between buying a new, stripped boat, compared to a used one with a lot of equipment. Whether new or used have it first checked out by the super sleuth of the boating world, an experienced marine surveyor of YOUR choice. If you buy your first big sailboat on impulse, expect many surprises, not all, pleasant. Sailing Illustrated

"Aikane" was the first of the new big cat breed. When two months old she won the 1957 Newport Beach to Ensenada, Mexico race breaking all records, leaving all committee power boats wallowing many miles behind her stern.

It was the product of a fascinating, stimulating, and often controversial designer Rudy Choy who developed his big cats with long lean displacement hulls which eliminated the monohull speed/wave trap, pgs. 140-141.

Soft water support permits a comfortable ride under ocean conditions with minimum water lift. Absence of a wake, yet a rooster tail at 20 knots with one finger steering, is an eyeopener. As to the big cat pointing ability of those designed by Rudy, they were able to outpoint and outfoot local 10 meters. In competition against a local 12 meter on a triangular course, the race was suddenly cancelled on the spinnaker leg when the 35 ft. cat less than 1/2 mile behind at the buoy was ready to pass the 12 meter . . . why?

For 15 years "Aikane" and Patty Cat II" were top contenders in stiff local competition. I was fortunate to spend some time racing on the big cat detailed when owned by Dr. Pursell with one of the best crews on the west coast.

As to the choice of a catamaran that will flip and float, or a monohull which will sink if holed . . . the choice is up to you. As wind increases, so does the monohulls amount of heel. While a big cat resists heeling, it uses a SHEET safety valve in puffy winds to release excess wind pressure by rapidly slacking the main sheet from 3' to 5', and sheeting back immediately.

When Rudy returned to Hawaii, most big cats also moved to Hawaii . . . except for one we found docked next to our boat, which was Rudy's own cat under new ownership. We wish we had 30 pages to cover the big cats designed by Rudy, but . . . if you want to know more about this field, read "Catamarans Offshore" by Rudy (Macmillan Co.) a big cat designer with no equal nor competitor. Fifteen years ago he taught me the unexplored potentials of performance in light hull construction, also for monohull ocean racing standards. . . a leader way ahead of his time.

the Big Cat

headstay bridle

jib tack method

sp topping lift

fwd safety net

bow crossbar

bridle

working jib traveler

sp foreguy

afterguy

LOA 44'0"
DWL 36'3"
beam 18'0"
hull draft 23"
boards down 53"

sp pole

running light

bridge deck

ROYCE

twin daggerboards

main topping lift

jib halyard

stbd backstay

main halyard

downhaul

sp. halyard to port, pole lift to starboard

shrouds

sp. halyard to port to starboard

reaching track

gennie track

topping lift

internal outhaul for roller reef

tiller bar

twin rudders

port backstay

sp sheet

Patty Cat II

aft safety net

main traveler

stern crossbar

Rudy Choy, President, Aikane Catamarans
677 Ala Moana Blvd., Honolulu, Hawaii 96813

Read "Catamarans Offshore" by Rudy Choy, published by
Macmillan Company . . . a must for multihull enthusiasts.

79

More controversy exists with trimarans than in other areas of sailing. On one side are many good, well built and well handled tri's, while on the other side we have seen many questionable backyard built tri's.

The tri dream appeared in the early sixties. Anyone could buy a set of plans and become a yacht owner. This was nothing new as an average carpenter could buy plans for a monohull and build a good wooden boat as all standards had been around for many decades.

The tri field was different as many of the concepts still had to prove themselves, many of the plans were sketchy, especially for backyard builders facing hull and other stresses up to 5 times that of monohulls, also with little understanding of ocean resistant metals.

We felt the '66 Multihull Transpac to Hawaii a practical method to prove the tri claims. Only one had the courage to show, the boat on the facing page, designed, built, and sailed by an aeronautical engineer. I spent nine days aboard helping prepare it for the race, also to understand this new concept. It placed 2nd in corrected time and 4th in elapsed time against stiff catamaran competition.

The wide deck platform on three lean hulls produced less underwater disturbance than a monohull, slightly outfooting and outpointing similar-length monohulls. When we turned the mark and raised the 1400 sq. ft. spinnaker it surged through the pack averaging over 12 knots to the finish way ahead of similar-length monohulls, at 8 knots.

Triple bow waves remove it from big cat competition, but downwind it easily passed all similar length monohulls. Upwind helmsman on a tri proved very critical.

The tri is a world unto itself. Collect as much information as you can, sail on a few tri's, and swap ideas with owners as considerable variables still exist varying according to the designer, without the look alikes often found in mono-hulls. You will have an excellent tri that sails efficiently and is comfortable and well arranged below, if you choose
80 your designer and builder carefully.

Trimaran

LOA 39'6"
LWL 33'5"
beam 22'0"
hull draft 2'4"
boards down 3'6"
working sails—
605 to 935 sq. ft.
spinnaker—
to 1400 sq. ft.

sp pole lift

club for self tending jib

fore guy

sp foreguy cleat

shroud arr'g't

sp after guy

daggerboard is adjustable from deck

ROYCE

downhaul

around headstay potential
of 1400 sq. ft. spinnaker.
(see page 128)

twinger

roller reef main

4 purchase main

spinnaker sheet

gennie sheet

gennie sheet

working jib sheet

main sheet

access to 35 hp inboard
with V drive, folding prop

sister hulls
called 'AMA'S

topping lift

traveler

81

The captain of a square rigger had to be a man of few words. His commands were specific, clear, and concise, as they had to be understood and put to use in seconds by crews from various nations barely able to communicate with each other. Thus the universal language of the sea was developed to fit this specific need.

Today's sailing vocabulary is a functional, colorful, spoken language developed from technical slang terms some more than a thousand years old. The term starboard comes from Scandinavian stjørn-bordi, the side (board) where the steering oar was hung. To protect it, ships were tied to docks lade-board, or "laddeborde" side later pronounced larboard. Since this term was easily confused in a storm with starboard, the British replaced it with the term port in the mid 1700's*.

Your sailing language is a spoken one ... rather than the written language of scholars. A puzzled newcomer as a result will find various terms used for one and the same function such as sail courses ... and according to choice writers may spell halyard one of three different ways.

Considerable effort is required to learn the sailing language, yet it is your only effective communication means to explain your intentions to other sailors, and to get exact answers from them. And without it you would feel lost trying to expand your sailing knowledge by reading books about Christopher Columbus, Horatio Hornblower, and other maritime gems. (*Thanks to Karl Freudenstein's

multilanguage research to redefine the definition of port.)

When sailing in the busy New York Harbor, we found airforce clock system more practical than traditional method above.

Beginner could soon report— "Tanker approaching 7 o'clock, and tug at 4:00. Change course right away to miss driftwood at 11 o'clock".

Sailing Illustrated   83

Sailing fundamentals may be divided into three groups. First is the foundation; second, the exposure; and third, experience by racing, hazing, etc., so you are able to handle a boat in tight quarters without undue concern, as most operations by this time are almost automatic.

● The FOUNDATION. The most difficult part of sailing is the new language. After a person becomes conversant with it, he is able to analyze and understand the operational functions of a sailboat underway.

We bought our first sailboat when I was 27. My background was Wyoming...far removed from the ocean and sailing. The only person available to help me learn to sail was 87 and almost blind. Our learning pains are still a major driving force to find better and easier ways to help future sailors adapt to the new world of sailing.

Our primary concern is to SHOW boat terminology and procedures so you can visually pick up the language and operation for various kinds and sizes of sailing craft. This method also works quite successfully for experienced sailors using our book as a review on recent techniques and ideas, or information on another type of sailing craft.

We developed a Basic Workbook which takes these basic steps in a programmed sequence, making it easier for a newcomer to find his specific answers. Other courses have been developed using 'Sailing Illustrated' as a basic text by various organizations stressing points they feel of most importance for local sailing conditions, etc.

A functional model sailboat for use in front of an electric fan provides a great aid to teach your family or crew the operational basics of sail raising sequence, coming about, jibing, wearing, backing the jib, spinnaker use, etc. The mast should be 12" to 15" tall. Lightest possible cloth should be used, such as silk required for model airplanes.

84

- The EXPOSURE. A few newcomers obtain their first exposure on the water with sailing lessons, yet most learn to sail by themselves, or have had previous experience by crewing on other sailboats.

A junior can readily adapt to a catboat-rigged dinghy under 12', yet an adult should learn in a sloop-rigged sailboat 14-26'. The larger size is more comfortable, and easier to pick up the feeling of sailboat handling.

We've taught on several 40' sailing craft, yet we feel a person should first have sufficient exposure & experience on a sailboat to 26', so he is able to handle it in most sailing conditions... without using an engine.

If it is afterwards necessary to sail a large boat with engine failure into a dock or slip, the sailor with enough exposure will find it a stimulating experience. Without this exposure it may become a terrorizing experience, with the boat soon afterwards put up for sale.

- RACING and HAZING. After a person knows the basic handling limitations and capabilities of his craft, the next step is to improve its handling in sail and hull trim by racing. Hazing or gaining experience in tight mooring and docking situations is also important so the skipper and not the boat, is the boss under all situations.

* * * * * * * * * * *

Man seems to learn more rapidly from his mistakes, so expect to make quite a few mistakes, the normal pattern followed by everyone when learning to sail. P. S., your author has contributed more than his share of mistakes which help to keep our book up to date.

The greatest fun in sailing, is to learn something new about nature, sailing... and yourself, every time you go sailing. The real reward for active sailors is this continual self-discovery process whether for long distance cruising, an afternoon on the lake, competitive racing, or producing our book called "Sailing Illustrated".

furling method

gasket tiedowns   hook   eye

shock cord tiedown

In the days when canvas sails reigned supreme, standard procedure was to stuff sails into a sailbag, being sure to leave lots of air pockets. If stuffed in too tight especially when damp, the canvas sails mildewed rapidly.

Common practice for many one-design owners today is to fold their dacron sails, using similar sequence to that shown at right. Reason is to keep wrinkle formation to a minimum, as some sailors feel wrinkles cause minute areas of drag, hindering racing performance, see pg. 88.

Folding a mainsail on a dock or lawn is not always an easy task. On some small boats, battens are removed, sail is rolled around boom, then boom and sail stowed.

On larger craft with mainsail stowed on boom, two methods are used. For those with standard reefing, see page 149, eyes are mounted on one side of boom with hooks on the other for a shock cord sail tiedown.

If hook and eye method were used with roller reefing, the sharp metal parts would chafe or cut sail. The older gasket procedure as result, is used to secure sail to top of boom.

When our new sails on the "Pink Cloud" were lowered, the luff rope of the main would fall out of the mast track, spilling mainsail onto the deck. We took the sail back to the sailmakers. Plastic slugs were installed on both the luff and foot, permitting storage shown at right.

When furling a sail for boom storage, pull AFT with each tug of sail so battens will lay parallel to boom and not be broken. Sail can be furled as shown upper left, or pocket made next to boom, then mainsail rolled and secured with either gasket or shock cord method, so it will stay neatly on top of the boom. The sail is ready to be raised in a few seconds, the next time you go sailing.

remove battens

folds

Accordian or loft fold
is shown so creases are
PARALLEL to foot since
horizontal folds disturb
less air flow than vertical
folds. For more information
see 'Junior Sailing Illustrated'

Accordian fold

head

clew

rolling-
luff to
clew

clew

Typical folding sequence for
mainsail after battens are removed.

When sail is stuffed into sailbag,
the corner you want to come out
first...is stored last.

Grommets and slugs are installed by sailmaker.
Sail is then installed on mast and boom.

Stops are inserted at bottom of luff slide track
and in slot below boom gooseneck.

Cloth gasket tiedowns in figure eight secure
sail to top of boom.

Sail cover added, Acrilon preferred, see pg. 91.

sail

gasket

gasket

slotted boom, also swedish track

Roller reefing gooseneck
is shown, see pg. 149.

Many sailboats over 20' have slotted aluminum masts and booms. Mainsail may
be stored on boom when not in use, and luff prevented from falling out onto deck
in heavy weather when a reef is applied, page 149, if slugs are installed on luff
and foot of sail by sailmaker. Carry spare slugs aboard as they break from
time to time needing replacement.

Lower centerboard or daggerboard before raising sails, to stabilize boat reducing chance of persons falling overboard.

Sailboat at right is on mooring, pointing into the wind. First sail to be raised is mainsail. For a boat to 15', the head is often secured to main HALYARD, then raised directly from sailbag. Pull foot of sail aft along boom setting OUTHAUL, then pulling boom down with DOWNHAUL.

Other sailors prefer to secure mainsail to boom before raising. Much depends on kind and condition of boat, though this method is usually second choice, as sail has more chance of falling into the bilge and/or being walked on.

On larger boats with mainsail normally stowed on boom, shock cord or gaskets are released, page 86, the head raised with main halyard, then the downhaul hardened and secured. Boom lift or topping lift is released, pages 61 and 97. A word of caution... have the sheet SLACK. Otherwise the mainsail may fill, and the boat start sailing on its own.

Sailmakers should stamp labels on corners of sails, or use coding such as ■ for tack, and ● for head. This helps to identify the part of the sail you are pulling out of the sailbag. If this hasn't been done, add markings to your sail, which otherwise might be raised 'upside down'. Somehow we feel the sailor who has not had this kind of experience, has never taken a boat from the dock.

Is it a clew, tack, or head?

Stow sails in REVERSE order to that in which they are raised. If they are lowered directly into the sailbag, areas will be stowed in correct sequence for raising directly from the sailbag the next time out.

If sails are stuffed instead of being folded, extra sailing time should be considered to smoothen out the wrinkles on the surface of your sails before a race.

Sailing Illustrated

Bending a Main

1. Check to see that halyard is clear aloft, then secure halyard shackle to eye in headboard of sail.

2. Fit slides on luff of mainsail into track on aft side of mast.

3. Add stop at bottom of sail track on mast to secure slides.

headboard

boom crutch

sail bag

4. Run slides out boom.

5. Secure outhaul to clew of sail.

6. Secure tack with pin to gooseneck fitting.

7. Add battens.

Sequence above may be reversed with mainsail first secured to boom on small open sailboat, yet it provides more tendency for sail to fall into bilge where it may be stained with dirt or water, or walked on by the crew.

rat tail   tabling

sail track slide

slides on luff

bolt rope

Sail track stop at right keeps slides from falling out of mast track before raising sail, and after sail has been lowered.

carriage or car   slides on boom

track

tack pin

pin

clew outhaul

boom

gooseneck fitting

downhaul

MAIN HALYARD is carried on STARBOARD side of mast.

headboard   head

batten pockets

1. haul up- 'haul yards'
2. haul out- 'out haul'
3. haul down- 'down haul'

Mainsail is being raised at left. Check for battens that may be missing or fouled halyards and sheets.

8. Crew is supporting boom while main is being raised or lowered so as not to unnecessarily stretch the luff.

9. Adjust outhaul.

10. Adjust downhaul.

Sheet should be slack during process so sail will not fill prematurely at dock or mooring.

clew   tack

Traditional mainsail raising method used for wooden mast and boom is detailed. Sequence is similar for the slotted aluminum mast and boom IF slugs have been added to luff and foot of mainsail, see page 87.

89

The flexible aluminum mast used on many classes, is designed to bend to a continuous predetermined arc, pages 114, 117, 119, 121, with the mainsail cut to fit this arc. On classes having the flexible mast, the sequence for raising the mainsail will follow either sequence discussed on the previous page. Some of the classes using a fixed boom position, will have the tack tension set instead of outhaul, see Int'l 14, Finn, Snipe, Star and Tempest details, using this method.

The three basic tension factors covered, plus vang and traveler, pgs. 116-121, are eased or increased depending on course chosen... and whether the wind strength is diminishing or increasing.

While beating to windward with wind strength increasing, all of these adjustments may be hardened. Tension increase on sail in addition to resulting bend of mast, helps to produce a flatter draft or flatter airfoil contour. If beating to windward and the wind is easing, the tension factors are often eased to increase the draft, or increase the airfoil or depth of the mainsail.

Various boats have been specifically detailed to help you study adjustments currently used... which will vary considerably from class to class, and to a lesser amount, within the class. Study and practice are required till you have the normal feel and touch of these adjustments.... part of the challenge and fun of sailing.

Similar yet different tension and draft factors result when comparing flexible and rigid booms. Those favoring the flexible boom feel it decreases leach pressure, helping minimize strong wind weather helm, pgs. 116-7, 132-5. Those in favor of rigid boom feel they can accomplish sufficient similar adjustments with leach line, pgs. 117-8.

At the end of the season, how about leaving your sails with your sailmaker? He will have more time to do a better job checking, repairing, and/or washing your sails than the following spring when he is swamped with rush orders.

Best way to check setting and trim of sails, is to take photos of your boat underway, from another boat.

Flexible Mast

Add snaps to ends of downhaul and halyards. Secure snaps to prevent losing halyards in sloppy weather.

Not enough downhaul tension.

downhaul

jib halyard

main halyard

Too much downhaul tension.

hard spot

snaps

Too much bend or 'overbend' in mast.

Not enough outhaul tension.

1

2

3

Add stopper knots to prevent your halyards from being pulled accidentally through their sheaves.

Too much outhaul tension.

hard spot

jib halyard

main halyard

ut location number on batten

Students broke so many wooden battens we had to buy them by the dozen. We prefer the 3 ply laminated fiberglass battens, as one ply fiberglass battens seem too flexible.

atten

batten pocket

batten in pocket

Worst enemies of todays synthetic sails are suns rays, and flapping in the breeze. Acrilan sail covers seem to have best resistance to weather, suns rays, etc.

91

Swedish snap hook   see below*   blackjack–AVOID!

Returning to 15' sailboat pointing into wind, after mainsail is up, bend on (secure) jib to jibstay (small boat), headstay a New York term, or the forestay, a Boston term.

The "Pink Cloud" jib is snapped onto jibstay at dock, page 96, without attaching jib sheet. It is dropped and stuffed into sailbag to keep from filling or falling overboard.

When time comes to raise jib, sailbag is removed and jib halyard raises head rapidly as practical. Jib sheet is then secured to jib clew with Swedish snap hook above instead of bowlines, customary procedure on large sailboats.

When approaching dock upwind in tight quarters, release button is pushed, disengaging jib sheet from clew of jib, preventing sudden fluky wind puff off buildings filling or backing jib at last critical moment when docking.

When dropping jib, we prefer to lower it directly into sailbag, to be raised directly from sailbag the next time it is used. If dropped to deck first then put into sailbag, chances increase for dirt, grease, footprints, etc., to stain jib. Sailmakers disagree with this practice using Dacron material feeling it adds extra wrinkles to sail cloth.

Swedish snap hook above is ideal for 20' to 28' sailboats. *NICRO FICO makes a jib clew fitting for sailboats in four sizes with load capacities from 3000 to 14,000 lbs. AVOID large snap shackle above . . . this author found it a blackjack when testing a new boat in a force 8 storm.

JIB HALYARD TENSION is critical varying in boat size. Jib halyard is set so luff wire tension is tighter than jibstay on most boats under 20'. On sailboats to 35', jibstay, jib halyard, and wire luff tension may be similar. On larger sailboats, major tension is carried on jibstay instead of luff wire and jib halyard.

92 *Nico Corp., 2065H West Ave. 140th, San Leandro, CA 94577

cure jib tack to bow fitting
to jib pennant if jib tack is
ised off deck, see pg. 61.

1

Jib luff snaps or sail hanks
are secured to jib stay.

The jib is being
'hanked on'.

2

Term HALYARDS originated from
'HAUL YARDS', or to haul up yards
on a square rigger, see pg. 285.

ter checking aloft to see that jib
lyard is clear, secure jib halyard
ackle to head of jib.

3

If jib requires battens
for leach, add them now.

Jib sheet is often secured
to clew with a bowline.

4

B HALYARD
carried
PORT side
mast.

'head'

clew

tack

5 Jib is raised at left for a
final check before casting
off from the dock or
mooring. See that sheet
is slack so sail won't fill.

4 Majority of jib sheet leads
are outside of the shrouds,
while others such as Star,
pg. 45, are sheeted inside
the shrouds.

AVOID
scallops!

Avoid SLACK jib halyard
on type of jib shown as it
destroys the shape and
draft.

This differs considerably
from the adjustable luff
jib pages 13, 33, 35, 45.

6 See page 12 for method used to adjust jib fairlead.

93

Suppose sailboat has centerboard or daggerboard down, rudder secured & sails raised. The next step may seem to be to cast off and start sailing. A note of caution at this point should be considered however.

Have you checked the sails to see if they are set properly; are the halyards stowed neatly yet ready for instant use; and have you checked the weather conditions. Following are some of our favorite stories about sailors in a hurry... forgetting that important last moment check.

We were just ready to cast off from a mooring at Staten Island when a storm hit. We had been so intent on raising sails that we overlooked the advancing storm.

Then we have the matter of a meticulous west coast sailor. He thought he had taken care of every detail... as he cast off from the dock to start an important three day race. It wasn't until twenty minutes later that a crew member realized the owners' wife, a very good cook, had been left at the dock.

A crew member pulled the wrong halyard and raised the jib in a crowded mooring area. The sail filled, & the bow swung to a broad reach before the boat finally responded to the tiller... after narrowly missing a new 50' cruiser.

The owner of a large boat decided to sail from the dock with a large group of guests aboard. Everything went nicely... until he found the hard way that a stern line was still secured to the dock.

Just before race time a Star skipper realized his regular crew member hadn't been notified of the race, so his friend who was head of the race committee volunteered. Since time was short, his new crew hurriedly raised the mainsail upside down. The sail filled and the boat sailed into the breaker line. After standing upright for two full minutes it finally toppled over... in full view of his race committee colleagues.

ower daggerboard or centerboard
BEFORE raising sails upwind.

aise the
ainsail
rst.

Raise the
jib last to
keep the bow
pointed into
the wind.

wind
direction

painter

Centerboard in
down position
provides resistance
to upset and upwind
directional stability,
see pages 88, 106-7.

Have your cushions out and any
preservers accessible BEFORE
leaving the mooring or dock.

Though SKI BELTS are NOT
Coast Guard Approved, see pg. 227,
we feel they are the most practical
preservers for most small boats as
they are easy to stow, take a lot of
punishment, and provide much more
practical flotation than cushions
which are CG Approved.

Jib is BACKED when its clew is
held to wrong or weather side,
pushing bow away from wind.

Purpose is to have sailboat on a
tack and under control within
a few seconds after leaving its
mooring. After mainsail fills on
new tack, jib clew is released
& sheeted correctly to leeward.
Also see pages 108, 109, and 168.

ROYCE

s your paddle ready if the wind
uddenly stops? When your course
s clear have crew cast off painter,
hen BACKWIND JIB shown at right
or a quick controlled start.

Put rudder hard over to make use of
sternway. When sailboat falls onto tack
crew will sheet in jib on correct side.
Give rigging, halyards a final check. 95

backstay

boom lift cannot release wind pressure

boom lift

topping lift releases wind pressure

w

Sailboats 22' and larger should have a boom lift to hold weight of boom when sails are not being used, and a topping lift or temporary line from outer end of boom to top of mast. Topping lift carrys weight of boom while sails are being raised and lowered, as weight of boom will stretch sail material, damaging sails airfoil; also pg. 149.

In a light breeze with bow into wind, mainsail may be raised with boom lift carrying weight of boom. After sail is up, boom lift is released. Use of boom lift is dangerous in strong or puffy wind as sail may fill before lift is released...causing a serious knockdown at the dock or mooring, and an embarrassing situation.

If weight of boom is supported by a topping lift instead, boom is able to swing to either side of boat releasing sudden wind pressures. After sail is up, topping lift is released, and downhaul hardened. On boats under 30', topping-lift boom-attach may be released and secured next to shrouds. Jib is usually secured to jibstay and put back into bag beforehand, pg. 92, ready for raising.

topping lift

sail raised

jib ready for raising

topping lift eased.. or secured next to shrouds

w

96

mizzen first

raising upwind

holding bow to wind

mizzen last

lowering upwind

jib first

raising downwind

wind

holding stern to wind

jib last

lowering downwind

Watch a wind indicator on a nearby home. It will catch an object on the aft side of the arrow, causing the other end to pivot and point directly into the wind.

An identical situation occurs when raising and lowering sails. You want to weathercock the boat so it will have RESISTANCE to TURNING or directional stability while sails are being raised ... and lowered. If above process is reversed, directional stability is lost. The boat out of control and out of balance may change course abruptly.

●

The BOW is weathercocked into wind with AFTERMOST sail raised first, the main second and jib last. Sequence is reversed for lowering with the aftermost sail the last to come down, also weathercocking the bow into the wind.

●

The sails may be raised DOWNWIND in light winds with the JIB first, the main second, and mizzen third, weathercocking STERN so the boat maintains downwind course.

The sequence is reversed for lowering with the JIB the last sail to come down, weathercocking STERN to the wind. This is seldom practiced except in light airs as slides stick and bind, the halyards get tangled, and sails may catch in spreaders breaking battens and ripping batten pockets.

st'b'd tack   port tack   wind   port tack   st'b'd tack
windward side   leeward side   port tack   port tack

Sailboat is on PORT TACK with wind coming over port bow, beam, or quarter. Sailboat is on STARBOARD TACK with wind coming over starboard bow, beam, or quarter.

When running with wind dead aft, sailboat is on starboard tack with BOOM carried to port... as boat is on tack OPPOSITE to side on which main boom is carried.

●

Course of sailboat is determined by angle at which it is sailing into, or away from the wind. We have included many course terms no longer used in todays' sailing but still found in square rigger movies. For todays' sailing we suggest the following terms:

● CLOSEHAULED (beating is preferred for racing)
● RUNNING (before the wind with sails wing and wing)
● REACHING (all courses between closehauled and running)

Man was able to sail up to a beam reach with his square sails for many centuries. Pointing, or ability to sail closer to eye of wind, slowly improved till square rigger could point about 20° higher, or 70° away from eye of wind if it had a clean bottom; 90° to 120°, with a fouled bottom.

Todays' cruising sailboats may point to within 50-54° of the winds eye, while many well designed fore and afters can steadily maintain a 45° course from eye of wind. Racing machines such as Int'l 110 and meter boats may point to within 30-35° from eye of the wind.

If fore and afters or square riggers point higher than these limits enforced by nature, the sails then become air BRAKES instead of providing propulsion. When sails hit this barrier they lift... their flexible airfoil breaks, with the wind pressure now hitting BOTH sides of sail, called luffing. Boat stops, goes into irons, then begins to drift backward.

Course is direction steered by a vessel either to a magnetic course... or its angle sailing into or away from the wind, or both.

Sail course terms originated with square riggers. Some are still used today, while others such as full and by or bye, have been replaced.

running

quartering

port tack

starboard tack

quartering

beam reach

beam reach

full & by

full & by

70°

wind

70°

Sail higher or lower to avoid blanketing jib.

STARBOARD tack

PORT tack

running
off the wind
before the wind
downwind
sailing free
scudding

broad reach
sailing large
off the wind
quartering wind

broad reach
sailing large
off the wind
quartering wind

beam reach

beam reach

reach
reaching

reach
reaching

close reach

in irons
head to wind

pinching

pinching

close hauled
beat, beating
work, working
on the wind
by the wind
full and by

60°

55°

50°

PORT tack

45°

40°

35°

30°

pinching

Sails lift and airfoil breaks in this area.

eye of
the wind

STARBOARD tack

99

sailboat is HEELING,
not keeling

Wind direction is of vital importance to sailboat operation. First factor to study is stationary TRUE wind indicators on shore which are flags, movement of trees, bushes, and grass, as well as smoke coming from chimneys.

Second factor is APPARENT wind direction found on your sailboat underway. For daytime, yellow/orange threads, or ribbons, and especially in light weather, feathers, are most effective for shrouds showing direction & strength of wind entering sails . . . especially in any kind of wave action. In smooth water the masthead telltale is effective but may produce a stiff neck if watching it constantly.

Night sailing finds white shroud telltales easier to see. Masthead telltale may be illuminated by turning on the masthead light directly beneath it.

A modern sailboat advances or works its way to windward on a closehauled course about 45° away from eye of wind. The sailboat changes wind to the other side of boat or changes tack by coming about, while advancing to windward. If the sailboat points above closehauled, the boom lifts, the vertical airfoil breaks, and sailboat slows to a stop.

As wind increases on upwind course, a sailboat heels which is a natural pressure-release valve. As angle increases you "hike" to the high side to reduce pressure being spilled from sails.

Most square rigger sailing was in the tradewinds with the wind aft to abeam, and as a result it could only sail at a shallow angle to windward. Instead of coming about to change tack, it was more normal for a square rigger to "wear about"*, or change the wind over the stern instead of across the bow while advancing to windward.

Fore and aft rigged sailboat adopted "wearing"* term for coming about for changing from one downwind tack to another, when jibing may be dangerous or impractical, see page 111.

100 Sailing Illustrated

roof top wind vane, page 97

masthead wind vane, page 119

smoke

Many methods may be used to indicate the winds direction.

jib luff telltale, see pages 12 and 119

wind blowing trees and grass

Shroud and backstay telltales should be standard equipment on most sailboats.

flags and pennants

Wear, wear about, wear ship. Various methods are detailed also for the lugger, pg. 277, and modern use on fore and aft rigged sailing vessels, pg. 111.

A square rigger is shown advancing to windward by wearing when changing tack.

sailing full and by

wearing ship

Probably 50% of todays sailing is closehauled, hard on the wind, beating or working to windward, about 25% of the time reaching, and the remaining 25% running or on a broad reach.

port tack

sailing upwind, closehauled, or beating

coming about

starboard tack

short tack or short board

coming about

port tack

coming about (racing term is called tacking)

starboard tack

long tack or long board

It was necessary in a square rigger for many centuries when changing tack while advancing to windward, to bring the wind across the stern rather than across the bow.

According to our information it was only in late stages that square riggers were able to normally change the wind across the bow instead of across the stern shown above called wearing.

Because of the difficulty in changing tack while sailing upwind, most square rigger sailing was intended for sailing before the wind or up to the wind abeam, with only a small percentage of time sailing full and by, page 99.

101

The airplane relys on a RIGID horizontal airfoil to keep it aloft . . . the sailboat relys on a FLEXIBLE vertical airfoil to provide upwind lift. While engine power provides air thrust for one, wind fuel provides lift and thrust for the sailboat. After the thrust is applied, it is the airfoil that provides LIFT to keep airplane aloft, and the sailboat advancing to windward.

The lift of an airfoil is developed from an increase in pressure on one side, and a decrease on the other. This condition is often inadequately described as SUCTION, which refers to a complete vacuum . . . instead of slight but adequate differences in pressure.

Between these two extremes are the high speed ice boat airfoil, and at a lower speed, the sailing catamaran. Due to greater surface speeds than sailboat, the full batten sails develop a SHALLOW semi-rigid airfoil for upwind sailing. (A May '68 Yachting article pg. 49, on full batten sail seems to indicate that they have many unexplored potentials for all kinds of sailing craft.)

Note how much greater a curve exists in LOW SPEED AIRFOIL of monohull sailing upwind. While the entire sail area is required, it is the shaded area having the maximum curvature providing the maximum upwind air-foil lift or propulsion for a sailboat going to windward.

The FLEXIBLE low speed sailboat airfoil performs two major functions. It provides PROPULSION for a sailboat underway both upwind and downwind. For sailboat about to stop at dock or mooring, the airfoils are broken to provide an AIR BRAKE to bring sailboat to a stop, 168-9.

A FLAT rigid wing without lift (without airfoil) . . would cause a vertical STALL on most aircraft. A sailboat trying to use a flat rigid sail above a broad reach will experience a parallel condition, a horizontal STALL. For downwind sailing it will be second best to the flexible sail retarded by rolling action of boat, causing unstable flow or air disturbance surging back and forth across flat surface and around its edges.

102 Sailing Illustrated

- **LIFT FORCE**
  AIRPLANE WING
  rigid horizontal airfoil

decreased pressure

increased pressure

- **LIFT FORCE**
  HIGH SPEED SAILBOAT AIRFOIL
  semi-rigid vertical airfoil

upwind airfoil
lift area

full batten
mainsail

airfoil

- **LIFT FORCE**
  LOW SPEED AIRFOIL
  flexible vertical airfoil

Draft area moves AFT in light
wind, and AFT in strong wind.

area of
maximum
draft

see pgs. 107, 118

1/2   1/3

maximum
curvature
area

upwind
airfoil lift
draft area

airfoil

wind

- **DRAG FORCE**
  RIGID FLAT SURFACE
  downwind only - plate
  stalls upwind, pg. 107

wind spillage
disturbance, pg. 120

small air pocket,
larger air pocket
desired downwind

stalled condition

downward
thrust only

sailboats
horizontal
stall

plane has
vertical
stall

see pg. 123, 128

wind

103

The flexible, sensitive and natural airfoil of your sails will provide propulsion or airbrakes. Example of latter is sailboat head to wind or IN IRONS, with laminar airflow past sails completely broken down.

When sailboat points close to wind as efficiency permits, and sails are trimmed as close as efficiency permits, vessel is on a CLOSE—HAULED course.

Slight course deviation is req'd to compensate for variables in strength & direction of wind. Due to sag of sail material, boom is trimmed closer on larger sailboat, see (2).

If sailboat points too high it is PINCHING. The boat slows down as drive area (forward half, pg. 9) is broken, becoming an air brake (also see sail telltale pgs. 12, 119).

If sailboat is on closehauled course yet sails are trimmed in too far, airfoil is in STALLED condition. Result is obvious by excessive heel & leeway (a condition similar to STALL angle of airplane wing).

If sailboat is on closehauled course yet sails slacked out too far, a LUFFING condition results helping to reduce a vessels speed when it approaches a dock or mooring.

Try operating just above a LUFF condition so maximum drive results producing minimum heel & leeway.

Sailing Illustrated

close hauled

wind funnel

All factors equal, a sloop has an advantage over catboat due to WIND FUNNEL or slot effect of wind flow past leeward side of main. As a result correct setting of a genoa jib is most important to avoid destroying the luff or drive area of main. Situation on ketch is increased as jib may backwind main, & main backwind the mizzen.

close reach

beam reach

Slack sheets & point bow a little lower so boat is on close reach, being able to steer a straighter course. From that & down to beam reach, sheets have to be let out to maintain maximum airfoil efficiency. If not slacked far enough, stall condition will result.

boom vang

high p.

low p.

high p.

low p.

broad reach

The boom vang, pg. 120, should be hardened to flatten mainsail by preventing boom from lifting when sailing downwind, and also sometimes when sailing as high as a close reach.

If vang isn't used, the boom will lift with mainsail developing into shape of a wind funnel, releasing useful wind pressure.

board
up

normal leeway

Any floating object can sail downwind... including gravel barge above, with drive force of wind pushing stern.

- **DOWNWIND THRUST.** Anything with buoyancy can float downwind. Sails should be at right angles to apparent wind (felt on the boat underway) with a slight cup to reduce air surge back and forth across sail area, pg.120.

  This world of sailing is noticeable in smooth water with a well balanced keel hull. Boat can operate through this range without sails up due to wind pressure on hull, mast,etc. Slightly below beam reach a barrier is reached in which hull stalls out, falls back to run to regain speed.

- **UPWIND AIRFOIL LIFT.** To sail higher to windward the sails become a major factor to provide upwind lift, with an opposing force of sideways drift compensated by hull shape, centerboards, etc.

  The higher a boat sails to windward, the greater becomes the increase in sideways force, with decrease in forward drive forces.

- **AIR BRAKES.** Sails at minimum angle to wind underway stall out with remaining forces producing leeway as forward drive is eliminated, hull also stalls out. Point a little higher and the sails lift, and airfoils break.... providing an air brake to stop your boat, 98, 102, 168-9.

  Designers are continually experimenting with methods to sail efficiently at a higher angle to windward without 106 losing speed. Closehauled sailing is a continuous challenge.

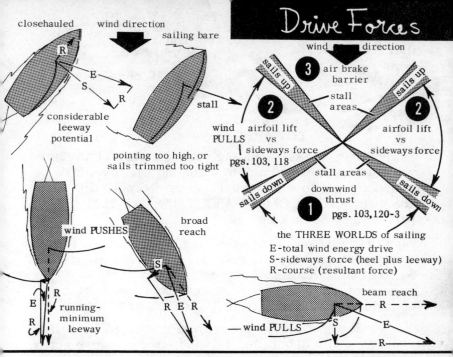

Drive Forces

closehauled · wind direction · sailing bare

considerable leeway potential

pointing too high, or sails trimmed too tight

wind PUSHES · broad reach

E · S · R

running-minimum leeway

R E R

3 air brake barrier

sails up · stall areas · sails up

2 airfoil lift vs sideways force · **2** airfoil lift vs sideways force

wind airfoil lift PULLS vs sideways force pgs. 103, 118

stall areas

sails down · sails down

1 downwind thrust pgs. 103, 120-3

the THREE WORLDS of sailing
E - total wind energy drive
S - sideways force (heel plus leeway)
R - course (resultant force)

beam reach

wind PULLS · S · E · R · R

Sailboat is 30' loa with 400 sq. ft. of working sail, wind force 5 with total wind pressure available of from **384 to 560 lbs.** (approximately .96-1.4 lbs pressure per sq. ft., pg. 137).

Wind pressure above is INCREASED by upwind <u>AIRFOIL LIFT</u>. The sails push the mast, pulling stays, shrouds, and sheets forward to <u>propel the boat.</u>

On the minus side are the sideways force factors of heel and leeway, parasitic drag of underbody, wave trap-pg. 141, also drag factors of mast, stays, shrouds, plus hull and cabin exposed to wind not providing airfoil lift.

SAFETY FACTOR. In sudden wind puff boat has heeling safety valve action to help spill extra wind pressure from sails.

Wind pressure is LESS since speed of boat away from wind must be subtracted.

<u>TOTAL AREA</u> of boat above waterline including sails, mast, shrouds, stays, hull, cabin, people in cockpit, which wind can push against, provides DOWNWIND THRUST for sailboat below, see pg. 120.

Minus factors are parasitic drag of hull, bow and stern wave trap.

Most DISMASTINGS occur sailing downwind as boat <u>doesn't</u> have normal method to <u>spill excessive wind</u> pressure which demands more awareness of crew.

boom and sail push against the mast

wind PULLS

upwind AIRFOIL LIFT

Dismastings often occur about 5' above deck due to <u>compression thrust,</u> also too many screws in mast at this point.

Breakage is now also occurring near spreaders with aluminum masts.

total area provides downwind thrust

<u>DOWNWIND THRUST</u>

wind PUSHES

tiller TOWARDS boom

(also head up–run to reach)

to cleat

jib

turn wheel TOWARDS new tack

Most winches turn RH or clockwise on boats under 30'.

Sailboat can only sail at an angle into the wind. Time comes when it must change tack by changing wind over BOW of sailboat going to windward. Procedure required is more commonly called COMING ABOUT, though in racing rules it is defined as tacking.

Page 104 defines wind as providing propulsion . . . or if the boat points too high, it becomes an air brake or wall. Sailboat must change course from one tack to other, by swinging bow across dead wind area, and falling onto new closehauled tack, till sails are full and pulling.

Variables are considerable in timing required for sailing craft to come about, due to wind strength, wave action, weight of boat, beam and underbody shape.

Traditional long, narrow HEAVY DISPLACEMENT craft normally has considerable inertia, permitting it to easily coast through eye of wind from one tack to other. On larger craft such as meter boats having large gennies difficult to winch in after sail is pulling, the sheet is often released and taken in on new side, BEFORE gennie fills.

Newer WIDE beam LIGHT DISPLACEMENT sail craft commonly found today in centerboard or the short keel weekenders, normally have minimum drive or inertia to take them through and past the dead wind area.

Light-displacement short-keel craft should change tack rapidly. AFTER mainsail fills on new tack, THEN release jib sheet and rapidly sheet it in for new tack . . . called "backing the jib". This method keeps sailboat under control while maneuvering in tight docking and mooring areas. We've taught on long keel motor sailers up to 50', also requiring jib to be backed continually when coming about while sailing in a harbor or on the ocean.

Coming About is method used to change wind's direction over bow of a sailboat going to windward.

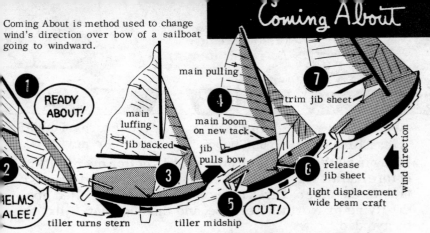

Command "Ready About" 1., is given to alert crew and passengers. Depending on size of craft, jib may or may not be uncleated and hand held. Helmsman 2., gives command "Helms Alee" moment he turns craft by pushing tiller TOWARDS boom.

After boat is slightly past eye of wind, the wind 3., starts to fill jib on wrong side, pulling bow over to new tack. Command "Cut" 4., or "Over", is given moment the boom swings to other side of boat, indicating craft is on new tack with main filling. Helmsman at the same time pushes tiller amidship 5., and jib sheet 6., is rapidly released and cleated at 7., for new tack.

Note: MAIN SHEET on monohull should automatically tend or adjust itself when changing from one closehauled tack to other when coming about. It is standard procedure on most multihulls to back jib and SLACK main sheet while coming about. Both sails are sheeted to new side after changing tack.

1. Same as above. 2. Same as above, except in larger craft head to wind, tiller 3., is pulled to midship position. Old backstay 4., is slacked, and new backstay 5., is taken in. Jib sheet especially with gennie on larger craft 6., is released, taken in, then cleated for new tack BEFORE jib can fill. Tiller is pushed over again 7., so bow will fall off from eye of wind, and sails fill on new tack, with tiller again in midship position 8.

(also bear off—
reach to run)

CRACK

| Will boom clear backstay? | Tiller AWAY from boom. | Wheel turns TOWARD boom or new tack. |

Jibing is method used to change wind direction over STERN of fore and aft rigged vessel, changing from one downwind tack to the other. Three types of jibing are controlled jibe, the flying or North River Jibe, and the accidental jibe to be avoided.

Controlled jibe is standard for down wind use in light to medium winds. In light airs boom may be pulled amidship, and pushed to other side as main fills. In stronger winds with rolling sea, main sheet may be temporarily snubbed around cleat to take punch out of boom swinging to end of its arc, on new tack.

Flying jibe is standard racing procedure when turning marks, and often used in afternoon sailing. In strong wind the rapid course change helps absorb punch of swinging boom, eliminating damage that otherwise might result. Flying jibe was developed to high state of perfection in upper reaches of the Hudson & North River, see pg. 274.

In strong or puffy winds it may be more practical to change from one downwind tack to the other, with wind changed over the bow instead. We have adapted the term "Chicken Jibe" to describe this maneuver.

In tight channel with strong wind, with insufficient room to wear, and jibing isn't practical, drop head of mainsail to avoid damaging uncontrolled accidental jibe.

Personal experience with endless students prompted us to use command, "Jibe-O-DUCK", which we feel is more practical than command "Jibe-O!" With sufficient practice jibing becomes as normal a method to change from one tack to the other, as coming about. The accidental jibe is discussed on page 122.

Sailing Illustrated

Jibing, Wearing

starboard tack

SET SHEETS VANG & OR PREVENTER

CONTROLLED jibe method

Fore and after jibes from one tack to another...by changing wind over STERN.

SET SHEETS VANG & OR PREVENTER

starboard tack

Boom swings freely from one side to the other during a Flying Jibe.

Mainsheet may be snubbed or cleated momentarily, reducing force of swinging boom...especially in strong wind.

JIBE JIB

JIBE-O-DUCK!

JIBE-O-DUCK!

As wind increases, boat may change its course considerably to reduce force of swinging boom in Flying and Controlled Jibe.

PREPARE TO JIBE

SHEET IN MAIN

FLYING jibe method

port tack

port tack

PREPARE TO JIBE

wind

SHEET IN

For STRONG and/or PUFFY winds.....

starboard tack

SET SHEETS VANG, PREVENTER

JIBE JIB

CHICKEN JIBE is method used to change a sailboat from one downwind tack to the other, by changing the wind over the bow of the boat instead of over the stern.

We had previously adapted the term WEARING to describe this maneuver.

JIBE JIB

back the jib

CUT JIB

EASE SHEETS

port tack

PREPARE CHICKEN JIBE

wind

111

Rigging must be tuned correctly so the boat can give its best performance. Job of helmsman and crew is to trim the sails and trim the boat for a wide variety of wind and weather conditions...so the boat sails itself.

Considerable differences exist between tuning standards of various classes, as to the degree of rigging tension required for best performance; opinions will often vary among owners having boats of the same class.

Most class standards are set by the reigning class champ, which are followed by the rest of the class. Specific information on tuning various class boats, can usually be obtained by requesting it from the class secretary, with many of them listed in our book.

Basic traditional methods are shown for larger boats. Set rigging with sails removed so tension will be equal on both sides of mast. Unequal settings underway with windward shrouds taut and lee shrouds slack, may produce a single or double mast curve, resulting in dismasting.

Jibstay and backstay on larger mastheaded sailboats, are usually set up with the theory that they cannot be set up too tight. Purpose is to keep the headstay from sagging, increasing backwind potentials of mainsail.

Avoid tension extremes on all kinds of sailboats. If the rigging is too loose, mast will jump around like a pile driver, especially in rough water. If rigging is too tight, it will try to push mast through cabin top, or through bottom of boat. It can also pull up and open planking on wooden boats, or break the mast or rigging, or pull the chain plates out of position on fiberglass hulls.

Many glass boats under 30' were produced with single lower shrouds. In areas of strong wind such as San Francisco, a pumping action developed, also dismastings. Several owners since then have changed to double lower shrouds for their boats, providing better fore and aft support to reduce pumping action and dismastings.

Rigging Tension

a single curve

a hazardous S curve

extreme arc aft

extreme arc forward

snug

snug

tight

STAYS lead fore and aft while SHROUDS lead athwartship to support the mast.

Slack jibstay destroys setting of jib which backwinds mainsail prematurely.

weather shrouds will be tight

Standard sloop rig tension methods are shown above.

Angle of shroud below and above spreader should be equal.

spreader

Droopy spreaders may lead to a dismasting!

Lee shrouds will be slack.

Though much extra work is required, it is better to varnish than paint a wooden mast so you are able to see cracks or strains which may be developing. Except for heavy black anodizing, we prefer to paint aluminum masts with vinyl paint every two years.

jumper stay

standard sloop rigs

tight

lower shroud

single spreader rig

jumpers or jumper strut

jumper stay

upper shroud

slack

lower shroud

masthead sloop rigs

upper spreader

intermediate shroud

lower spreader

tight

slack

medium

double spreader rig

slack

Royce

Wooden masts, standard since the dawn of history, are becoming increasingly scarce, especially those made from evergreens such as fir and spruce, due to the publics yearly demand for Christmas trees. It was predicted by Herreshoff before the turn of the century ... as he tried his best to discourage the use of trees for this purpose.

We were told Vikings grew trees for several centuries to be used for masts. They planted a tree, then shortly afterwards, a circle of trees around it. The circle of trees acted as a wind break to help the center tree grow straighter, also reducing number of lower limbs as the center tree tried to outgrow the trees surrounding it.

What is most interesting, was to find that until the new aluminum mast, no two wooden masts in history were ever supposed to be identical. Advantages of the aluminum mast common today, are standardization which produced predictability ... with controlled flexibility. John Powell of Sparlight Ltd., was the aluminum mast pioneer in large boats, Ian Proctor, the leader in one-design classes.

It was interesting to watch the change in the Snipe class when the Proctor aluminum mast was first tested against Snipe wooden masts. When a puff moved in, the boat with a wooden mast heeled first, then started moving, while those with flexible aluminum masts heeled less, adding more effort to accelerating forward speed. In a stronger wind the slot opened more with the flexible mast, which reduced chance of jib backwinding mainsail.

While both advantages in the aluminum Snipe mast may seem small, a flexible aluminum mast provided the edge, the extra few feet at the finish line separating boats that placed ... and those which also raced.

Major cause for dismasting a couple of feet above the deck is the same for both kinds of masts ... too many screws and fittings in that area, providing a weak spot in the mast. Internal halyard pulleys should be staggered vertically to reduce a weak spot in this area of the mast.

Use carpenters level to check fore & aft trim on your sailboat underway.

Hull Trim

An Int'l 14, a 12 meter, and an 80' ocean racer are floating teeter-totters making fore and aft weight distribution and hull trim more critical than many sailors realize.

Boat should be kept on its fore and aft lines on beat, reach, and run, to present minimal frontal area with minimum hull resistance, going through the water. If stern or bow is down, frontal area increases reducing speed, producing erratic steering action sometimes due to changing bow entry. Check fore & aft trim underway with carpenters level.

Have hull weight trim distribution near center of boat while beating. We trimmed sails on a 25 year old 40' ketch for self steering. A half hour later its 125 lb. owner walked a few feet forward bringing bow down, and pulling bow up into the wind. If he'd walked aft, the bow would raise slightly, and swung further away from the eye of the wind causing lee helm.

Sailing downwind with spinnaker, pg.123, move weight aft to counteract bows downward thrust as wind increases, also to keep bow from digging in on smaller craft. If boat has up/down movement downwind, it may be reduced or dampened by moving weight apart.

Best athwartship trim while beating is _7° to 15° heel_ .... check with inclinometer, & neutral helm. Weight may be shifted slightly to leeward in weak breeze, and moved to windward in strong breeze to maintain the same ideal heel angle. If monohulls heel more, the lee bow wave pressure increases, page 133, increasing weather helm drag which should be kept to minimum for best hull trim weight distribution.

HULL trim vs SAIL trim vs HEEL trim=performance (balance)

115

light wind   medium wind   strong wind

—————————traveler adjust closehauled—————————

Due to twist of material, mainsail should be trimmed half way up sail. 12 meter boom closehauled as result is almost amidship, while dink carries boom over quarter.

Start with reference point on transom to trim boom. In light wind traveler car may be carried upwind increasing airfoil, and to leeward in strong wind flattening mainsail and reducing heel. Downpull of boom by vang may also be used to minimize twist of sail with large roach.

Traveler is normally eased to leeward for reach through run. Tension is increased on vang to reduce sail twist, with depth maintained by easing outhaul and downhaul.

Flexible rig with mid-boom sheet attach, provides built in draft variables. The flexing can provide fuller draft for light winds and rougher water, or flatten main trim for stronger winds and smoother water ... with variables between for a wide range of wind and wave conditions. Shallow draft gennie (pg. 13), excels for closehauled, while the fuller-cut reaching jib is more efficient for a reach.

Masthead rig with end boom attach, uses traveler and vang shown right, to adjust main for varied conditions. Draft can be flattened by using zipper or reef points on foot of sail, and by easing leach line (roach line) pg. 118.

40' sloop "Dolphin" uses loosefooted main for racing. Wide variety of draft conditions are possible using outhaul, and topping lift. This main is restricted to an afternoon race as rules permit only one mainsail for a long distance race.

flat camber
or
flat draft

vang

vang

————— beam reach ————— run

Flexible curvature of sail is called draft or camber.

end boom attach

end and center boom pull

mid-boom attach

rigid boom support

aft traveler

aft traveler

mid-cockpit traveler

take up on topping lift

ease outhaul

full draft

loose-footed main on 40' sloop

slack off topping lift

take in outhaul

flat draft

Foot reef provides ideal adjust for a wide variety of winds. It has full length luff upwind when reefed in, and when let out, has extra area for reaches, runs, and beating in very light winds.

The foot reef * is also called 'Cunningham Reef' differing in purpose from standard reef, see pg.149.

full draft

Harden leach line, bending leach to windward, increasing draft in light wind.

flat draft

Ease leach line in strong wind, so leach trails straight back in upper part of main. It helps reduce heel & resulting weather helm.

foot reef off

foot reef on

(* also called Hooligan Reef)

end boom sheeting

cam cleat

e tensioning hod sewn foot of nsail

full draft

mid-cockpit sheeting

flexible mast

Various methods are shown to change draft of mainsail for various wind and wave conditions.

See March '68 Yachting for the history of the 'Bendy Rig'.

harden in on backstay if class permits

Outhaul, downhaul, bend of mast and boom, absorb fullness to flatten draft as wind increases on flexible rig.

Leach tension is eased automatically, reducing weather helm.

117

1/3

1/2

Draft is further aft in light winds and strong winds. Areas of your sails supposed to provide the maximum amount of upwind airfoil lift have been indicated at left by shaded areas. Major factors involved in closehauled upwind sailing are efficient sail trim and hull balance, 115, 133.

trim jib first ●

Yarn telltales on jib luff are very important when beating, to tell if sail is trimmed correctly, if boat is sailing lower than necessary, or pinching. Sailing below this on a reach, the speed indicator and shroud telltale become primary factors to watch. For broad reach to run, the aft telltale and speed indicator should be checked. . . . if you are to obtain best sail trim for maximum speed.

Numerous adjustments are required to produce the best jib and mainsail shape and trim under a wide variety of wind and wave conditions. In light winds they help to increase draft of the mainsail, or to flatten it in strong winds . . . with a wide variety of sail settings and trim which may be used between the two extremes.

Major consideration as wind increases, is to keep weather helm to a minimum. To accomplish this, the "Daring" uses a saddle to move centerboard aft, while "North Star" pulls the jib stay forward. Leach line is found on some racing sails to cup the leach, increasing draft for light winds. In stronger winds the leach line is slacked, letting upper part of main trail directly aft to reduce heel which causes weather helm, pages 132-135.

The Barber Hauler was invented by the Barber twins of San Diego. It was first used on Lightnings to open wind funnel between sails, for best laminar flow on reach, just above point at which boat was able to carry spinnaker.

Hauler also helps reduce backwinding of main in strong wind. Star has considerable use of the Barber Hauler, to control and adjust the jib trim and resulting wind flow between sails, which is considerably different between light and heavy winds, see page 34.

118   Sailing Illustrated

closehauled

Sail trim and hull balance with minimum rudder drag, major factors closehauled.

Laminar air flow between sails in Lightning, pg. 34.

reaching

Sail shape, rudder trim, major factors for reaching.

Maximum rake of mast aft to reduce weather helm.

light wind full draft adjustments

see pg. 29 for details

Ease clew & tack downhaul.

deck sweeper rigid boom

mast step fwd

Masthead telltale is useful in smooth water, oscillating excessively in wave action.

e aft wind

rake fwd downwind

Extreme mast bend helps to flatten sail.

jumper tension eased

Major advantage of flexible boom is to automatically ease tension of leach as wind increases.

Fluttering leach on main with rigid boom disappears by hardening built—in leach line. If too tight, a cupped leach may result.

Jib luff telltales are major factor sailing closehauled.

strong wind flat draft adjustments

Tack downhaul & clew hardened.

d boom/mast djustments

Watch shroud telltale and speed indicator when reaching.

black nylon yarn

t wind—firm h. Ease as increases.

Boom thrust is adjusted forward to increase mast bend.

cb not raised in Finn Class.

mast step aft

Mast step moved aft induces bend in mast.

strong wind   light wind

harden backstay

flexible boom

vang

10" to 12"

Rudder raised in light wind to reduce drag.

Without saddle, pg. 26, cb is raised as wind increases.

Maximum cb angle can be maintained as wind increases, with saddle pulling cb aft to compensate for weather helm.

119

HULL trim vs SAIL trim vs HEEL trim = PERFORMANCE (same as BALANCE)

vertical

preverter/vang
combination

boom without vang

boom using vang

When sheet can no longer provide vertical pull on boom beyond end of traveler, the boom will lift and the sail twist, spilling useful wind pressure. Boom lift tendency is obvious on monohulls from beam reach to run, and on a reach in stronger winds. The Int'l 14, pg. 26, requires a vang to be used most of the time even when sailing closehauled, with its full roach.

Illustration at right shows extreme twist of main on beam reach without vang. Only the small shaded area provides drive, the remaining confused sail area spilling wind pressure from head to clew to tack due to extreme twist, with sail disturbed by continual movement of boom. A VANG is required to provide vertical pull to stabilize the boom and the boats movement, which increases sail drive because of the additional thrust area.

Mainsail rides on lee shroud downwind in Thistle and FD classes, breaking sail surface into two areas, producing unnecessary chafe. This tendency is minimized by allowing lee shroud lever release shown at right. Plastic tube or bicycle type handle reduces shroud chafe against boom.

PREVENTER is a line leading forward to oppose aft pull of sheet, to prevent an accidental jibe when sailing downwind, pg. 123. We usually prefer a combination preventer/vang shown above and at right, eliminating the need for a person to go forward to set or release a bow preventer.

Sails provide airfoil for upwind sailing drive, and wind cup or bag for sailing downwind with thrust areas shown below. Due to rolling action, outhaul and downhaul are eased to help cup effect, reducing disturbance of wind spilling to either side, pgs. 102-3. Total exposure of sail area is major downwind performance factor.

Backstay tension is slacked, and jumper tension is increased in classes such as Int'l 14, and 5.5, permitting top of mast to move forward, increasing drive and easing helm.

120

Vang limits vertical lift of boom, also producing thrust of boom and gooseneck against the mast. English prefer to use the term kicking strap instead of vang.

Vang downpull on boom improves shape of sail, and efficient vertical trim. Result is maximum drive area with minimum wind pressure spillage.

minimum drive area

ain without vang s considerable ist, spilling nd pressure.

Maximum twist with minimum drive area.

It you want to improve your racing record, it's a good idea to start analyzing your use of the boom vang.

boom lifts

sheet tension only

Minimum twist, large drive area results.

boom downpull

gooseneck thrust

vang

sheet

boom chafe preventer, see pages 31, 46-47 Rake mast forward especially in light wind.

Jumper tension is hardened on some classes such as 5.5 & Int'l 14, especially in light wind to pull mast fwd.

prevang is a combination vang/preventer

gunwale

Lee shroud lever slacked downwind to prevent crease across mainsail.

halyard tension adjust holes

Increase depth by hardening leach line.

tension lever on upwind

Ease outhaul, downhaul, foot reef, for reach and run, to develop depth or cup in center of main.

slack backstay

aft telltale is in free air for sailing downwind

raise cb or db

harden vang

whisker pole

standard preventer

bow

main boom

prevang

down and fwd pull

standard vang midship downpull

main sheet

Total useful sail area is major factor in downwind sailing. Check your sail trim against speed indicator.

121

Check pages 22-56 for specific boat details which vary according to class rules.

Now that's what I call a jibe!

Jibing is as normal a sailing procedure as coming about, yet as our friend above found out the hard way, not all jibes come out as planned. While vang and preventer help reduce potentials of accidental jibe, main factor is skipper awareness to avoid one in the developing stage.

Skipper should be aware of dangers when running before the wind and swells, since rolling and broaching could lead to an accidental jibe. Avoid sailing by the lee in a cb or db boat, see right, which can contribute to jibe with upset. Storms also take unnecessary toll often due to sudden violent winds and windshifts, pages 206-213.

Disturbed wind flow can also cause anxious and some-times humorous moments. If you sail close to high bluffs, steep hills, or tall buildings, sudden wind shifts and/or DOWNDRAFTS may result. Not aware of this we sailed too close to a support pillar of the George Washington Bridge one peaceful afternoon. A knockdown with two accidental jibes resulted... rearranging the furniture.

We expected a drawbridge to open as we approached it near Jones Beach without success, requiring our boat to jibe in a strong wind. The boom jibed... but the top of the mainsail didn't jibe, producing a GOOSEWING jibe. It was necessary to rejibe the boom and make a second try to produce a successful jibe.

When running in light wind you may sometimes find the faster course between two points by tacking downwind. As wind increases, the boat sailing straight downwind may finish earlier than the sailboat tacking downwind.

Spinnaker is a lifting sail, yet pull on mast, sheet, etc., depresses bow, lifting stern. Move weight aft in strong wind to improve rudder control, and to keep bow from 122 digging in... especially critical on centerboard boat.

Spinnaker is a lifting sail, which lifts the stern & depresses the bow.

a HALF jibe

If only lower half of mainsail jibes — the result is a 'goosewing' jibe.

WHA HOPPEN?

LADY HILDA

a 'goosewing' jibe

wind

start

broad reach

running wing & wing

preventer

by the lee

preventer

light breeze-tacking downwind

strong breeze-running downwind

downdraft

vertical whirlpool

port tack

stbd tack

finish

123

The "Sphinx" broke out a triangular sail in 1886 for running. Due to huge size it was called "Sphinx's Acre", slowly changing to todays term spinnaker. It might be described as a large drifter with pole often dragging in the water. Early flat "Sphinnaxer" eventually developed into the lifting parachute spinnaker used today.

Spinnaker development has been rapid in recent years. Basically we start with a full cut chute with wide shoulders limited to running. A flat cut reacher with narrow shoulders may be used from broad reach to a beam reach. A storm chute, similar but smaller without shoulders, reduces oscillation, cause of many spinnaker wraps around jib stay. One design classes permit only one chute, a compromise version with major emphasis on reaching.

The star cut chute fills the awkward area between the reaching spinnaker and the gennie for sailing closehauled as it operates up to a close reach. Some find it useful as a heavy weather chute for running because of its flat cut which reduces oscillation, also its strong construction.

Then enters rapidly changing technology of tonner and twelve meter competition. In the 1974 twelve meter trials, "Intrepid" introduced the new tri-radial as an all purpose chute, out maneuvering "Courageous' which continually lost ground as it had to change reaching and running chutes.

"Courageous" then used the tri-radial in the American Cup Series. This is a complex spinnaker to develop and build. Stresses theoretically fall on the thread lines, loading and unloading throughout the entire chute at the same time.

Loose side of chute is trimmed with sheet, while pole side is trimmed with after guy leading aft from pole, a foreguy leads forward from pole end on most boats over 20'. Pole weight is supported by spinnaker topping lift. Above a broad reach with spinnaker pole well forward, a reaching strut is used to reduce chafe of afterguy against shrouds. After dealing with the spinnaker off and on for twenty years,
124 it can best be describe as an "emotional" sail.

Spinnakers

Sven Salen used the first parachute spinnaker in 1927 on his 'Maybe', helping him win the Seawanhaka Gold Cup. A few months later he introduced the 'Swedish Jib' at a race in Genoa, Italy, nicknamed the genoa jib'.

topping or pole lift

fixed side

spinnaker pole

sheet

foreguy

afterguy

Undisturbed edge on pole side is important.

Reaching strut keeps after guy off shrouds to reduce chafe potential, also to eliminate an abnormal pressure against shrouds.

old fashioned flat spinnaker

1 narrow shoulders — flat cut

reaching spinnaker

2 storm spinnaker is smaller, stronger

3 broad shoulders — full cut

running spinnaker

4 pole carried low, flat cut, small shoulders

star cut—wind forward of the beam

5 diagonal — crosscut bottom

miter head

6 crosscut bottom

radial head

7 all stress loads fall on thread lines

tri-radial

125

sheet
halyard
swivel
pulpit
head
port
stbd
jibstay or headstay
spinnaker bag
spinnaker pole
foreguy
foreguy bridle
older turtle
raise spinnaker BEHIND jib
topping lift
Drop jib after chute is raised.
afterguy
eye on mast
headstay
teflon ring
shock cord
*The starting point to begin trimming spinnaker pole.
apparent wind
foreguy
126 **sheet**
afterguy

For larger sailboats . . .

LIGHT WINDS. Majority of sailboats to 50' set spinnaker flying, by raising it directly from spinnaker bag secured to the pulpit, forward of jibstay or headstay as shown.

STRONG WINDS. Raise chute behind the jib, or set up in STOPS before raising. After chute is up, it opens and fills after tug on sheet and afterguy. This method is important with large spinnakers which may fill part way up, if set flying. Pressure may make it difficult to winch halyard rest of way .. or may pull crew member up the mast,

* * * * * * * * * *

Net is required to reduce chances of chute wrapping around headstay. Two slides are often used, secured to mast with shock cord. This permits slide to ride to top of headstay when gennie is used . . . then drop down as shown by gravity, for spinnaker use. Rope spinnaker net page 128, may also be used.

* * * * * * * * * *

To set spinnaker flying. Rig lines as shown with pole carried to windward side for new tack. When order is given . . . . . .

1, 2. Raise HALYARD and pull back on SHEET simultaneously to reduce wrap.
3. Start winching AFTER GUY aft when chute is about 2/3 up, so pole is parallel with boom, at right angle to apparent wind. Experiment with varied settings as this is just the starting point, due to variables in wind and wave action, kind of boat, etc.

4. Adjust and set TOPPING LIFT.
5. Adjust and set FOREGUY.
6. Adjust SHEET so luff is full without reverse curve or spillage, referred to as 'sailing just above a catastrophe'.

A trained crew goes through this sequence so rapidly a new sailor must watch closely to follow the sequence listed above.

Considerable practice is required to become good friends with a spinnaker. Use a stop watch to check raising, lowering & stowing time so chute is set for next use. Light, medium and heavy sheets and guys, are used for different wind strengths. Light ones are used in light winds to keep chute clews from drooping.

Much practice will be required to perfect spinnaker handling. Have well defined jobs, and stick to basic terminology. Talking should be kept to a minimum when flying spinnakers . . . or expect snafus.

Raise jib to blanket spinnaker. Ease fore-guy, then release tack from foreguy.

pull in sheet

afterguy forward

slack halyard rapidly

pull chute in rapidly

head

stbd

arms length folds

head

port

stbd

nnaker bag   EDELWEISS

Royce

head

If a spinnaker carries too much pressure <u>in a strong wind, slack</u> the <u>spinnaker halyard</u>, and lower the spinnaker pole, to help stabilize steering action of your boat.

* * * * * * * * *

Procedure to take spinnaker down....

1. Change course to blanket spinnaker behind the jib.. spilling wind pressure.
2. Slack AFTER GUY so pole goes forward.
3. Release CHUTE from pole end.
4. Pull in SHEET so CLEW of spinnaker comes into hands of crew.
5. Slack HALYARD as rapidly as crew can stow chute in cockpit, or through hatch or companionway, so it is out of way.

* * * * * * * * *

Correct and careful stowing and resetting of chute is important to eliminate chance of wrap when spinnaker is being raised.

One or two crew members are required to bag the chute underway in a tight cabin. On larger boats two persons do the folding, and a third stuffs the folded material into the spinnaker bag.

Pull both clews together, stuffing foot into the bag with clews hanging over the side. Taking hold of the sides as shown, work up the sides towards the head, till all material is stowed, with the 3 corners outside bag.

Port and starboard clews are folded into the bag, then the head folded over. The top is secured over the spinnaker bags metal ring on top for stowage, or reset on pulpit.

* * * * * * * * *

The spinnaker set in stops can be raised well in advance of time it has to be used.

Tie light cord at regular intervals starting from the clews ... working towards the center, then at regular intervals, toward the head. Position chute in bag same as previous method for stowing and raising.

Precautions must be taken to see crew won't accidentally pull on sheet or after-guy before time to open chute. A large powerboat wake with a resulting rolling motion of sailboat ... may also break the stops prematurely. The chinese fire drills which sometime take place as a result ... often in tight quarters, seem to grow with each telling.

Physically and mentally plan spinnaker action way ahead of time it is raised or dropped.

clew
(free clew)

ring

sheet

twing

bridle

plunger pull

plunger

ring

tack
(fixed clew)

pole end

plunger

fixed
afterguy

twing

running
guy

prone to chafe,
see page 202

sheet

afterguy

foreguy

twing

Some sailors prefer traditional "tack" and "clew" terms for lower corners of spinnaker. The terms "free clew" and "fixed clew" are finding acceptance by many new racing sailors.

spinnaker
rope net

pole lift

bridle

(free clew) clew

tack foreguy

twinger*

(fixed side)

(fixed clew)

tack

foreguy bridl

tack foregu

downhaul
(facing page)

*Twinger pull has to be DOWN not out to be effective.

Double-ended pole, or end-for-end jibing method is used for most boats to 40'. Larg boats may use the dip pole method shown pg. 130. Method shown right, is used for op one-design boats, with pole downhaul coming back to lower part of mast.

Similar jibing method is used on boats to 40', except foreguy must also be changed secured to ring on corner of chute. Foreguy coming to bridle under the pole, elimina this extra operation. Running guy seems used on majority of boats for short races. long ocean races, afterguy is secured to ring on chute, reducing chafe on afterguy.

Discussion of "twing" or "tweaker" will produce varied reactions. We've had considerab luck with it on wide beam monohulls over 30' to make chute trim changes in preferenc to sheet, yet with little luck, on narrow beam hulls. We used a stout shock cord 'twing' on wide deck "Tri Star" pg. 81, providing better trim, also eliminating spinnaker net. Wra potentials are maximum on rolling monohull, running in sloppy seas with puffy wind while multihull beam reduces rolling, minimizing wrap in same conditions. Spinnake net made of rope above has stowage problem, minimized if it is wrapped in a cloth roll

Balance of sailboat carrying spinnaker is critical in all winds, yet most obvious o monohull rolling considerably in strong winds with tendency to bury bow, pg. 123 causing erratic steering action. Steering action may be reduced by moving crew af to level hull under these conditions, see page 115.

When people wander around the deck with spinnaker up, extra rudder compensations are required, reducing boat speed. If twinger & foreguy adjustments may be made fror cockpit in a short race instead of on the foredeck, it may improve your racing record

Double ended or end for end pole jibing method is detailed for smaller boats without foreguy, views shown looking aft.

tack

pole lift or topping lift

ring

continuous plunger pull line

mast track

slider eye

plunger

swivel snap

spinnaker pole
Pole angle to start with is level with water surface, or 90° from mast.

1. Pull plunger at mast end.

2. Push pole to other side of boat.

running guy shown above

3. Secure end to new guy.

4. Jibe main.

Pole downhaul is used on - - - - -

Int'l 14, pg. 25
Thistle, pg. 31
Lightning, pg. 37
Flying Dutchman, pg. 39
Int'l 110, pg. 47
M 20, pg. 63

5. Release end from previous guy.

Starboard tack changing to port tack.

Double-ended pole jibe method is basic for most sailboats. Boat detailed is under 22' with pole downhaul coming aft to bottom of mast, jibing itself. Larger boats have foreguy and twinger changing sides during jibe.

6. Push pole outboard.

7. Fit end into eye, lock plunger. Plunger pin is normally carried on upper side of pole end fitting.

shock cord?

8. Reset new sheet, and new running guy.

tack

shock cord?

Pole lift in some classes is made of shock cord; in other classes, the downhaul instead. When ring is released from spinnaker pole, shock cord elasticity pulls both topping lift and downhaul back to mast, where it is out of the way for windward operation.

running guy (afterguy)

Dip pole method for sailboat 40' or larger, with pole dia. from 4". Steady, well trained crew accustomed to this method should be considered.

stbd

pole lift

socket

hollow spinnaker pole

trip line
stbd outhaul
port "lazy" outhaul

foreguy

afterguy

st'b'd
(tack)

sheet

free side
port (clew)

fixed side

capsule locked in pole

lock inside

capsule lock

locking end

"lazy" outhaul

foreguy

raise topping lift

ease foreguy

Somewhat similar method with pole of smaller dia. may be < used on boats 24' to 36'.

Single ended pole is used having outhauls secured to both ends of spinnaker.

"lazy" outhaul

capsule

spinn
sh

slack topping lift

course of
pole end

jibe main

stbd
outhaul

port
outhaul

Foreguy may be taken in.

Trip line is pulled, releasing stbd capsule pole end, while spinnaker afterguy and sh are released to predetermined amount fi cockpit, marked on both lines.

Foredeck crew hauls on port outhaul. Jus before reaching midship, other crew ease topping lift so pole can clear headstay, pulpi gennie on deck, etc., which often requires t socket fitting on mast to be raised.

After passing headstay, pole is raised by hauling on topping lift, then port outhaul taken in till engaged by locking means. Sheet, foreguy and afterguy are trimmed, while "lazy" outhaul may act as "twinger".

Additional crew on foreguy, can reduce chance of pole flopping around in seaway.

starboard

Terminology with this jibing method is confusing. Commands "Take in port side, and ease starboard", seem to reduce snafu potentials.

capsule

130 sheet
"Lazy" outhaul can double as a "twinger"

trip line
port outhaul
"lazy" stbd outhaul

port

Wind Steering

"twin spinnakers"

raffee

squares'l

ACRILAN "sail" vane floating freely on beam reach

vane shaft

tab shaft

tiller

pendulum tab paddle

Man has dreamed of self-steering mechanisms using only the forces of nature for centuries. Twin jibs dubbed "twin spinnakers" are shown above for trade wind sailing. When boat wanders off course or wind shifts, pressure differential pulls jib sheet, changing course till sheet pressures are again equalized.

While autopilot holds a magnetic course, the wind vane maintains a course with apparent wind felt on a boat underway. Say's Rig is detailed, 2277 Alamo Pintado Road, Solvang, CA 93463.

Suppose you want your boat to sail a beam reach. Put boat on beam reach manually, letting vane point into apparent wind (1) shown at right. When boat is on course and sails trimmed correctly, lift course setting captive pin (2) so clutch link falls down, then (3) put course setting captive pin into desired pin hole. Mechanical clutch linkage in base then locks vane "sail" to tab paddle, to maintain course the boat is on.

While many vane systems have been produced, we detailed Saye's pendulum tab system which is simple, stronger than auxiliary rudder system, also has more power in gale when self steering is most needed. It is easily removed for stowage.

2 manual steering

vane shaft

captive pin out

clutch link up

vane stop

vane crank

vane gear wheel

clutch link

tab crank

trunion

tab shaft

swivel axis

yoke

3 vane steering sail and tab locked together

captive pin engaged

base

keeper wire

adjustable mounting bracket

131

extreme lee
bow pressure

Monohull balance of hulls and sails trimmed for closehauled course is very delicate and continually changing, due to amount of heel with resulting change in immersed shape of hull, see above. Imbalance due to increasing heel can be compensated for with rudder, producing unnecessary drag... or corrected with sail changes, to produce self-steering neutral helm.

A new sailor, depending only on rudder trim corrections for heel, soon finds the rudder produces tremendous drag which reduces boat speed, due to water density being over 800 times that of the air.

Under light conditions closehauled, DOWNWIND lee helm is produced if sloop is only sailed with jib; and UPWIND weather helm, with boat wanting to go up into the wind or into irons, if only sailed with the mainsail up.

(1). Sloop closehauled is carrying gennie for self steering, replaced by a working jib at (2)., as wind strength and heel increases, to still maintain neutral helm.

(3). At considerable heel angle in strong wind, unequal bow pressures and CLR moving forward as result, have increased tendency to force bow up into the wind. It is time to reef main for self steering, to balance boat.

(4). In an April '65 storm in the Catalina Channel moving from a force 6 to 9, our 24' sailboat maintained self-steering neutral helm on reach to close reach, with a working jib for over five hours ... requiring a fishermans reef over most of jib at peak of storm. The tiller was held in place and adjusted, while secured by shock cord. This experience plus endless questions by students prompted our reevaluation of storm operational conditions, especially with the popular, small, wide beam craft.

CLR-hull Center of
Lateral Resistance

CE-sail Center of Effort

mbined CE

CLR — lead

an drawings show boat in
right condition, sails trimmed
idship... with 'lead' between
mbined CE and CLR.

hen boat heels, sails trimmed
rmally, lead disappears and
aft is BALANCED with CE
line with CLR. As wind
creases, CLR moves forward
quiring sail adjustment &/or
trim to be balanced again.

Upwind sail/hull balance is critical
and delicate. IMBALANCE between
the two is corrected with RUDDER
TRIM, producing considerable drag
after rudder angle exceeds 4°-5°.

DOWNWIND
(lee helm)
STABILITY

Imbalance causes
turning moment,
boat wants to turn.

tiller
downwind
(alee)

ce

ce

wind
direction

clr

tremendous
TURNING
moment

tiller upwind
(aweather)

UPWIND STABILITY
(weather helm)

clr

As keel boat heels, water pressure is reduced on
weather bow, and INCREASED on LEE BOW...a
major factor seldom discussed. Imbalance can be
compensated as CLR moves forward, to also move
sail area forward and down at same time.

1 LIGHT BREEZE

ce   gennie

clr

tiller amidship

for fishermans reef see pg.147

3 STRONG WIND

reefed
main

ce

clr

Boat maintains course when
CE/CLR forces are in balance.

Reefed main and
gennie may balance
just as adequately
as full main and
working jib.

2 MEDIUM WIND

ce   working jib

tiller amidship

clr

4 extreme
STORM CONDITIONS

also see pages 146-148

working jib

raise tack
for
drainage
pg.232

extreme lee
bow pressure

ce

Boat may steer it-
self using shock
cord with balanced
CE/CLR, depending
on wave action.

clr 133

not enough heel

balanced helm

excessive heel

inclinometer

heel angle	wind pressure left
10°	-98%
20°	-94%
30°	-87%
40°	-75%
50°	-65%
60°	-50%
70°	-32%
80°	-15%

Many sailboats are designed to have a neutral balanced helm between 7° to 15°. In lighter wind with less heel sailing upwind, boat becomes cranky producing downwind helm. When heel increases beyond ideal angle, underwater shape of hull, pg.132, wants to force it to go up into irons if compensation isn't made. drag — rudder

With too much heel comes a little tiller pressure.... which exerts tremendous rudder pressure, the only way the boat out of balance can fight back. Rudder beyond 5° produces tremendous drag due to water density being over 800 TIMES that of air. This drag reduces boat speed and pointing ability, as well as producing very strong & unnecessary pressure on rudder and its fittings.

When forces are in balance you can trim sails and hull so the boat sails itself. Crew of 60' 10 meter "Branta" prefer tiller to wheel. They watch tiller continually trimming sails for neutral helm. If rudder were lost 'Branta' could sail triangular course relying on sail choice and hull trim. Turns would naturally be wider around buoys without rudder to provide rapid change of course.

wind
low p. lift
high p.

We often hear weather helm helps to provide maximum upwind lift for sailboat going to windward. Due to leeway, water flowing around windward side of keel or board and rudder, helps provide lifting action with balanced helm.

After sail/hull balance, try minute changes with rudder trim, sail trim, weight trim, and adjusting standing rigging while checking against speedometer or other boat of 134 class to find your boats peculiarities for maximum speed.

ler points upwind · into irons

boat wants to head downwind

boat wants to head upwind into irons

tiller points downwind

cessive UPWIND ather helm 'ABILITY

downwind

excessive DOWNWIND lee helm. STABILITY

mast raked too far aft

mast raked too far forward

normal cause-too much heel, or weight too far forward

● normal cause-not enough heel, weight is too far aft

see pg. 97

see pg. 97

main is too large

main is too small

jib is too small

jib is too large

Star opens slot, pages 44-5

Star closes slot

move weight aft

move weight forward

ce

ce

raise board

clr

lower board

clr

ve saddle aft (pgs. 19, 26, 119)

saddle forward

drop jigger

1

2

cb down maximum

combination keel and centerboard method to provide hull/sail balance

raise cb

force 4-5

breeze

FORCE 5, full sail

lower FORCE 6 needs sail reduction

mizzen first

reef mizzen

ease main

See Wind Force Scale definition page 137.

standard keel sailboat

135

The key to racing performance is BALANCE . . . with even minor variations highly critical in competitive one design classes.

After the wind force pressure patterns and variables are understood and applied, the ocean and lake sailors have a useful tool. It makes sailing more fun, easier and safer, as wind changes become obvious in developing stage

Our wind force pressure scale was developed by Admiral Beaufort of the British navy in 1806. His purpose was to first record the rudder action of square riggers in light winds when trying to develop steerageway. At force 5 his square riggers reached hull speed, and above that a reduction in sail area shown at right, was required.

While weather bureau reports wind speed in mph, the sailors primary need is know wave action (RESULTANT) and (CAUSE), wind pressure strength. Once understood it may be applied to a 9' or 190' sailboat.

● Memorizing this scale is easy . . . forces 1-2, ripples; 3-4, waves; 5-6, whitecaps; 7, whitecaps and swells — the small craft warning (see page 139).

This wind pressure scale was developed for use on the open ocean. It is a flexible yardstick with variables that need to be understood for our use. In currents, the wave action will be greater blowing against than with the current, while ground swells also develop wave patterns to be compensated for. '

Suppose a force 6 wind suddenly starts blowing across a smooth stretch of ocean, then several hours later quits abruptly. It takes time in the beginning for the wave action to catch up with the pressure pattern. Afterwards it takes time for the old seas to smoothen out.

On inland lakes where wind pressure has insufficient area to develop this visual ocean pattern, one or two forces are often added. While wave action may be force 5, you have force 7 pressures acting on boat, sails and rigging.

Wind FORCE or pressure scale is probably the most important, yet the least understood item facing the new sailor IF he wants to stay out of trouble.

Wind Pressure

Shown below, to provide accurate admiralty records of time required for voyages as well as wind strengths and storms that were encountered during the voyage.

RIPPLE PATCHES	light air	wind speed 1-3 knots	pressure per sq. ft. .003-.03	bare steerage	**1**
OVERALL RIPPLE PATTERN	light breeze	4-6 knots (4-7) mph	.05-.12	20' to 25' sailboat upwind steerage	**2**
SMALL WAVES 1/2' to 3/4'	gentle breeze	7-10 (8-12)	.16-.33	moving easily, gennie upwind	**3**
LONGER HIGHER WAVES 1'-3'	moderate breeze	11-16 (13-18)	.40-.85	ideal sailing all courses	**4**
FEW WHITECAPS 3'-6'	fresh breeze	17-21 (18-24)	.96-1.4	spirited, change to working jib	**5**
WHITECAPS OVERALL 6'-11'	strong breeze	22-27 (25-31)	1.6-2.4	reef main	**6**
WHITECAPS and SWELLS 11'-17'	small craft advisory	28-33 (32-38)	2.6-3.6	working or storm jib	**7**
HIGHER/ LONGER WAVES blown foam	gale warning	34-40 (39-46)	3.8-5.3	storm jib	**8**
	whole gale	41-47 (47-54)	5.6-7.3	bare poles	**9**
	storm warning	48-55 (55-63)	7.6-10.0		**10**
	violent storm	56-63 (64-73)	10.4-13.2		**11**
	hurricane	OVER 63 knots	OVER 13.2 lbs. per sq. foot		**12**

RIPPLES

WAVES

WHITECAPS

SWELLS & WHITECAPS

CONFUSED WAVE PATTERNS

In 1958 a new type of storm warnings were introduced, that have proven quite successful when correctly used. Of most concern to us is the small craft warning...for vessels under 300', that is calibrated in wind force.

Page 137 covers the cause of wind PRESSURE, with the resultant action upon water. The pressure as you notice, doubles per square foot from force 5 to force 7 .... requiring a reduction of more than half in sail area.

From force 7 to 9, the pressure again doubles. This will not only require another half reduction in sail, but the dynamic action of the water has greatly increased.

Force 12 which originated with square riggers not being able to carry any sail, the axiom still applies as the pressure on the hull, spars, etc., is enough to keep a boat going. In one case we checked, it was sufficient to put an elderly gaff headed sloop without sail on a plane during a white squall. Their only protection was to start dragging anchors to slow the boat down to a safer speed.

One night in an ocean race, we experienced a sudden wind increase from force 6 to 10 or 11; only 3 of 13 entries finished that race. We had a knockdown and were unable to carry any sail. With the engine on, we had excessive sternway & a wild rolling boat without rudder control.

Finally I analyzed the pressure . . . and the high doghouse. Turning the Newporter Ketch beam to wind, it took off like a scared jackrabbit. We later referred to it as a "doghouse reach", a sensation you'd rather read about.

Another time we moored in an open roadstead with a force 5 wind increasing to force 8 after dark. Following the USCG advisory broadcast the next morning . . . the two pennant signal was raised! While the system is good, it is up to the sailor in the final analysis to anticipate stormy weather and protect himself . . . secondly to rely on the storm warning signals. P. S., the new owners hair color changed from black to gray during that wild night.

See page 136 for definitions of Wind Force.

Small Craft
Advisory—
Force 7

~~Fresh~~ Gale*
Warning—
to Force 9

Storm
~~Whole Gale*~~
Warning—
to Force 11
*changed Jan. '68

Hurricane Warning-tropical
cyclone with winds Force 12
and above is forecast for
the area.

red

storm signals for .... daytime .....nighttime

P.S. .... due to lack of space elsewhere, we would like to mention a few causes of head failure which seems a major factor in sailboat sinkings.

Basic parts used in the head have a practical yet limited useful life span. For a boat used year-round, all parts contained in a repair kit should be replaced every two years.

Avoid putting water-resistant facial tissues into the head. We've found they ball up in the overboard valve, permitting water to back into a boat underway. Carry a coat hanger to unplug overboard valve from outside.

A tennis ball should be standard equipment for boats with heads, as it can usually plug bowl opening when everything else fails.   139

0 · WL speed→0.5　　　1.0　1.34⌐ 1.5　surf　2.0　plan

lb/ton pressure →4　10 15　30 60 120 150　180

If hull speed of a light planing hull is exceeded, the boat will lift and increase its speed. A light displacement hull may temporarily reach surfing speeds in the same situation while a heavy displacement monohull may be sailed under if its speed exceeds $1.6\sqrt{\text{waterline length}}$.

— 30' —
— 20' —
— 27' —

←deep trough
little free-
board

wave wave
speed -len.
knots feet

knots	feet
6	20.0
7	27.2
8	35.6
9	45.0
10	55.6
11	67.3
12	80.1
14	109.0
16	142.4
20	222.5
25	347.7
30	500.6

$1.34\sqrt{\text{waterline length}}=\text{max.eff.hull speed}$

Nature made strict limitations for ocean operation, a primary one being HULL SPEED or speed/length ratio. Hull speed of sailboat with 20' waterline is 6 knots. This coincides with 20' wave length speed...going 6 knots.

Increase speed to 7 knots...crest to crest distance is now approx. 27'. Unless boat has tremendous overhangs, a deep TROUGH develops. Without water support, boat may sink lower...and eventually sail under.

Some square riggers may have disappeared being unable to douse sail quick enough in a storm. As speed increased, the hull floated lower...and sailed under.

According to WAVE SPEED SCALE at left, a heavy disp. sailboat requires 220' waterline to maintain efficient 20 knot hull speed.

Wave length/boat-speed scale, has plagued man for centuries in his use of monohull power & sailboat hulls. Todays oceangoing vessels are not only restricted to speeds caused by WAVE trap...but RESISTANCE of water. Most tankers & freighters will seldom exceed 0.7, or liners 1.0 waterline length speed as fuel consumption becomes prohibitive.

As hull speed is reached, a PRESSURE pocket develops UNDER vessel, causing monohull bow/stern wave trap. As wind increases, pressure must be sufficient to lift and plane a light hull, or dig a deep trough and sail heavy vessel under. "Sailing Theory and Practice" by C.A. Marchaj has

140 detailed information on sailboat hull hydrodynamics.

Heavy displacement monohull sailboat speed is limited by its basic hull design with the resulting water resistance. Skin friction is major resistance factor to $0.8\sqrt{wl}$.

0.6 to $0.8\sqrt{wl}$

stern wave   bow wave

Freighters and tankers cruise around $0.6\sqrt{wl}$, moving easily at this speed with minimum fuel consumption. Maximum speed of liners and battleships is about $1.0\sqrt{wl}$, after which friction and wave action produce excessive fuel consumption.

The 'theoretical' maximum efficient hull speed is reached at $1.34\sqrt{\text{Waterline Length}}$. The controlling or limiting force is the bow/stern wave trap.

$1.34\sqrt{wl}$ speed (approx.)

stern wave crest   trough amidship   bow wave crest

Water pressure pocket under hull, produces hydraulic action with bow/stern wave trap as resultant.

The 'Patty Cat II' hull design, pgs. 76-79, practically eliminates water pressure buildup. Wave action is nil at 20 knots.

As speed and wake increases, bow and stern wave pattern moves aft, developing a deep trough between. Stern squats due to minimum water support aft.

$1.5 - 1.6\sqrt{wl}$ speed

Freeboard generally reduced.

stern wave crest   deep trough aft   bow wave crest

pressure pocket

Hydraulic lift results in planing of light craft, after displacement speed has been exceeded.

wake reduced

pressure leakage

The water 'hardens' as resistance increases rapidly with boat speed, providing water lift. Water density providing this hydraulic lift, is approximately 835 times that of air.

hydraulic water lift

Separation point should be sharp to avoid drag!

attack angle

ROYCE 141

PRESSURE TRAP

PRESSURE LIFT

* For additional information on power vessel speed limitations, read 'Naval Architecture of Small Craft' by D. Phillips-Birt.

planes easily   planes later   Cal 25

A.   B.   C.

A. Light sailboats with ample sail area and good bottom support such as Int'l 14, 505, Finn, Thistle, FD, etc., may permit planing speeds to 5.0*, limited by crew experience, condition of equipment, and wave action.

B. Light keel Tempest, Int'l 110, centerboard Lightning, etc., are heavier with less relative sail area, which may produce speeds under normal conditions to 3.0*.

C. We've had our heavy 24' sailboat exceed the bow/stern wave trap on a beam reach, hard on the 10 knot peg for over an hour, which was exhilarating but uncomfortable. Yet we have been able to make the Cal 25 surf easily with little fuss. The Cal 40 was the first of the large ocean racing fleet to surf consistently for long periods in the Transpac to Hawaii. In recent years many large ultra light dinghies up to the 70' 'Merlin' consistently exceed the heavy displacement bow/stern wave trap.

•

Sequence details method to put FD on plane in adequate wind. Keep boat flat and watch jib luff closely so sails are full. Bear off rapidly as speed increases, not to run out of apparent wind moving forward. Weight is important factor to keep boat on planing lines, while vang tension becomes critical to produce a flatter high-speed airfoil.

Another planing method is to have boat on course. As puff hits, pump and/or trim sails rapidly, and if possible catch a good wave to keep bow up and out of front wave ... so bow won't dig in and stop with stern still moving, the cause of broaching, or cartwheeling and boneyarding.

The FD automatically drops off plane while jibing, as it rounds the mark. If you want to drop off a plane earlier when not racing, use the methods shown. Planing methods detailed, are similar for other classes.

* Speed factor refers to $1.34\sqrt{\text{waterline length}}$, pgs. 140, 146.

ACTION—
wind pressure

REACTION—water lift

Monohull Planing

Hydraulic water lift pushes hull to surface of water after displacement speed has been exceeded. Planing action can be accomplished and controlled by method shown below.

s puff approaches, prepare to lane using following factors.

- keep sails full
- have minimum heel
- adjust traveler to match gennie

FD rudder is raised in light wind to reduce parasitic drag. Rudder should be all way down for maximum steering control when planing.

FD methods are shown, which may vary with other classes.

s puff hits —

hike rapidly to keep boat level

bear off or sheet in to keep sails full on apparent wind pulling forward as the boat speed increases

trim vang

Constant sail trimming is all important to keep boat on plane.

Jib luff is critical — watch luff closely!

Bow will be up from 5° to 15°, with heel at minimum.

oat automatically drops off plane rounding nark in race, making jibe easy due to speed.

f you want to drop off plane earlier—

release vang and luff sails by heading into wind till boat drops off plane.... then sheet in again. AVOID luffing up with spinnaker.

or ease vang and sheets

sheet in again

143

jams under pressure!　　can be released
under pressure
jib sheet
main sheet

Quick release cam cleats　should be
standard on cb and db boats, reducing chance of upset.
See various kinds in the SPYGLASS reference book, pg. 30.

CB and DB boats upset when equipment fails, operator doesn't recognize changing weather conditions, or come about too slowly and are caught in irons. After sails fill their forward lift has changed to sideway thrust, and the boat trips over cb (see Big Splash, pg. 37, Dinghy Sail. Illus.).

Boats using boards for leverage stability have inverse ratio to keel boat. Hull form provides more initial stability. After 45°-50° is reached, the centers pass each other, and the boat becomes more stable in upset position. The C of G can be changed if a person puts his weight on the centerboard or daggerboard.

When boat has 90° upset, check crew, then have them lash all floating objects to boat. Slack main halyard, then swim to top of mast. Unshackle head of sail, secure float to main halyard to prevent 180° upset (turning turtle) while sails are being dropped. For wind or current situation it might be advised to drop anchor. After boat is righted PLUG centerboard or daggerboard well ... start bailing.

In 180° upset, check crew, then slack sheets all way. Rig line across bottom of boat, use body as righting lever. Drop sails, plug well, start bailing. Metal daggerboard should be secured to boat after leaving dock, as it can sink in capsize. After salt water upset, hose down metal parts, then dry and wax them to reduce corrosion. Boat may be dismasted during recovery if towed in upset condition, or righted without sheets being released.

The further a keel boat heels, greater effect of keels weight to restrict heeling ... but it can sink if boat fills.

● Movable ballast can hasten upset chances----------
fresh water weighs approx. 8.3 lbs. per gallon; regular
gasoline, 6.6 lbs. per gallon; diesel oil, 7.3 lbs. per gallon.

the Upset

SELF RESCUING Laser, Kite, Finn, Snipe, Lightning, and Pacific Cat may be upset, righted with sails up, and continue race while self bailing.

KNOCKDOWN-slack sheets or drop a sail.

CofB-Center of Buoyancy
CofG-Center of Gravity

righting force

upsetting force

C of B

C of G

C of G

C of B

of G

balancing factor

upsetting factor

90° UPSET
emergency measure

Secure float to main halyard

float is needed to prevent 180° upset

Plug centerboard or daggerboard well before you start bailing!

r sailboats NOT SELF RESCUING-

Lower sails, then use force factors below.

float

Boat will float broadside to wind or current—anchor may be required, see pg. 217.

Secure your metal daggerboard to boat before leaving dock.

180° UPSET-cast off sheets all the way!

force vectors

Righting 20-25' twin hull after upset.

Dismastings may occur if sheets are not released.

inclinometer

UPSET

SAFE RANGE

UPSET

If you are discouraged after an upset... remember that it has happened in the best of sailing families.

Can you use an inclinometer on your boat marked to operational limits by the builder?

Upset potentials multiply if you sail cautiously in strong wind... keep speed up for maneuverability and stability in strong wind

*Heavy disp. hull speed scale based on boats waterline length

1.34 maximum eff. hull speed   *danger zone   surfing planing

```
0            0.5           1.0            1.5          2.0
|----+----+----+----+----+----+----+----+----+----+----|
     lb/ton pressure 4    10   15   30 60  120   150   180
```
water resistance in pounds for each ton of vessel weight

Yawl and sloop sail reduction methods are quite similar.
At force 5 they carry sufficient wind pressure (.96—1.4 lbs.
per sq. ft) to maintain maximum efficient hull speed.

When wind increases it is necessary to reduce sail area
to still maintain same total pressure in sails as before.
If the wind jumps from force 5 to 7, the wind pressure
DOUBLES, requiring sail area reduction to half of #2.
In a sudden temporary puff, use FISHERMANS REEF by
easing or releasing main sheet, also heading higher to
reduce heel producing abnormal upwind helm, pg. 133.

In a sudden violent storm a *heavy displacement sailboat
such as narrow 10 meter, may be sailed under in its own
wave trap... the probable cause of many unexplained
square rigger disappearances, page 140.

Current light to medium displacement wide beam boats
have little chance of being sailed under. When overpowered
past wind pressure to reach hull speed, they may heel
excessively, have equipment failure as the sails try to
go faster than the boat... or temporarily surf or plane
as they exceed the speed trap (see graph above), an
exceptionally rare phenomenon before 1960 in ocean
racing sailboats larger than open one-design craft.

Some of todays glass boats are cranky at surfing speeds,
others under certain conditions are quite efficient. When
instructing off Santa Barbara in '68 on a Cal 25, the wind
suddenly increased from force 5 to a weak 7. The main
was dropped and we returned to the harbor under jib
alone on beam reach never under 10 knots, and often up
to 14 and 15 knots. Conditions were ideal to produce this
wild and wonderful experience to our students who were
not novices, wanting this type of exposure. Larger boats
such as Cal 40, "Windward Passage", "Blackfin", and others
in increasing numbers surf in favorable conditions.

Reefing

SHERMANS REEF
used in sudden
[str]ong wind puff.
[Ea]se or release
[m]ain sheet to reduce
[ex]cessive upwind
[h]elm caused by
[h]eeling, pg. 133.

[Ea]se main sheet,
[h]arden in on
[ji]b sheet

Force 5, main and genny

[f]or #1, see page 135.

Twin headsails (see upper right).

[W]ind force pressure **DOUBLES** when
[th]e wind force changes from 5 to 7,
[7] to 8, etc., requiring **HALF** the total
[sa]il **AREA** to maintain the same
[w]ind pressure on sails required, see
[W]ind Force, pg. 137.

mainsail
first
reef → double
headsails

4

[F]orce 6 at #4. Wind pressure increases by
[h]alf, requiring a 1/3 sail reduction in
[a]rea to maintain similar pressure as
[a]t #2, not to overpower boat and cause
[a]bnormal pressure on sails, hull, rigging.

[F]orce 7 at #5. Wind pressure doubles
[th]at of #2, requiring **HALF** sail area of
[#]2 to maintain same total sail pressure
[a]nd not overpower boat.

mainsail
second
reef → small
jib

5

Reefing method shown below is for a 40
yawl with a 27' waterline to develop a
maximum normal hull speed of 7-8 knots
(see pg. 140). At #2 it is carrying a
force 5 wind with jigger down. As the
wind increases (see pgs. 14, 15) the first
change is to DOUBLE HEADSAILS at #3,
reducing wind flow on lee side of main.

As wind pressure increases, sail area
has to be decreased proportional amount
not to exceed sail pressures of force 5
required for 7 knot hull speed.

Loosefooted storm trysail to take
sting out of jibing, is laced to mast
so sail cannot pull out mast track in
sudden blow. On the other hand it can
only be raised to the first projection
on mast such as lower spreader.

spitfire
jib

6

Both sketches #6 and #7 show yawl riding
to storm sails in force 7 through 9, with
different trysail methods.

Switch track permits main to be lowered
and storm trysail raised immediately.
In rare instances to prevent being
becalmed in deep troughs the sail
below can be raised higher
than at #6.   storm
trysail

7

When overpowered at #6 or #7 on light,
wide beam hulls the next step seems to
be to sail under jib alone, page 133.

If wind still increases and boat cannot
carry any sails, see pages 154 to 157
Also study pages 150 on heave to methods,
and pg. 152, the broach to be avoided.

147

2. clew reef line

tack reef line

5. tie in reef poin

1.

3. halyard marker

cheek block   cleats

4. tack cringle   6. harden downhaul

"Quick Reef" appeared in '68 permitting main to be reefed underway without dropping or using roller reef. 1. Pull clew reef line tight and cleat, raising boom to #2. Drop halyard marker #3 to predetermined point. 4. Snap hook secured to boom through luff eye cringle, or haul down and cleat tack reef line. 5. Tie reef points or zipper shut to secure bunt. 6. Harden downhaul, sheet in main.

First demonstration I saw required 3 seconds to complete. For single 1/3 reef we feel it has no competition. For larger boats or heavier booms, add winch to clew reef line. Aft pull of clew reef line flattens airfoil for strong wind, wire may be sewn into sail across reef area for extra support. Reef lines dead end on other side of boom.

long tacks   short tacks   dinghy

cutter

For long tacks on ketch, it may sail straighter course easier under jib and mizzen, yet for tacking up narrow harbor it may turn easier under main alone. Cutter often operates under inner jib (forestays'l) in storm.

Dinghy has little defense in strong wind. If boom is removed and sailed loosefooted, damage from accidental jibe is reduced. Next step is to slack halyard to reduce sail luff efficiency. Final step is secure sail and mast to bow line and use it as a storm anchor.

peak halyard

Gaff rigged sail can be SCANDALIZED in a strong puff reducing sail area by half. After topping lift is set up, release PEAK halyard 148 (on port). This is a temporary measure only.

lift →

full main

leach earing

2nd reef

1st reef

1/4 to 1/3 reduction– first reef

tiedowns

additional 1/4 to 1/3 reduction– second reef

Practice of tying reef points around bunt instead of tying around boom, was started to prevent chafe on varnished wooden boom.

tack earing

main halyard, stbd side of mast

See pg. 87 for another view of roller reefing gooseneck on aluminum boom shown below.

topping lift

first reef   bunt   slip knot or reef knot

luff earing tiedown

each earing tiedown   regular boom vang   roller reef winch

*main tiedown supports

Standard reef above is tied into sail at dock or mooring before raising. Three sketches above show mainsail area with single reef, and double reef. Details show tiedown method for single reef with slip knots tied around reefed material or bunt. Tie luff lashing through luff earing, next tie leach lashing through leach earing, then secure individual lashings. If a second reef is required, tie a second reef on top of first reef. Raise mainsail, ease topping lift, harden sheets.

When boat is underway and sail reduction is required, topping lift is hardened, mainsail is luffed, halyard is eased and mainsail cranked down around boom like an upside down window shade using a roller reef, steps 2, 3, 4 below. After desired area is reduced, ease topping lift, harden mainsheet so sail fills.

We feel a boat 22' and larger should have standard AND roller reefing. Standard reef can be tied in at dock or mooring before raising, preventing sheet snagging and sail filling prematurely, which may happen if steps 1, 2, 3, and 4 below are used.... this may be hazardous in heavy weather. Roller reef is ideal underway as sail area can be reduced while still up and pulling, without being dropped to apply standard reef. Positive locking roller reef mechanism is required which cannot pull out when coming about, releasing sail accidentally. AVOID boom lift, use topping lift, see pg. 96.

main halyard winch

downhaul

raising main

supports boom   AVOID using boom lift!

LUBRICATE periodically

2 main raised

better leach support in these areas

3 roller reefing main

topping lift supports boom

cranking down main

continuously pull leach aft by hand

main halyard eased

4 roller reef finished, then topping lift is eased

boom vang saddle is required on sail

149

Before stout parachute surface anchors pgs.156-7,160-1, sailboats in storm were forced to run downwind under bare poles towing lengths of chain or hawser as canvas storm anchors were often prone to failure.

The other method was to HEAVE TO, maintaining drifting position with sails and rudder counterbalancing each other. It was common practice making lunch in light to medium weather, or for single handers riding out storm.

Above we see the aft sail which enables lobster boats to go into irons and stay head to wind in wind condition while their operators pick up or replace their lobster pots. The aft sail on a ketch or yawl can also accomplish this by providing upwind helm or directional stability, pg. 97.

Illustrations at right show balancing method combining sail and rudder trim fighting each other. Their purpose, to cancel forward movement of vessel in deep water as it slowly drifts to leeward without coming about.

Practice heaving to in good weather to understand the basic principles involved if it must be used in storm conditions. We enjoy trolling for fish under sail. Main difficulty was learning to heave to on short notice.

Long keel cruising boat pg.152, can heave to and look after itself for long periods of time if need be. This is a wonderful way to ease movement to reduce the noise factor and make the boat more comfortable. Heaving to may cause abnormal rudder pressures so check rudder and fittings periodically for wear or potential failure.

The popular wide-beam light-displacement sailboat with short keel isn't generally able to look after itself in a storm or confused seaway if hove to. It should LAY TO parachute anchor using methods shown pgs. 156-7, 161, 150 providing it is sufficiently offshore to do so.

square rigger is hove to with sails aback to maintain position.

The ancient art of "heaving to" to maintain position in good weather or survive a storm in bad weather is by balancing the sails AGAINST the rudder.

The boat is balanced so that the bow will fall off, then point up a little as the boat gathers headway, and fall off or fall back to original position without coming about.

The reason, is to reduce sailboats speed till it is making little or no headway. The boat is then able to ride up and over the waves off her bow, yielding to them easily so they don't break aboard. It permits her to "roll with the punch".

Try heaving your boat to in good weather to understand the factors involved. First start with jib backed, tiller pointing the other way or to leeward #1.

Now raise the main and rig a preventer so the mainsail acts as a wind vane to help hold boat in this position.

Two masted boats are generally easier to "heave to" due to a wider variety of sail combinations.

Older boats may often be easier to "heave to" because of long keels, see sketch at top of page at left which will resist turning in bad weather, 20,152.

Many of todays glass boats with short keels which are excellent for easy turning in tight harbors are difficult to "heave to" except in conditions which are ideal. Because of the short keel they are too active and can easily be thrown around by wave action in a storm, instead of being able to maintain position by ability to "heave to".

Much of the present edition is devoted to ample coverage of the popular, wide beam, light displacement craft. See following pages for heavy weather operational methods.

Robert Manry has delighted thousands of Americans by sailing his 14 foot "Tinkerbelle" from Falmouth in the U.S. to Falmouth, England.

At night he 'parked' his boat to a canvas bucket with a 150' length of 1/2" nylon. A float with a 15' line was secured to the bucket to keep it from sinking any deeper.

jib is backed

wind direction

tiller to leeward

slowly drifting off to leeward

mainsail pointing into wind

jib is backed

main may rig in

jib in sheet

preventer

tiller to leeward

jib is backed

trysail to leeward

tiller to leeward

rudder is moved

rough riding—
turns too easily

easier riding
resists turnir

Tremendous wind and wave pressure potentials exist in
a seaway. Up and down bouncing, chafing of sheets, gear,
and sails, plus abnormal pressures against rudder and
rudder fittings bear close observation and study.

If headway can be maintained, jog along an easy 2 to 3
knot forward speed to ease action, reducing boat rolling.
It also minimizes chafe which is always present, also
reducing pressures on rudder due to forward motion.

Action won't be as pronounced on long keel cruising boat
above. Popular wide beam light displacement sailboat
with short keel will be much more active in storm. If
latter should heave to, abnormal wave pattern may knock
bow off course. Boat may jibe or come about with tiller
and sails lashed down at worst possible moment, pg.151.

By its very nature light displacement craft wants to go
faster than heavy cruising boat in storm, and must be
slowed down. This type boat is more subject to surface
wave action which is a great safety factor as it allows
boat to roll with punch. On the other hand the lively action
may be more fatiguing on crew, requiring shorter watches.
If waves are short and steep, an upwind course may be
desired as downwind course may present more hazards.

With majority of cases a downwind jetty entrance should
be avoided in considerable wave action. In other instances
a "Mexican Hat" pg. 162, towed behind a sailboat with a
little chain and trip line, may provide sufficient drag to
permit steerage control to enter some jetties without
broaching or other similar problems.

trip line

Mexican Hat

chain

Wave action provides drive downwind, resistance upwind.

1

An easy BALANCED helm is important in good weather . . . yet more important in bad weather to protect the rudder and its fittings, also to not unnecessarily fatigue the helmsman.

(continuation of pg. 147)

If boat can still efficiently carry storm sails, keep boat jogging along moving easily so it is always able to respond to rudder. If the boat points too high, it rapidly loses rudder control at the worst possible time, till it is able to fall off and fill sails to again be able to respond to rudder.

Short watches are best as fatigue can produce bad judgment at critical moment. We recommend Bonine® or Bucladin® (a prescription pill) to avoid seasickness. Avoid pills that make you sleepy . . . and avoid OVER MEDICATION as it is the worst time to fight side effects produced.

2

Avoid sailing a beam reach in cresting wave action as a large wave breaking aboard may roll the boat.

Lightning, Snipe, etc., can broach and upset in smooth water if wind rapidly increases over stern.

BROACH TO. Boat above is sailing downwind with main up . . . out of balance. Boat wants to slew around into wind, catching a wave on the beam and rolling. The boat should have downwind helm, jib only. If steering is difficult and boat still wants to slew around, add drag such as rope, chain, or Turboflow element shown lower left.

3

POOPED—
wave breaking over stern

4

PITCHPOLE—
bow trips digging in, coming down steep wave

Stern may keep going as it pivots around or over bow.

bow stops

Both situations above are product of sailing downwind in a storm. If pooped, stern may slew around beam to wind, producing a broach and roll. Causes are boat going SLOWER than wave speed, or shallow water with steep waves.

PITCHPOLE is often caused by boat going FASTER than wave speed, coming over top of steep wave, and having bow dig in before flotation can lift bow. How far the bow digs in, and if boat is rolled by the next wave depends on situation. The narrow beam deep draft hull seems more prone to bow digging in, pg. 155. Avoid sailing downwind especially in shallow water where vertical development increases.

WAVE ACTION. Try to stay in deep water where waves may look mountainous but boat can often ride them like a duck. As waves move into shallow water they become steeper as they are retarded at their base. When crest to trough ratio is 7 to 1 they break, releasing considerable energy. They are most dangerous at 8 or 9 to 1 ratio just before breaking with steep almost vertical fronts. Read 'Ocean Sciences', Annapolis.

Mariners Library, Rupert Hart-Davis Limited, (London) publishes over 40 books . . . the classics of long distance cruising, heavy weather, etc.

5

7 to 1 or less

crest to crest   trough

breaking crests
steep front

Boat must respond to rudder—don't overly reef. Downwind sailing in storm has many hazards, upwind sailing more protection.

<u>The seaworthy boat</u> is one that will take care of you, after you can no longer take care of the boat. A bottle can ride out the wildest hurricane if the top is sealed, and if the bottle doesn't hit a solid object.

Heavy weather sailboat operation is almost identical. Seal the boat, then keep it in deep water so boat cannot be thrust against solid objects such as a rock, heavy driftwood, a shoreline, etc.

If boat is holed in collision, use sail as shown above, so pressure of water against hole helps seal opening. Before shoring up inside, have everything ready, then shove rapidly into position. If done slowly, inward pressure on sail ceases, with water beginning to flow between sail and hull.

Hull form and keel length is critical in storm as longer keel resists turning, while popular short keel boat can be overly active, fatiguing helmsman. Keep body warm and dry as possible. If you are cold and wet, it drains body heat, which increases mental fatigue, decreasing analytical ability

<u>An ocean boat should always be prepared</u>, so when a storm hits, the boat is ready <u>to take care of itself.</u> Avoid wood screws, bolting everything possible such as cleats, bitts, lifeline supports, etc., with corrosion resistant metals

<u>Shock cord mounts</u> should be provided to secure movable objects, and bunk straps provided to keep you in your bunk in a seaway... also to <u>contain BATTERY</u> in a roll.

It is a good idea to use <u>double clamps</u> on most hoses, or replace clamps periodically, including stainless clamps. Pay special attention to <u>maintenance and care of head</u>... which we feel has been major factor in boat sinkings. The positive action sea cock valves on the head are preferred to gate valves without positive sealing in closed position.

MASTHEAD LIGHT may provide maximum visibility in questionable situation, as deck mounted side and stern lights and vessel silhouette are almost impossible for lookout on large vessel to see looking DOWN at water.

flat areas

wind

Keep jogging along on reach or close reach if possible, with water draining easily under high-tacked jib.

BOW ENTRY is better prepared to take storm, wind and wave action, due to minimum flat surfaces for nature to thrust against.

If broad reach or run are chosen in hurricane, waves have flat areas to thrust against, which can cause dismasting, pitchpoling, etc. Stern is also open to waves breaking and filling cockpit.

In the spring of '64 off Carolina coast, 39' keel/cb yawl "Doubloon" ran under bare poles with winds 60-80 knots. Changing to broad reach, it had a beams end knockdown.

After righting, course was changed 60° to 70° from wind, later experiencing two 360° rolls and one beams end knockdown.

Makeshift sea anchor was then used comprising sails, sailbag, and anchor, to keep bow 50°-60° from wind with 45° desired, mattresses lashed to stern pulpit to help weathercock bow into wind.

A couple of months later owner of "Mambo" purchased a "Para-Anchor" for use in a similar situation. Both boats are practically identical to "Finisterre", pgs. 66-69.

Shallow draft boats are drier and more active, responding faster to surface wave action. Designer/builder Bob Derecktor, Apr. '67 Yachting, pg. 122, states.."..a deep keel boat is more likely to trip on a steep wave and roll over" (see pg. 153). Main cause of "Doubloon" roll probably was to tripping over centerboard in down position.   155

Unsolicited letter from Mambo owner tells first use of "Para'Anchor" in Gulf Stream with winds 40 to 60 knots, with seas probably 25' high. 120' of 1" diameter nylon line, and similar length 5/16" dacron trip line were used.

Main problem was <u>chafe</u> of nylon line going through chock. Owner said only one man was required in heavy seas afterwards to take in "Para-Anchor" with trip line. No knockdowns or 360° rolls experienced by "Doubloon", were encountered by "Mambo" in similar weather.

Within its first year "Para-Anchor" was used by fishing fleets worldwide. After a severe loss of fishing vessels in a '64 typhoon, it was tested by and became standard of the Japanese fishing fleets; also see pages 160-161.

In '69 we tested the "Two Pennant Storm Anchor*". Though only 6' dia. storing size of a pillow, its heavy nylon open weave made minute bleed holes, releasing small streams of water for stability, producing minimal drift. We call it a storm anchor for heavy weather, though it could be broken open in light weather under power.

Traditional iron hoop, canvas storm anchor is shown at right which should be restricted to powerboats providing <u>considerable backwards drift</u> with bow into wind.

Sailboats generally have large rudders only designed for forward motion. Traditional storm anchor may produce excessive sternway tearing rudder loose... or causing abnormal pressures on rudder fittings. <u>Sail craft should consider parachute</u> surface <u>anchors</u> providing minimum drift <u>to protect their rudders</u> under severe conditions.

Bucket makes ideal dinghy anchor going into lee shore through breakers. Secure bucket to bow line so dinghy keeps bow into breakers... without turning sideways, rolling, broaching, or pitchpoling.

*Lissaur Co., 2529 Chambers St., Vernon, CA 90058

Four quart oil can designed to be carried inside a storm anchor is made by Atlantic and Pacific. Oil chosen should spread rapidly... consider light vegetable oil.

STORM anchors for surface use are detailed. The 'Para-Anchor' pgs. 156, 160-1, is also used worldwide for this purpose.

manila rope (minimum strength, mildew prone)

trip line

iron hoop (corrodes easily)

canvas cone (mildew prone)

TRADITIONAL storm anchor with iron hoop and canvas cone permits considerable drift, especially useful for powerboats having large open cockpits and small rudders. Oil dripping from container on bow helps to keep waves from breaking next to boat.

See Jan. '68 Yachting pg. 92, for use of Fenger Type drogue.

oil slick   swivel

The TWO PENNANT Storm Anchor recently developed provided minimum drift, may be a lot more practical for sailboat use as it has much better holding power. Chute has heavy nylon thread with open weave. (Protect chute from suns rays when not in use).

float   trip line

sixteen 1/4" nylon threads

Sailboats have large rudder and rudder fittings having little or no protection when drifting backwards rapidly using traditional storm anchor.* Two Pennant Storm Anchor has a much better bite on waters surface, producing minimum drift to protect rudder and rudder fittings. Bow cleat or bitt must be strong, ample size, and bolted through deck as shown page 190. Chute collapses and is easily taken in with its trip line.

wind direction

pull on bow bitt is considerable

*or heaving to, pgs. 150-1.

Check continually for chafe where anchor goes through the chock.

add swivel

Many kinds of drags (drogues) may be used on sailboat for downwind use when waves otherwise would hit transom causing boat to slew around broadside to waves, producing excessive roll, or 360° roll. Methods used may be overturned dinghy, tire, long rope or chain warps., with distance to drag an important stabilizing factor. Single or double Turboflow element, pgs. 152, 162, with chain and trip line seems worth a try for this use, also entering downwind jetty under sail or power in some situations, pg. 152.

water flowing aft protects rudder

AVOID too much drag!

157

History of the mud hook or bottom anchor requiring thousands of years of development is shown on the facing page. If todays' modern anchors were available centuries ago, world history would have changed tremendously.

DANFORTH and NORTHILL anchors due to tremendous purchase power with light weight have much to recommend in todays use if properly dug in. The PLOW anchor seems to be favored by many of our cruising sailors today. Obtain sizes, specs., from the anchor manufacturers listed.

Paint all of these anchors WHITE so they are easier to see if properly dug in underwater... fouled, or wrapped around a rock, as the gray galvanize finish rapidly disappears as it merges with color of rocks, mud, etc.

Large MUSHROOM is a pivot center for chain to swivel on, as permanent mooring in all but loose sandy bottoms. With sufficient chain and properly dug in.. it has good holding power. Enough chain, scope, etc., required, pg. 167, for hurricane high water, yet must be compromised with local restrictions in New York area. Our only use for the small mushroom is shown page 161, not as an anchor.

Grapnels are used for anchoring in rocky or, coral formations, or to pick up mooring chain in the spring of the year if left in the water year round.

STOCKLESS or Navy type is used on large vessels with purchase depending mostly on WEIGHT. If a ship were shelled(WWI thinking) the vessel could steam out dragging anchor due to its inefficient holding power. Until modern lightweight anchors were produced, the YACHTSMAN anchor was preferred due to light size and easy stowage.

Care should be used to see anchor pin doesn't unwind when anchor line is shackled to anchor. For temporary use, monofilament fishing line is more practical than hemp, wire, etc. To lock pin for permanent use, a punch may be applied to cut the threads which lock the shackle to the pin.

Some anchors don't require stock, others require one to prevent rolling sideways.

DANFORTH anchor, also pg. 162;
Navy lightweight (LWT) anchor.

crown
shank
anti-roll stock
pivoting flukes
add rubber crutch tips

folding
NORTHILL
anchor
crown end
folding stock for stowage
arm
fluke
shank
sharp bill

stockless *swivel*
fluke

Woolsey PLOWRIGHT anchor

(excellent light burying anchors)

For specific information on Danforth and Northill anchors write to Danforth, Portland, Maine 04103; for the Plowright, Woolsey Marine Industries, 201 East 42nd St., New York, New York 10017.

Three anchors shown are excellent for temporary anchoring, while large mushroom is used in many areas for a permanent mooring, pages 166, 167. A good anchor has imitators with varying quality, so check look alikes closely. The shear pin anchor is questionable as we've seen the pins shear too often at the wrong time.

The Danforth is used by many sailors. Danforths' Bob Ogg uses the twelve pound Hi-Tensile for all purpose use on his 64' Huckins, with better strength for weight ratio than their Standard anchor. Large party fishing boats in our area which anchor numerous times daily seem to prefer the Northill.

The plow anchor designed by an Englishman is better known and more widely used in Europe. As more Americans are exposed to it, they are also developing a strong preference for this anchor.

Contact manufacturers above for the best light lunch hook, working anchor, and storm anchor, along with their recommended anchor rode specs., (combination fiber line and chain) for your boat.

Ground tackle term includes anchor, chain, line, shackle assembly.

head
stock
shbone
voting
ikes
grapnel

tripline eye on crown end
stone
5 prongs

killick

early Greek
stock

Roman
stock

the firstanchor

Hawaiian coral hook

stockless, babbitt

mushroom anchor, see pgs. 166-7

head
to 40,000 lbs. on carrier Midway

stockless navy type stows easily in hawse-pipe of large vessel

crown end
arm
shank
stock

After 4000 years Chinese anchor is still used.

old fashioned
wooden stock often used
shank
stock
ring end

yachtsman (Navy term is old fashioned)
key lock
bill
shoulder
arm
crown end
palm of fluke
stock

159

Size of anchor depends on type of boating area. If boat is over 18' in an exposed sailing area, two anchors are preferred. One may be a light lunch hook handled with minimum effort; the other one larger permitting your boat to ride out any kind of expected storm in your area.

Follow anchor lowering procedure shown, yet consider emergency heaving method discussed pgs.162.-3. Carry more than enough anchor line for a strong blow in your area. In many locations it means 15' of heavy chain, with 300' of anchor line. Length is to provide enough scope in shallow area, so anchor will dig in deep and stay.

A 3 or 4 to 1 scope is common for good weather, while in deep water say 600', a 2 to 1 scope is supposedly sufficient also if enough chain is used. The 8 to 1 scope theory often provides wry remarks in our area with 1000' to 3000' depths a short distance off shore. The volume, weight, cost, etc., make the 8 to 1 scope quite impractical.

Are your anchors painted? We've seen white anchors we felt dug in correctly, fouled at depths to 100', yet still visible in clear water. In murky water we've seen white anchors visible to 20', galvanized ones, to 4'. A scuba diving course proved invaluable to check anchors, which might be a good winter project to consider. The training not only proved ideal for this purpose but provided a lot of fun for underwater sight seeing. Friends presented us with an elderly anchor drag alarm. Anchor and weight dragging at same time, actuates battery-powered alarm.

The "Para-Anchor" and "Two Pennant Storm Anchor" were developed and tested by your author as a result of several unpleasant heavy weather experiences on power-boats and sailboats. The 'Para-Anchor' at right is an ideal all-purpose deep-water surface anchor known and used worldwide, pg. 156. While we've found 50' to 75' of anchor line and trip line sufficient for good weather, both lines should be considerably longer for heavy weather use, pages 155-156.

An anchor may be fouled by swinging around her anchor when the wind, tide, or both change direction. A two anchor system may be used to avoid this, page 162.

...p anchor slowly and gently to reduce ...nce of fouling anchor or line in all but ...ergency conditions, see pages 162-3.

...OPE is ratio of anchor rode, page 159, ...d out, to water depth which changes with ... tidal stage.

A scope of 7 or 8 to 1 is usually recommended for storm action in SHALLOW water, while less scope may be sufficient for deeper water.

... l scope may be ...ficient for light ...ather, temporary ...horing.	We often find that a 4 to 1 scope is adequate for many anchoring conditions.	
... holding ...er	1/2 holding power	7 or 8 to 1 scope — maximum holding power — chafe

...e lower end of fiber anchor line to ...uce chafe from sand rocks barnacles.

Heavy chain should be used on anchor end of line to improve anchor digging angle.

← chafe area

...hor line was traditionally called a CABLE, generally 120 fathoms or 720 feet long, named ...anchor to which it belonged as the SHEET cable, Bower cable, etc., on square riggers.

... a buoyed trip line ...n anchoring in a ...ky area. This will ...ke it easier to ...ate anchor if ...ght in rocks.

...loat or plastic bottle

Alarm indicates anchor is dragging.

BRRRRING

If you have to anchor with short scope in rough weather, use as much chain as possible, and/or send weight down anchor line to reduce pull angle on the anchor, also easing shock on anchor line in wave action.

sag (catenary) in line
weight is about half way down anchor line

light line

Traditional name for weight above on anchor line was called 'kellet' or 'sentinel'. Small mushroom anchor is practical for this use.

Check for chafe where the anchor line goes through chock.

float

trip line

anchor line

swivel

24' diameter parachute

...ara-Anchor' is a deep water ...rface anchor for light weather ...nditions as well as riding out ...major storm, pages 155-6.

The rock and roll of a bad anchorage is good to mix martinis, but difficult on tempers. We use ROCKER STOPPERS* ("Mexican hats") with chain, secured to our boat amidship, to reduce the excessive motion. If distance between them is doubled, the motion is again reduced by a half.

A Tahiti ketch entering a Mexican port ahead of a storm, had engine failure just before reaching the jetty. The owner heaved a 5 lb. hi-tensile Danforth which dug in immediately. It saved the boat, while holding for 18 hours with winds 35 to 50 knots, and ground swells often breaking under the stern. P. S., it gave the anchor a bent fluke.

Majority of boats put ashore or sunk in the South Seas, seems due to a minor unexpected engine failure such as the one mentioned. In '66 our engine quit in the breaker line. I heaved our 5 lb. Danforth using double braided anchor line, in a similar manner to our heaving line. The anchor dug in immediately, saving our boat.

A light Danforth ready for heaving in a tight spot, may also save your boat some day, but it requires special practice. As 3 strand has more tendency to kink when heaving, we recommend braided line stowed as discussed on page 186.

We enjoy taking the neighborhood kids fishing. The anchor line is led through the bow chock and back to the jib winch. The anchor is lowered from the cockpit, and raised by cranking it in with the jib winch.

Twin bow anchors can hold a boat in a changeable condition of tidal current or wind, as either anchor will hold the boat. The boat is first anchored bow and stern, then the stern line walked forward and secured to the bow cleat.

*Pastime Prod. Inc., 419 Park Ave. South, New York, NY 10016

162

It is easy to forget to secure the bitter end of the anchor line.

Stories about the 'bitter end' of the anchor line are hilarious ... if they happen to another person.

the bitter end

In an emergency, how far are you able to heave a light high-tensile Danforth anchor?

Use braided line only which has been stowed correctly, page 186.

secure bitter end first

bucket with anchor line

A person should make at least twenty practice throws with the heaving line on page 194, before attempting to heave an anchor. You can throw it farther without chain, or with a minimum amount of chain on the anchor.

For boats without an anchor winch ... if the anchor is difficult to take in due to a wind or tidal current, use the halyard or jib winch which adds leverage to winch in the anchor line.

halyard winch

jib winch

float supporting coiled anchor line

If anchor is stuck under rock, take in anchor line, coil and secure it to a float. Using a second line, tie a bowline around anchor line, letting knot slip down till it encircles anchor shank. Pull in the opposite direction to break anchor loose.

Use line which will not stretch .. AVOID nylon.

163

For the sailor having luxury of ample mooring area, the only problem is to know right moment to point bow of boat into wind so it will stop next to mooring can. Forward inertia will carry boat to stop close enough so crew may grab pickup ring with his hands or with a boat hook.

In crowded areas, sailboat when possible should be luffed up to mooring instead, so if swimmer or other obstacle appears at last moment, the boat may be brought back into control by pulling in sheets. Otherwise the jib has to be backwinded before boat will respond to tiller.

The skipper at right has choice to approach mooring on either beam reach or close reach, the idea being to approach mooring upwind, using the sails as an airbrake at required moment, to stop forward motion. If downwind approach is made in any type of wind, the sails should be lowered to reduce inertia, then drop a BUCKET off stern at last moment to act as a water or hydraulic brake . . . if it is secured to the boat.

Always remember to have constant lookout for any other boats that may intercept your course though they may be temporarily hidden behind another boat.

When going through single moorings, the SAFE side to approach a boat or mooring is on the boats STERN . . while its bow is the DANGEROUS or windward side. If a sudden puff hits, it may blow your boat into the mooring, mooring line, or bow of moored boat. If you are close to its stern, a sudden puff of wind will blow you away from the moored boat; the exception, is a sudden wind shift.

If you have to cross in front of moored craft and your boat can't point high enough to clear it, get as much way on as possible. Now turn into the wind and coast until it is safe to pay off on a tack. This is called SHOOTING, and should not be tried unless your boat can easily clear the obstructions, mooring float and chain. Shooting should be avoided in small light sailboat that has minimum inertia.

164   Sailing   Illustrated

Crowded Mooring

TOO CLOSE TO MOORING LINE

WIND DIRECTION

SHOOTING TOO CLOSE

INSUFFICIENT MOMENTUM

WATCH FOR MOVING BOATS

SHOOTING

THIS ILLUSTRATION GIVES A GENERAL IDEA OF PROBLEMS INVOLVED IN APPROACHING A MOORING OR SAILING THRU A CROWDED ANCHORAGE.

WATCH FOR STERN LINES

Royce

APPROACH MOORING CLOSE HAULED

PICKUP RING

ROUND UP INTO THE WIND

165

Give your permanent mooring serious attention. This is especially important if your area is subjected to winds of hurricane strength and its resulting abnormal tides, and also if your boat can only have a limited amount of area or arc to swing through.

Plan the needs of your mooring on east coast, so that it will be able to take your boat through the above situation, yet still have a little slack left. The combination of high tide and strong winds blowing over a wide expanse of water can make an anchorage difficult. Add a strong current and the situation becomes quite serious.

The mushroom anchor has little holding power when first dropped. Have a rowboat riding to the painter for a week or so for the mushroom to have time to dig in. Since it is basically a pivot instead of anchor, the heavy chain is the mushroom anchors greatest need. If it has adequate chain, the snap of a boats pull will be absorbed by the chain, the mushroom will be most difficult to break out.

A good mushroom anchor in a good holding bottom with adequate heavy chain, is the best boat insurance. Main area to watch for is the painter, and as storm seasons approach, always try to have two painters to a mooring. Examine and replace any worn links, shackles, and pins once a year. Since the pins are able to work loose and set a boat adrift, always wire them, taking into due account the corrosion with eventual breakage of the wire.

Makeshift anchors such as locomotive wheels, chunks of concrete, etc., are wonderful on a calm day. When a storm hits the area, your boat may take that weight for a very expensive ride through a crowded mooring area. The cup shaped mushroom anchor that is properly dug in will be most difficult to break loose . . . IF the boat has sufficient heavy chain with adequate scope, to swivel on.

Hurricane High Water

pennant (painter)
float

Spring Neap Tide
Mean High Water

attach pennant
directly to chain

Chain weighs about 40
times as much as rope
of similar diameter.

scope of
3 to 1

Chain length required is a 3 to 1 scope of water
depth at Mean High Water; if water depth is 20'
the chain should be at least 60' feet long.

swivel

boat length	chain size	anchor weight	pennant length	strength	notes
up to 15	5/16"	100 lbs.	4'	400 lbs.	Anchor weight
16' to 20'	3/8"	150 lbs.	8'	600 lbs.	is increased at
21' to 25'	3/8"	200 lbs.	10'	800 lbs.	the rate of 10 lbs.
30'	1/2"	300 lbs.	10'	1200 lbs.	per foot on boats
35'	1/2"	350 lbs.	10'	1400 lbs.	26' and over.
40'	5/8"	400 lbs.	10'	1600 lbs.	Safe working load
45'	5/8"	450 lbs.	10'	1800 lbs.	of pennant is four
50'	5/8"	500 lbs.	10'	2000 lbs.	times the weight of the anchor used.

Specifications shown above are the MINIMUM standards for the Port of New York,
also including the areas of Western Long Island to Larchmont and Huntington Harbor,
excepting narrow Sheepshead Bay which requires two anchors for each mooring buoy.

Mooring must be raised at intervals not to exceed TWO years, so it can be inspected
for damage from bottom chafing, corrosion, and destructive water conditions.

Authors note: Shackles with screw pins require the eye of the pin to be secured to
the shackle (see page 158) to prevent pin from unwinding. After mooring is in water
a couple of months corrosion generally expands galvanized steel screw pins, also
shrinking the eye of the shackle, making it more difficult for screw pin to unwind.

Periodically check mooring fittings from the surface to five feet below. Corrosion
rate is usually more rapid in this area due to warmer surface temperature and a
larger oxygen content in the water. Stainless fittings are ideal for above the waters
surface use, but they should be AVOIDED at the waters surface and below. Due to
oxygen starvation crevice corrosion may result with stainless shackles, etc., which
is indicated by stress cracks.

167

1. head to wind

2. luffing

On the facing page we see how ideal a three sided dock is for sailboats. Providing it has enough draft for sailboats, it can be approached with wind coming from any direction. At the proper moment a boat can point into the wind, turn on the sail airbrakes, and stop at the dock.

If one or two sides of the dock are blocked, or a boat has to come off and return to a lee dock, it becomes more of a sporting proposition. These variables are covered in the following pages.

When approaching dock or mooring under ideal conditions, the skipper usually has a choice of two approaches. In one he will round up into the wind breaking the airfoil, or putting the boat in irons. This will reduce the inertia so the sailboat will drift up and stop at the desired spot next to dock or mooring. Since the boat is weathercocked into the wind, page 96, all sheets must be slacked.

For the second approach, the mooring or dock will be directly on sailboats course. The airfoil is broken by luffing or slacking off on the sheets. To balance the boat the jib sheet is let fly first, then the main slowly slacked as the boat reduces speed.

In crowded areas it is especially important to keep a boat under control all way by luffing up to a dock or mooring. If a swimmer, boat, or other object has to be avoided, the sheets can be trimmed in for immediate rudder control.

Suppose a sailboat approaches a dock or mooring buoy by turning head to wind, losing inertia and response to rudder. The quickest method to get under way again, is to have crew member back the jib on opposite side to the tack you want to put boat on, see page 95.

THE SAME FLOAT WITH
WIND COMING FROM
DIFFERENT DIRECTIONS.

HEAVIER THE BOAT
THE FURTHER IT
WILL COAST.
(FOREREACH)

SAFE
SAFE DANGER

WIND

SAFE
DANGER DANGER

WIND

SAFE
DANGER SAFE

WIND

SAILBOAT HAS TO HAVE
SUFFICIENT HEADWAY TO
ROUND UP INTO WIND
AND COAST TO A STOP
AT THE DOCK, USING THE
WIND AS A BRAKE.

Royce

SAFE
SAFE SAFE

WIND

169

The lee dock has many variables to be considered all the way from methods to approach it, and the individual response of a boat due to weight and hull design.

In the first situation a sloop has to sail into a downwind dock. The main is the first sail lowered some way out, followed by the jib to keep it weathercocked on downwind course. Enough steerageway must be maintained so boat will respond to rudder all way into slip. The boat is then stopped by dropping a bucket off the stern to provide a momentary hydraulic water brake.

In the second situation a sailboat rounds up head to wind with jib lowered first, followed by main. A bucket is dropped over bow, so boat will slowly drift backwards stern to dock. The galvanized iron bucket with a stout handle is recommended for both situations, instead of a weak canvas bucket, or a small storm anchor that only has a purchase on the water in heavy weather.

The third method of anchoring and backing into an adverse dock has a lot to be recommended if you want to go sailing shortly, and the anchor doesn't foul or drag during this maneuver.

While variables exist on facing page due to hull inertia and design, it becomes even more obvious stopping in tight downwind slip at left.

Under normal conditions a light 14' sailboat may sail into the slip, stopping boat at last moment by suddenly turning the bow 180°. This kills its minimum inertia & the boat suddenly stops.

A heavy keel boat same size or larger on the same course usually approaches same dock with bare poles Lower main first, later jib to weather-cock boat downwind. The craft is then stopped in slip by suddenly turning the bow 180°.

DROP JIB

DROP MAIN

DROP BUCKET OR BUCKETS

HYDRAULIC (WATER) BRAKES STOPS BOAT IN SLIP.

WIND

BACKING INTO A DOCK. A BUCKET CAN SLOW THE DRIFTING AND KEEP THE BOW POINTED UPWIND.

WIND

DROPPING AN ANCHOR AND BACKING INTO AN ADVERSE DOCK.

Royce

WIND

171

With the wind straight on to a one sided dock, about the best way to leave it is kedge out, raise sails, raise anchor, back jib and sail away.

On a three sided dock with ample sailing water, the same sailboat can be towed by hand to either side, sails raised, and the boat sailed away.

If the wind is coming directly off the dock, or on the sailboats quarter, you have to weathercock boat, page 96, from the bow. This means that it will be sailed from the dock under jib. Out a ways the boat rounds up into wind, main is raised, then sailed away.

Especially when encountering a lee dock to be sailed from, study the existing cleats, buoys, etc., that if used correctly will take you away from dock with minimum fuss. Quite often by towing a boat to another cleat, or turning it around with spring lines, lee dock problems may be eliminated. A heaving line requires little space can be used as a lead line to test depth, & provide method to take sailboat from lee dock across into windward dock.

To be sure the tack a catboat will take when leaving a dock or mooring, back the mainsail to opposite side. This unbalanced force will shove bow out. Approaching a dock from a downwind course provides a couple outstanding variables. In a light racing hull such as the Finn, the daggerboard must be down for it to round up and stop at the dock. A heavy cruising cat on same course, may raise centerboard, pivot 180° so boat will settle right up to dock . . . due to different inertia and hull design.

Slip lines may prove to advantage for pivots, etc., to take a sailboat out from a lee dock under power or sail, or to pivot boat at dock by hand. While slip lines have many uses, they should not have knots or other increased dia. at end that might catch in a cleat, causing more than a normal share of undocking comedy.

UNDER MOST CONDITIONS A SMALL BOAT CAN PADDLE OUT OR SAIL OFF A LEE DOCK WITH MAINSAIL.

Leave Lee Dock

This is a DOWNWIND leeward dock.

KEDGING OUT FROM AN ADVERSE DOCK.

WIND

This is an UPWIND windward dock.

WIND

USE ONLY JIB WHEN LEAVING A DOCK DOWN WIND. HOIST MAIN LATER WHEN YOU CAN POINT INTO THE WIND.

BOW LINE

WIND

BACKWIND THE JIB, CAST OFF BOW LINE AND PUSH OFF WITH A BOATHOOK.

QUARTER OR STERN PIVOT.

Royce 173

1. Bow line, 2. stern line; 3. after bow spring, 4. forward stern spring.

The bow line leads forward from the boats bow to the dock; a stern line from the stern or aft quarter to the dock.

Spring lines are used that lead forward from the stern, or aft from the bow. Purpose of these are to reduce fore and aft movement of boat at dock without strapping boat too close to dock. Another advantage of spring lines, is to act as pivots for turning a boat at the dock by hand, under sail, or under power.

shock cord

Our first sailboat was too active at its mooring, especially in a tidal current. In many conditions it wanted to climb up and over the float. While it damaged the paint, the continual banging and clanging through the night was hardly pleasant.

Our first attempt to drop a bucket over the stern worked with great success for two nights keeping the boat off the mooring float. The pressures soon pulled the cleat out of the deck, the bucket disappeared, and we were back where we started... banging against the metal float.

A temporary bowsprit or holdoff pole lashed to your boat, with a shock cord extending from its outer end to the mooring can, is a practical method to eliminate the problem. Since it sticks out beyond the buoy, it stands a good chance of being hit and/or broken by another boat. This practice may be reduced by carving a rather sharp point on the outer end of the temporary bowsprit or pole.

About the only disagreeable aspect of the holdoff pole, is that it usually goes overboard when you cast off from the mooring. If not picked up for a couple of weeks, it may collect a considerable barnacle and grass growth if it has not had a coating of bottom paint.

short dock   stern in   bow in

174

boat, dock markers | midship dock line

After adjustment, add permanent markings.

Sailing through tight mooring areas may become quite challenging. If a person isn't adequately trained, it may also be expensive since he is self convicted, if his boat underway collides with another that is moored.

It is easier to go through sailboats swinging to single moorings than double moorings. Since the moored sailboat

dangerous

wind

safer side →

will point into the wind or current whichever is stronger, the safest side to pass is usually under its stern.

If a sudden wind puff hits, it should blow your boat away from the moored ones stern. If you were passing near the bow or danger side, a sudden wind puff might lay your boat over right into the moored one.

Another factor to consider, is that sailboats and power boats do not always lay the same to a mooring. A sailboat with more wetted area usually swings to the current while a nearby powerboat with more windage and less bottom area, may swing with the wind and be more restless.

In areas having little mooring space, boats often have to tie up between double moorings. Instead of sailing under the stern of these, you sail between the mooring buoy lanes. Again you have to sail closer to the windward one than the leeward, to protect your boat in a sudden wind puff.

While sailing through tight anchorages, you also have to take into account the wind variables. In a light wind on a centerboard boat with little way on, you must stay farther away from moored boats than in a stronger steady breeze.

Our boat above has three sets of docklines mounted on both sides of boat, which are a great aid while instructing students in docking under a wide variety of conditions. Markers on boat and dock make it easier to position a boat having a short dock or slip, such as shown above. 175

torque tilt	prop wash tilt
stern walks to stbd RH prop	pivot
forward	reverse
Maximum flow across rudder, maximum steering response.	Minimum flow past rudder, minimum steering response.

Especially when accelerating, a boat doesn't track straight ahead. RH prop _walks stern to stbd_, pulling bow to port, note hull pivot. Compensate, correct with rudder.

When accelerating in reverse with minimum flow across rudder, the major factor is rotary prop wash pushing up against stbd hull bottom depressing port side, producing list which _pulls stern to port_, bow to starboard.

Back your boat for 100 yards. After reaching speed in reverse, inertia overcomes prop wash forces. Port stern pull may temporarily reverse or neutralize itself. For a sailboat steering with rudder, RH prop on outboard motor locked so motor won't turn, it also follows inboard pattern.

LH prop produces opposite stern walking/pulling factors. Offset and folding racing props are more individualized and complicated to understand.

Boat left is using _bow pivot_ line to pull stern out from dock to compensate for stbd prop wash. Bow line is slipped when stern is far enough out from dock.

Off center stern pivot line may be used to walk stern around dock. Pull line in rapidly when slipped not to foul prop. Use forward spurts till dock is cleared to minimize fwd stbd stern walking potential when accelerating.

RH prop peculiarities are detailed, LH prop factors are opposite.

Single Screw

boat-forward

prop-reverse

stern-walks to port especially **when accelerating**

boat-reverse

prop-forward

stern-may swing to stbd if wind or current isn't present

▲ <u>Expect</u> walking/pulling <u>variables</u> due to weight, hull underbody, size of propeller, windage, current, etc.

boat-forward

prop-reverse

rudder-to port

stern-first stbd, then rapidly to port.

boat-reverse

prop-forward

stern-rapidly to stbd, bow may hit the dock

Approach slowly with less angle to dock

boat-forward

prop-reverse

stern-to port, straighten out with short bursts fwd throttle

boat-reverse

prop-forward then reverse

stern-rapidly to port

bow-rapidly to stbd, bow may hit dock

Boat/prop in reverse-stern only to port, bow to starboard.

Boat below is backing out long slip. Stern pulls to port in reverse. Counteract with short sudden burst of forward swinging stern to stbd. Then reverse again, drift out in neutral. While boat is still backing, use rudder, prop forward to pivot boat in short turning radius.

Carbon Monoxide

The average person living in modern society has been exposed to more carbon monoxide than he realizes due to theoretical training in high school physics that carbon monoxide is tasteless, colorless, and odorless.

Develop a positive attitude that you will recognize the smell of exhaust fumes coming from all gasoline engines. This is the smell from partially burned hydrocarbons. Any time you are able to smell these fumes...carbon monoxide is also present inside a garage, car, boat, or plane.

You have to be continually on guard for this deadly, sweet, gentle, numbing, mind crippler, as its awareness will only last a short time before the scent organ loses its sensitivity.

Carbon monoxide is a DEOXIDIZER since it is absorbed into the blood stream to 250 times faster and easier than oxygen. It unites with the hemoglobin in the blood... to prevent oxygen from going to the skin tissues.

SYMPTOMS. If you wake up with a 5 martini hangover yet you haven't had an alcoholic drink for several days, check for carbon monoxide. If your boat is underway and you feel like you have had a stiff drink, are drowsy, or irritable, yet the strongest drink you've had is coffee, check right away for the carbon monoxide source.

As a victim becomes sleepy, he may have a red face, headache, dizziness, and loss of balance or vertigo. As he becomes sleepy the heart may pound or flutter, and the oxygen starvation may soon cause irreversible damage to the brain. A person may be confused or incoherent in the early stages, similar to drinking too much alcoholic beverages.

upwind

boat cover

downwind

Powerboat carbon monoxide problems are shown as they are similar, yet more obvious than on a sailboat. When you smell these gasoline exhaust fumes in a cabin going upwind, open a forward hatch, or if downwind, stay out of the cabin. Check for the source such as exhaust clamps, hoses, and manifold leaks.

If you have had a bout with carbon monoxide, blood transfusions may help, but be sure none of the donors have hepatitus, making it worse.

DIESEL engines produce unpleasant fumes, yet no carbon monoxide. The proof... only diesel engines are permitted deep in mines. Though they use up precious oxygen, carbon monoxide exhausts for miners in confined areas aren't classed as a health hazard.

The 4 cycle low-performance sailboat engine operating at displacement speeds may operate almost troublefree for many years if it is adequately understood and properly maintained.

As compression isn't critical in the 18 to 40 hp engine, the 35' sailboat above normally uses a 25 hp engine, they are able to operate on lower octane fuel than needed for many autos. The main problems though are sporatic operation, and then often at full throttle for long periods, is that of fuel storage, and condensation inside the tanks, especially if stored out of the water during the winter months. Check with your dealer, engine manufacturer, and refiner, for the latest products to be used in this rapidly changing field.

The schematic shows a diesel engine exhaust system for a 40' sailboat. When flanges are used, it is necessary to make a BYPASS to carry water from one water jacket chamber to the next. Exhaust gases rise in the muffler while water is sprayed into the exhaust chamber through a series of holes or orifices. The engine water and exhaust gases finally combine to drain overboard.

The sailboat engine often operates cold, sometimes under 135°, using the free flowing outside water cooling source, without causing boiler scale to precipitate in the water passages, which can build up, strangle, and cause severe overheating in raw outside cooling water with thermostat temperatures above 150°.

Since the low water cooling temperature also causes insufficient heat to boil off oil contaminents of sulfur, condensation, and sludge, more frequent oil changes are required to reduce sulfuric acid, a product of sulfur and water.

The full length DRIP PAN is seldom found on inboard power boats, is a commendable item to keep a clean bilge. They are often found on ocean-going sailboats requiring clean bilges for food and storage on a long race or cruise.

The 7 1/2 hp long-shaft "aluminum spinnaker" installed in the aft lazarette of our "Pink Cloud" required much time to install, proving more practical than we had anticipated.

The motor is seldom used during instruction, except if the wind goes down. On trips to Catalina over 26 miles away, we call our boat a motor sailer, as the motor is used about half the time if we are to follow a schedule.

A plate form-fitted to the outboard motor, is bolted to the top of the outboard well to seal off the compartment from ocean water. We wish outboard manufacturers had templates showing contour of outboard at this intersection.

Correct fuel is important for 2 cycle operation. We use a good premix outboard fuel and run it out of carburetor after use, so motor starts with a couple of pulls.

Ventilation of the closed compartment is important to pass USCG requirements. Ventilation is also required to retard corrosion rate on bottom of metal outboard fuel tanks, detailed at right. Frame on platform restricts horizontal movement of tank, while stout shock cord restricts up and down movement in a seaway.

Maintenance of our motor left in the water year-round is rather easy. It has a yearly tuneup and the water pump is replaced yearly. Check grease level in lower end occasionally, and lubricate exposed connections often with WD-40®. Three or four times a year an organic bottom paint (TBTO) is painted on the immersed portion of the outboard motor to retard ocean growth which is quite rapid . . . AVOID corrosive copper bottom paints.

We feel a 7 1/2 hp long-shaft motor most adequate for our sailboat. Due to the extra 5" shaft length, the prop stays submerged even in considerable seas. When towing a heavy 28' powerboat with engine failure, we had about a knot loss in speed while towing it both with sail and outboard power.

air intake vent

exhaust vent

RUN
OFF
kill button stops motor

idle exhaust

organic bottom paint

neutral
forward
reverse
warmup lever

Single lever controls both shift and throttle.

It is a good idea to AVOID most bottom paints containing copper and mercury, as abnormal corrosion may occur on lower unit in areas where painted surface has been scraped and/or damaged.

Air vents reduce condensation corrosion on bottom of fuel tank.

forward

drainage

drainage

Water drains FROM powerhead above,
while at right water in cooling system may drain back INTO powerhead, causing expensive corrosion damage to crankshaft, bearing, cylinders, etc.

Outboard motor at top is enclosed and protected in aft engine compartment, see page 61.

Outboard mounted on a bracket at right may be swamped in rough water, with stern mount at left a lot more practical.

For more information on outboard motors, see Royce's 'TrailerBoating Illustrated'

Much information in the present edition resulted from our full-day year-round sailing lessons offered locally since 1960. Basically they serve a wide variety of needs as no two groups of sailors desire the same kind of information.

These sailing sessions permit us to enjoy the stimulating and fun-filled company of new sailors, as well as an excuse to go sailing. Majority of customers are from our area, several from the northern part of the state, and especially during the winter months we enjoy the company of many out of state sailors temporarily fleeing the cold and snow.

The new crew comes aboard 'Pink Cloud' from 8 to 9 a.m. With a silent prayer to the wind gods, we cast off from the dock. The boat is underway with customers filling in the workbook language and terms... while they also ask various specialized questions they may have.

Before noon we enter the ocean with students handling the boat for the rest of the day. The next two hours they try to hold a closehauled course which takes considerable practice.

We return to the harbor afterwards with the rest of the day spent sailing upwind through the harbor and moorings. Several attempts are made to stop at a mooring, usually followed by several tries to stop at various docks. Eventually we return to our dock with students making most of the landings. After a brief idea session, our tired but happy (we hope) customers leave for home.

Many customers feel a day instruction ample, while others spend two or more days, depending on the amount of specific information they may desire.

This information is provided to give our readers a better idea of how our continual sail instruction forces us to seek new ideas and better methods to benefit our students, also providing vital research information for our book.

Our major interest is to see sailing in the eyes of our customers who may want a 14' sailboat, a 24-30' weekender, a 40' cruising sailboat, a catamaran or a trimaran. Most sailing sessions are conducted on our boat, yet we also teach on other boats, helping to provide us with a wide and continually varying year-round exposure to sailing.

The flexible sail triangle of man, nature, and machinery, is always with us. The weather is usually kind, though at times, difficult. Yet lessons are seldom cancelled except for rain or lack of wind. Two days before writing this page we had a family aboard, overly concerned with the 'hazards' of boating safety. The wind increased till in the early afternoon we had a double reef.. yet still taking quite a few 30°−40° knockdowns. To our happy surprise . . . they found this type of sailing ideally suited for the type of family recreation they had been seeking.

Our normal concern is to hope for a little more wind, though we find the training to keep a sailboat sailing itself under very light conditions . . . providing a much better foundation for heavy weather sailing than if the winds are strong.

●

Enthusiasm and stimulation of our sailing customers seem endless. This kind of instruction is so much fun that it is often with regret we find our sailing day coming to an end. 183

fibers | yarns right lay | strands left lay | rope right lay | cable left lay

end, fall

bight

overhand loop

overhand knot

standing part

underhand loop

figure 8

The navy defines ROPE as wire rope, LINE as fiber rope. Our sailing fraternity defines rope as becoming line only when used in boat operation including standing and running rigging, anchor line, etc., and rope when used to secure an object. See glossary pg. G25 for square rigger rope terms.

SYNTHETIC vs ORGANIC rope. Many changes have taken place since our book was first published. Synthetic rope obsoleted manila having more resistance to the elements, with greater strength for the same diameter rope.

Three strand nylon became popular for anchor lines, yet chafed easily and became brittle when subjected to the suns rays. Its elasticity proved a disadvantage for towing, and even hazardous when taking in anchor during storm.

During continuous testing of boating products we found BRAIDED rope equal and superior to three strand nylon in all areas except waist lifeline, pg. 229. Braided line is also easier on hands for sheets and halyards than three strand Dacron or polypropylene.

● Best photographic book of three strand knots and splicing we've found is "The Art of Knotting and Splicing" by Cyrus Day, pub. by U. S. Naval Institute, Baltimore, Md. 21402.

● For 1819 knots, splicing, gaskets, mats, blocks, tackles, and other methods, extremely well illustrated to fully rig and operate square riggers is "Lever's Young Sea Officers Sheet Anchor", Sweetman Co., Box 1509, Largo, Florida 33540.

184

Strength shown is new rope under test conditions.

diameter metric	inches	traditional 3 strand manila	controlled stretch 3 strand nylon	controlled stretch braided Gold-N-Braid	minimum stretch 3 strand Dacron & polypro	minimum stretch braided Yacht Braid	galvanized chain
6mm	1/4	600	1850	2100	1750	2300	2700
8mm	5/16	1000	2850	3500	2650	3450	3700
9mm	3/8	1350	4000	4800	3600	4950	4600
.5mm	7/16	1750	5500	6500	4800	6600	6200
12mm	1/2	2650	7100	8300	6100	8600	8200
14mm	9/16	3400	8350	11200	7400	11700	10200
16mm	5/8	4400	10500	14500	9000	15200	12500
18mm	3/4	5400	14200	18000	12500	19100	17700
22mm	7/8	7700	19000	26500	16000	28300	24000
24mm	1"	9000	24600	31300	20000	33600	31000

Braided rope strength provided by Samson Ocean Systems, Inc.; variables exist with 3 strand rope specifications.

Rope and chain strength table listed above is "minimum" or lowest tension under which it may break at any given point, exclusive of damage from chafe, sharp edges, etc.

The safe working load of rope is computed with a safety factor of 5 to 1, providing maximum security where life and property are involved. A rope with a safe working load of 2000 pounds without chafe should require one with a ratio on the above table of 10,000 pounds or more.

This large safety factor is recommended by rope manufacturers due to unusual conditions of extreme wind and wave action, sudden jerks, or strains your boat may be exposed to from time to time.

While chafe such as a dock line going through a small chock with sharp edges will rapidly reduce its operational strength, pg. 188, the safety factor may also be reduced to 80-85% by an eye splice...and to 50% with a square knot with compression and shearing action. A bowline on braided rope may reduce rope strength to 70%, and to 60% with a bowline on 3 strand.

The cost of quality synthetic rope increases daily, yet it is still a bargain in strength, chafe resistance, and long life, if compared to manila rope which was the standard in 1960.

high points

chafe areas

minimum bearing surfaces

continuous bearing surface

Nylon rope is three times stronger than Manila which deteriorates rapidly, losing strength in boating use. _Braided_ rope is up to 15% _stronger_ than three strand synthetic rope of same diameter, varying with rope size.

Rope diameter shrinks as it stretches. At about 50% stretch 3 strand nylon may part, a hazard as end snaps back under load. A cleat pulled out under tow, snapping back to kill Coast Guard operator providing rescue tow service. Braided rope has _30% less stretch_, reducing snapback in same situation, making it easier to tow another boat.

More time is required to know if anchor has dug in with 3 strand anchor line. 'Rubber band' action makes anchor difficult to break out in storm, or if caught under log it may fly back towards boat when suddenly released.

A major surprise came when testing 3 strand and braided anchor line. HIGH POINTS of 3 strand chafed rapidly against rocks, coral, chocks, breaking threads, reducing strength from minimum bearing surface. _Resistance to abrasion_ of Samson Gold-N-Braid was surprising.

Age hardening is a factor to analyze when buying rope. We've seen imported synthetic rope which hardened and became brittle in two years, yet after considerable use Samson Braid still seems to have excellent flexibility... though both may look the same at boat shows when new.

Braided Dacron is preferred to 3 strand Dacron for sheets and halyards with longer life, easier on hands, 50% better gripping surface on sheaves, plus stronger for same dia.

Avoid coiling braided anchor line like 3 strand due to NEUTRAL LAY. We drop our 300' 7/16" braided anchor line into a plastic bucket to avoid hitches.
We store another anchor line in a nylon sail bag with GROMMETS added for ventilation and drainage when stowed wet, also useful for storing wet storm

186 anchors, pages 156-7.

drains beneath   grommets

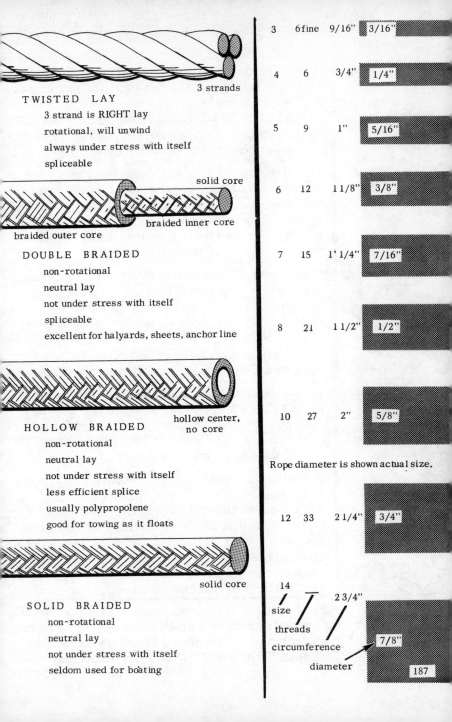

TWISTED LAY

3 strand is RIGHT lay

rotational, will unwind

always under stress with itself

spliceable

DOUBLE BRAIDED

non-rotational

neutral lay

not under stress with itself

spliceable

excellent for halyards, sheets, anchor line

HOLLOW BRAIDED

non-rotational

neutral lay

not under stress with itself

less efficient splice

usually polypropolene

good for towing as it floats

SOLID BRAIDED

non-rotational

neutral lay

not under stress with itself

seldom used for boating

3	6 fine	9/16"	3/16"
4	6	3/4"	1/4"
5	9	1"	5/16"
6	12	1 1/8"	3/8"
7	15	1' 1/4"	7/16"
8	21	1 1/2"	1/2"
10	27	2"	5/8"

Rope diameter is shown actual size.

| 12 | 33 | 2 1/4" | 3/4" |
| 14 | | 2 3/4" | 7/8" |

size

threads

circumference

diameter

187

tremendous
chafe..
AVOID!

skene
chock

leather gives
maximum
protection

Take braided rope from freely moving spool letting it fall into container pg. 186, so neutral lay will be maintained without kinks. Three strand rope is removed from coil by pulling inside end. Failure to do this, and coil three strand rope clockwise, will result in kinks.

Razors, knives....and <u>small chocks,</u> are basically <u>cutting wedges.</u> Too many boats are lost at anchor or at the dock when the anchor line or dock lines have been chafed and cut through as a result of wind and wave action...setting the boats adrift.

Good rope is expensive. With normal care it may have a long useful life. If sharp edges are present for it to rub or chafe against, the useful life may be shortened considerably. Manila chafes easily especially if wet, while nylon has more chafe resistance. Braided rope has considerable resistance to chafe.

Adequate size skene chock lower left, of a larger size than first considered will not only reduce chafe action, but it will also help to prevent dock and anchor lines from jumping out of the chock in wave action.

A manila dinghy painter chafed, breaking twice in three days on a vacation. After resplicing, area was wrapped with <u>plastic</u> electricians <u>tape.</u> Very little chafe was evident at the same spot when we returned to the dock two weeks afterwards. We recommend you tape the eye and first two feet of anchor line, to extend its useful life and maximum strength, pg. 186.

First practical dock line chafe kits we've seen with sized/punched leathers, needle, thread, are manufactured by Svendsen Products, Box 1465, Torrance, Calif., 90505. They are excellent!

The fishermans knot is used to join fishline, twine, and small rope.

The sheet bend is used to join light and medium ropes.

The double sheet bend is used to join light to heavy ropes...

while the fisherman's bend is used to tie a rope to a ring.

Seizing may be required.

The carrick bend is used to join heavy ropes, hawsers, and cables.

Rolling hitch is used to provide a lengthwise pull to a mast, spar, etc. A stopper knot may be needed if tow line has slippery surface.

loop thru . . . over top . . . then pull tight

avoid wood
screws

Deck hardware has been improved considerably during recent years. Bronze and stainless cleats and bitts are preferred due to strength, and we recommend you choose a larger size than first considered. Avoid mixing of metals to reduce corrosion potential.

bolt thru
is better

Stronger dock lines of smaller diameter are used, which due to light weight often jump off cleats and bitts. Instead of the single loop, come through cleat (upper left) then put loop over top as shown. Use two loops around bitt to overcome tendency to jump off small bitts.

Wood screw cleat installation should be avoided on wooden and glass boats since the cleat can be ripped loose.

bolt thru with
wood block is
recommended

Cleats and bitts should be bolted into deck with wood block backing, & using washers of different sizes so stress will be spread over larger area, both on wooden and fiberglass boats.

●

If you have a sailboat 24' or larger, it may be a good idea to add a midship cleat for a spring line. With three dock lines looped as shown at top of page, and backed up correctly, a boat owner can recover a lot easier from a docking misjudgement . . . . which occasionally may happen to the best of sailors; see illustration top of page 175.

190

"ballit" (bollard)

bitt

cleat

Use two or three half hitches on cleat with three-strand synthetic line.

Use several half hitches on cleat with braided line, especially in the smaller diameters.

dock line

k cord

Elvstrom compensator eases dock line pull in a surge.

slippery hitch

the adjustable hitch

One or two loops are often used around object, when making the adjustable hitch.

1

2 clove hitch

a slipped clove hitch

1 The jam hitch... it does the same job as a rolling hitch.

2

3 a figure 8 knot

The sheepshank is used to shorten a line. It must remain under tension to avoid slippage.

191

The BOWLINE has a wide variety of uses.

"MAN OVERBOARD"

The BOWLINE STIRRUP i an excellent method to tak a person aboard a small h (same purpose as a perso using a saddles stirrup to climb aboard a horse).

1 UNDER **2** OVER UNDER UNDER **3** UNDER **4**

The SQUARE KNOT was originally called a Reef Knot.

We've found ropes having slippery surfaces such as nylon, polyethylene, etc., slip and unwind with both the square and bowline knots. We haven't had the "double square knot" with three overhand knots slip, page 194.

　Read "Lever's Sheet Anchor", pg. 284, for 1819 marlinspike practices.

standard coiling method for three strand

1

2 loop thru and behind the coil

loop over top

3

4 loose end goes back thru coil

pull end

COILING FOR STORAGE

2 cleat halyard then coil line

3 loop behind, then pull pull loop thru center

4 rotate loop 2 or 3 times

5 pass loop over cleat

COILING A HALYARD

add twist

COILING BRAIDED LINE

Due to NEUTRAL LAY (pg. 186) braided line coiled same as three strand for halyards, sheets, etc., usually produces figure eight loops.

If a twist is added with right hand above the figure eight loops can be eliminated.

6 shock cord

Halyard cleats seem to be smaller each year. In sloppy weather add shock cord around mast to keep halyards in place.

Your boat should carry a practical heaving line such as the one above which requires little stowage space. We have pulled tired swimmers to our boat with it, we've towed dinghies and rowboats, and used it as the method to pull across a heavier tow line from another boat. It is also useful on a crowded launching ramp for handling a trailerable sailboat or powerboat.

The yellow polyethylene line is easy to see and handle, and it floats, protecting the prop. The "soft" softball is heavy enough for heaving, yet soft enough not to hurt a person hit by the ball.

We use two heaving lines, the first with 50' of 1/4" polypro braided line with 1100 lbs. breaking strength which uses the ball above. The second, is 75' long of 1/4" polypro which uses a heavier small fender which can be thrown further.

The secret of a practical heaving line is to use braided rope with a NEUTRAL lay or resistance to coiling. If you drop braided line into the container at left, the line will stow itself ready for use without producing snarls and snafus though being stowed for a long time. It can also be thrown as easily by left handers and right handers.

AVOID 3 strand heaving lines. They require much practice, often producing kinks and hitches when used by weekend sailors. Fouling seems unavoidable if coiled by a right hander then used by a left hander. If professionals coil a heaving line in the morning, yet find they won't use it till the evening, they often recoil the line to eliminate potential half hitches.

Ocean racing and cruising sailors have found the best way to avoid drowning, is to stay on the boat. Many deep water sailors prefer the shoulder harness for maximum protection in stormy weather, while the waist lifeline is easier to use and is less confining for a short summer squall, we carry both kinds on our boat.

Start with a ten foot length of 1/2" three strand nylon, and a #3 bronze boat snap. The eye splice end should go through the eyel of the snap twice. Add whipping to the other end, burning any loose fibers.

The waist lifeline should be tied long enough so it can encircle the waist a second time, yet remain snug and out of the way when snapped on itself when going below.

Use the double square knot, page 192, made of three overhand knots instead of a bowline which may have slipping tendencies when used on nylon rope.

Double braided eye splice method is considerably different from the three strand eye splice sailors have been making for centuries, After studying the following items listed below, then use splicing sequence detailed on the next pages.

Practice ONLY with NEW ROPE when learning to make a braided eye splice as tension on used line tends to shrink its diameter in use, increasing friction between cover and core. This makes it difficult to splice, requiring a smaller size fid, tapering point, after lubricating internally with "Fluid Film", or similar product.

TAPE. Plastic electrical tape is ideal. Limit to two wraps as additional tape makes splicing more difficult.

FID. Be sure it is CORRECT size. Next larger size will be almost impossible to push through rope, and smaller size fid hardly provides sufficient opening to PULL inner and outer core and cover through.

MARKING PENS. The bamboo tip pen is ideal. Use TWO colors though second pen is only used for step 5 in the beginning... which is important to locate point for step 20.

Angle of PUSHER and FID is important. A slight angle provides best leverage to pull cover and core behind fid. If push is almost parallel to fid, pusher may instead go through tape or rope, only pushing the fid. We feel this awkward holding/ pushing action the most difficult part to become accustomed to when making a double braided eye splice.

Order a SPLICING KIT from Samson Ocean Systems, Inc., Pleasure Boating Division, 99 High Street, Boston, MA 02110; or buy 18' of 3/8" braided rope which can be cut into three 6' lengths for six smaller diameter eye splices, plus a fid and pusher. An ice pick makes a good pusher, yet always watch out for the sharp point.

The important idea is to make your first braided eye splice soon as possible. If you follow the steps detailed methodically as shown, they will seem puzzling yet you have at least an 80% chance of making a good braided splice on your first try.

During a free for all discussion at Avalon one afternoon the topic switched to splicing. The four guests aboard reluctantly admitted to each other making a perfect splice the first time using the following sequence, after unsuccessfully trying other braided eye splice methods.

outer cover | double braided rope

inner core |

Anchor line-Gold-N-Braid*(nylon core, nylon cover),
Running rigging-Yacht Braid*(polypro core,polyester or
Dacron cover) *Samson Cordage terms. Puritan splicing
methods are similar.

red dot   fid

DETERMINE EYE SPLICE

1. Tape end. 2. Measure back fid length, make mark.
3. Add thimble for size of loop. 4. Mark this X. 5. Count
seven pairs of threads forward of mark 2, make red dot
on cover. 6. Tie slip knot 4 to 6 feet from eye.

core

MARK and EXTRACT CORE   cover

7. Bend rope at X shown right, separate
strands with pusher and pry out coure.
8. Mark core I at this point.

marker   If thimble has
locking ears add
now

core

MARKING INNER CORE   X

9. Pull out core. 10. Tape core end. 11. Measure back from I
amount of fid shown, mark it II. 12. Measure a fid length
from II, add an inch, mark it III. 13. Cut taped ends for taper
to fit eye in fid. 14. Retape cut ends with electrical tape.

INSERTING FID INTO CORE

15. Insert fid into core at II, out at III. 16. Insert taped end of cover into eye of fid. 17. Angle taped end forward locking cover into fid eye. Push fid at slight angle BEHIND taped cover end at 18, till the cover comes out of core at 19, see below.

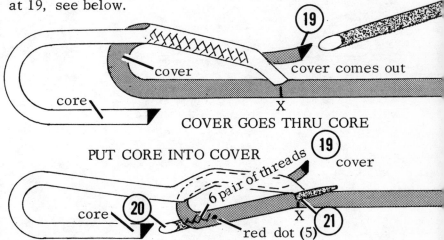

COVER GOES THRU CORE

PUT CORE INTO COVER

20. Insert fid 6 pair threads after RED dot, coming out at X.
21. Push core into fid so it comes out at X, by using the same holding, pushing method shown 16, 17, and 18, to pull the core through the cover (see next page).

Sailing Illustrated

22. Pull core thru till the two ends become one.
23. Remove tape. 24. Tease, spread threads on cover end then cut groups of strands at intervals for taper.
25. Pull both directions at crossover to eliminate slack.
26. Pull direction shown so cover barely disappears into core. If not pulled tight at 25, cover may go in too far to cause bunching, see 29 below.

BURYING CORE INTO THROAT

27. Put slip knot around peg, hook, etc. 28. Hold eye splice with one hand, pull other hand towards eye splice so cover slides over marks II, III, and crossover, so core is buried into throat at 30.

When bunching occurs...

A. Pull on core tail as shown.
B. Pull out loop to smoothen crossover area.
C. If it doesn't bury, insufficient pull was made at #25.
D. If it still doesn't bury, open at D. Pull out core to bury bunching, then pull in direction of #28 to bury core at D.
E. If it still doesn't bury, pull out cover, return to #20.

31. Open loop and position thimble.
32. Close loop after thimble is in position.
33. Count 6 pair threads out on core tail, then cut at angle leaving small tuft.. not to pull core inside making a hollow.

(34) whipping — (33) the core tail   end of tapered
                  tuft shows   cover (26)
(32)

throat

34. Pull needle thru as shown burying knot.
35. Wrap throat several times with Dacron (polyester) for halyards, sheets, etc., or nylon whipping for anchor line subject to stretch. In periods of extreme pressure, thimble with ears, pg. 196, has less chance of jumping out of the thimble as anchor line stretches.

36. Needle goes thru/around twice as shown, pull tight.
37. Cut whipping with ample tail. Burn it back to splice which will lock whipping in place with a good anchor.
38. For anchor line, tape eye plus a foot or more of throat with plastic electricians tape to reduce chafe, page 161.
39. Untie slip knot and have a "Compōz'®". or a martini.

We hope you will try to make a braided splice soon. If sequence is followed exactly with NEW rope, you will be able to make a professional splice the first or second try. For USED rope, wash thoroughly to eliminate salts and sand. Then lubricate thoroughly with FLUID FILM or WD-40, let set for a while to soak through to reduce the internal friction between core and cover, and splice. 199

Traditional whipping thread found in marine stores is quite practical for many applications.

Nylon whipping thread is useful for other applications such as found in the excellent sail repair kit from West Marine Products, 850 San Antonio Road, Palo Alto, CA 94303. Send for catalog.

Double Thread Whipping will take tremendous punishment, the reason it is recommended.

whipping end of braided line

short matches have insufficient heat for fusing

1 Tape line an inch from the end.

2 Cut end about 3/16 from tape.

3 Fuse end with long matches rolling melted end to maintain same diameter.

4 After end cool remove tape

The extra steps above eliminate chances of burning whipping twine if end is fused AFTER it has been whipped, using synthetic line. If you don't decide to whip end of line, soldering iron can fuse strands or double braid together. In some instances the 12" match may provide sufficient heat for permanent fusing.

5 square knot

through strand

Pull through one strand.

6 through strand

Enough wraps with or against lay, same length as diameter.

Pull end A out from lay.

7 through strand

Over, under, and through next lay, then pull tight on all three lays.

8 down first lay

end B

cut

end A

Fourth tuck is through first lay, then cut as is shown above.

9 inner end B

outer end A

Pull end B tight.

10 cut close

Tie inner & outer end with square knot, cut whipping tails close to knot.

Eye Splice

add seizing

bight

standing part

3 unlay strands

3 fix ends (burning, tape, twine, etc.)

4 1 under 1
middle strand first, 2 and 3 then fall into place

5 2 under 2

6 3 under 3
remove

7 pull snug

8 under over
over under

Continue over..under.. over..under.....for
MANILA — THREE tucks
SYNTHETICS- SIX tucks

All tucks are AGAINST the lay of the rope.

All strands must have EQUAL tension.

9 remove excess

10 burn ends of synthetic strands

For specialty splicing methods especially hard laid rope write —
McGrew Splicing Spike, 8120 Rio Linda Blvd., Elverta, CA 95626.

1. Fuse ends of small dia. synthetic strands and/or tape large dia. strands.

2. Unravel as many strands as desired. . add extra turns for slippery synthetic line.

3. Tie off at these points to prevent further strand unwinding.

seizing

marlinspike fid to open strands

seizing

4. Splice ends together using sequence below . . . one tuck only.

5. Pull strands together so they are snug against each other.

6. Tie seizing around meeting point of the six strands.

7. Remove seizings at #3.

8. Continue over . . . under . . . over . . . under to end of strands, remove seizing #6.

9. If taper is required, cut some threads back, otherwise have ends show.

10. Roll and pound on hard surface.   11. Add whipping if desired.

thimble

shackle

leather required

202

Major causes of equipment failure in equipment busting 1969 monohull Honolulu Transpac were----

1. Metal overloading or metal fatigue.

2. Spinnaker cloth failure . . . chafe and too much wind.

3. Eye splices NOT USING THIMBLES on spinnaker sheets, guys, etc. (for location see page 129), as acute angle of metal eye pulling on unprotected line after several days of hard racing produced continual chafe at this point with failure, not obvious on round the buoys or overnight racing.

To reduce this kind of failure in eye splices not using thimbles, have leather sewn around loop of eye splice. The leather spreads the contact area, and is tremendously resistant to chafe. Boats using leathered eyes with well trained crews who knew their boat continually checking for chafe, avoided this kind of failure.

Tugboat Hitch

First loop around bitt, cleat, or post, then over, around and back under.

Towed boat using Tugboat Hitch is no longer at the mercy of the towing boat if this hitch is used. It can be released on towed boat without slowing down or stopping, as it is almost impossible to jam, and easy to release or cast off.

Pull half hitch tight, then add as many extra half hitches as required.

The boat at lower right is aground on a lee shore. A second boat has come to help, but it must stay at least 100' off shore or it will also go aground.

A fishing rod with a two ounce sinker can cast up to 200' to the boat aground, or to a victim in shallow water or heavy surf. A tow line is then secured to the fishing line, then pulled across from either boat.

Leverage is required to work against, in order to pull the boat off the lee shore. One method is to dig in your anchor to pull against, providing your boat can stand the strain.

Another method is to secure an anchor to the tow line, permitting the stranded boat to kedge itself off the lee shore; also see pages 222 and 223.

fishing pole   sinker or float

Water is a continually changing dynamic surface.... making weather study much more important on the water than on land. Storms send advance physical warnings .... IF a person knows what to look for. Many of the impending weather changes are written in the beautiful and ever changing cloud patterns. Latin derivatives are used to clarify basic cloud terminology.

●

UPPER

CIRROCUMULUS (ringlet-heap) resembles fish scales called Mackerel Sky. It has no shadow and indicates a weather change. CIRROSTRATUS (ringlet-layer) is white, frozen, cobwebby fog that may mean rain. CIRRUS (ringlet) is thin, stringy "Mares Tails" that make a beautiful sunrise and sunset, due to light refraction through ice crystals.

Cirrus and cirrostratus make a HALO (ringlet) around the sun and moon, that may predict change in day or two.

●

MIDDLE

MIDDLE clouds are ALTOCUMULUS (middle—heap), forming lumpy patterns of flattened globular masses. High grayish sheet ALTOSTRATUS(middle—flat) may thicken to nimbostratus, but does NOT have halo around sun & moon.

●

Nothing is more beautiful nor more dangerous than the CUMULONIMBUS (heap-storm) with high vertical develop- ment. Look for anvil top and take no chances as it may be weak or strong... but will soon pass, in most instances only covering a small area, see pages 206 and 207.

LOWER

The NIMBOSTRATUS (storm-layer) cloud is flat, uniformly gray, ragged and wet looking. It often indicates steady rain over a wide area.

STRATUS (layer) is low and of indefinite shape giving water a hazy appearance. If on the water surface, it is called fog, see pages 218 to 221.

CUMULUS (heap) clouds are clean, fluffy, & dome shaped on the upper surface. If one grows tall enough to reach elevation where temperature is below freezing, it develops into the tall, dangerous cumulonimbus (heap—storm).

Cloud formations

CIRRUS

HIGH CLOUDS
(ICE PARTICLES)

ANVIL TOP

CIRROSTRATUS

CIRROCUMULUS

20,000 FT.

MIDDLE CLOUDS

ALTOSTRATUS

ALTOCUMULUS

6,500 FT.

LOW CLOUDS

STRATOCUMULUS

CUMULONIMBUS
THUNDERSTORM
THUNDER HEAD

CUMULUS

ROLL CLOUD

STRATUS

NIMBOSTRATUS

CATSPAW

An ANVIL TOP develops when the CUMULONIMBUS cloud climbs above 15,000' where moisture particles are permanently frozen. The higher the vertical development, the greater the intensity of the approaching storm.

Is your boat PERMANENTLY protected from lightning?

For temporary storm protection—

bolt heavy copper wire to mast going to copper plate in water.... DON'T attach to shrouds.*

storm cloud shreds

Weather is cool and refreshing.

D A N G E R

Dangerous strong shifting winds can be found

A simple 24 hour pocket size weather radio should be standard equipment for your car, van, camper, and boat.

STATIC developing on your radio may be first warning of a thunderstorm anywhere from 25 to 100 miles away. It is a good indication that a storm can hit within one to four hours.

First visual signs will appear on horizon from the west, southwest or northwest. It will be a high cloud formation with a DIRTY BOTTOM that has a tall thin and stringy cirrus ANVIL TOP.

The wise boat operator must always expect the worst and prepare accordingly as this type of storm may be light or severe, and more than one storm may be coming through. Scientists have estimated the power of a severe THUNDER-STORM, CUMULONIMBUS, THUNDERHEAD, or SQUALL

The ROLL CLOUD shown is supposed to give 3 to 5 minutes calm before the storm, however the roll could is not as common as many people believe.

*Aluminum has 2/3 the conductivity of copper, the reason the copper plate should be bonded directly to the mast so if your boat is hit by lightning, the surge can be easily dissipated. Stainless shrouds with 1/50th the conductivity of copper may cause too much resistance resulting in confused, dangerous side flashes of lightning.

advancing **COLD FRONT**

ANVIL TOP

CIRRUS

Direction of storm moving at approx. 25 miles an hour.

32°

STATIC

STRONG DOWNDRAFTS

ROLL CLOUD isn't always present.

A R E A   Quick, sharp temp. drop

Weather is hot & muggy.

anywhere in the danger area shown above!

The thunderstorm usually lasts for a short time and will cover an area less than 200 miles. However a whole series called a SQUALL LINE or LINE SQUALL may be advancing across a large area.

As rank beginners, we admired these beautiful cloud formations from our kayak on the Hudson River on July 4, 1948, a day that will long be remembered. What we were watching is exactly what you see above except the anvil top must have gone up over 100,000'. The violence of the 100 mph and over hurricane force winds that hit us in our small kayak will be remembered for a lifetime.

Because one thunderstorm has hit, don't expect that the potential is over. We were hit by three thunderstorms in one afternoon off Staten Island, two were very vicious.

If a storm is on its way don't try to outslug it, head for a protected area with plenty of time. If you are stuck, use a bucket or any kind of a drag attached to the anchor line and sit or lie on the bottom of the boat.

Many people have drowned in storms because they stood up, swung their arms (USCG help wanted signal?) and then hollered for help. After the storm had passed the boat was floating peacefully without occupants ... they had fallen overboard and drowned.

Advancing warm front is climbing up slope of cold front beneath. Cold air moves slower due to ground friction.

halo around sun and moon

cirrus ice particles

--------------------- 32°f ---------------------

ribbed or mackerel sky

WARM AIR

altostratus

COLD AIR

nimbostratus

24 to 48 hours

static ?

barometer dropping;

Advancing front of STABLE WARM AIR

When weak fronts pass with almost identical humidity and temperature, only a mild wind shift may occur.

A strong advancing warm front usually moves at HALF the speed of the cold front. Another difference, it sends cloud warnings a long way ahead of the front. As it moves in on you, the cloud sequence shown above may be observed.

First notice is the CIRRUS (ringlet) that produces a ring around the sun and moon. As the cirrus thickens, it changes to cirrocumulus or ribbed Mackerel Sky.

The cirrus messenger may be from 24 to 48 HOURS and up to 1000 MILES in advance of the front. After lowering, the ringlet disappears as temp. rises above 32°f. In this middle or alto layer, cloud forms change to altostratus or altocumulus.

When this lowers, precipitation begins with rain pattern depending on intensity of advancing warm front. If the barometer dips little, a nimbostratus bank may follow. If it dips considerably, unstable warm air with a hidden violent cumulonimbus (heap-storm) may follow.

STABLE WARM AIR. With little barometer drop, a high stratus bank may exist to produce heavy rain in the beginning...but it decreases steadily.

Advancing front of UNSTABLE WARM AIR

UNSTABLE WARM AIR. With considerable barometer drop, hidden cumulonimbus or series of them may often be concealed behind advancing cloud wall. Thunderstorms and/or lightning may advance before the front. Rain may be variable, alternating between heavy downpours and slow drizzles ... with occasional thunderstorms.

Pattern of strong warm front sequence is first told by physical change in clouds... next by drop in BAROMETER. When front passes, barometer climbs as sky clears.

Greater the barometer drop, the stronger will be the strength of WIND and WAVE conditions as front MOVES THROUGH. After the front has passed, it does not necessarily mean that the wind & wave action will cease.

●

What other physical signs exist of an approaching storm or low pressure? BIRDS for instance find it increasingly difficult to take off and fly. If you see them sitting along the beaches or bluffs looking miserable and sluggish, the chances are that a low pressure area exists or has been moving in. The ART PENS used to illustrate this book start to leak as internal pressure is greater than the surrounding air pressure. When a high pressure area moves in, the ink pressure is less internally so the ink flow is sluggish.

The fore and aft rig was developed to make use of the land and sea breezes prevalent along our seacoasts and on the Great Lakes.

When the land warms up around noon, a SEA BREEZE starts flowing toward the land. It normally increases to midafternoon, disappearing about sundown. The greater the difference between water and land temperature, the stronger the land and sea breezes will result.

From dusk to midnight with land & water surface temp. about the same, a breeze is usually nonexistant. After midnight when land temperature is cooler, the wind starts blowing seaward increasing to about dawn when the temperature differences are equalized and it stops.

The sea breeze is generally steadier, stronger, and more predictable coming across a level surface with relatively constant temperature. The LAND BREEZE is more puffy and changeable due to going over hills, etc.

●

Wind plays many tricks on the sailors. When coming off a high bluff a DOWNDRAFT may occur with sailboats short distance apart going same direction on opposite tacks. When the wind is blowing onto a bluff, it must rise, which often causes a dead air pocket close to the bluff, pg. 123.

●

Wind FUNNELS bear close watching. The canyon at right funnels down, increasing the wind velocity. If the canyon makes a slow turn, it may also change direction of wind flow up to 90°. Where two wind funnels converge such as found at Lake Mead (facing page), the overall wind pattern may be 15 mph, but up to 45 miles per hour . . . where the two funnels converge!

Wind funnels also exist when sailing past rows of buildings from which the wind is coming. The greatest velocity may be found flowing down the streets. Downdrafts may also exist when sailing close to buildings.

WARMED AIR HEAVY
WITH EXPANSION
TARTS TO DESCEND

CYCLE OF <u>LAND BREEZE</u>
BEGINNING AROUND MIDNIGHT
ENDING MIDMORNING,
STRONGEST AT DAWN.

WARMED
AIR RISES

WIND IS OFTEN PUFFY

WARMER AIR
ABOVE WATER

50°

AND IS COOL

60°

BLANKETED AREA

RISING AIR
HEAVY WITH
EXPANSION
STARTS TO
DESCEND.

WARM AIR
RISES

CYCLE OF <u>SEA BREEZE</u>
BEGINNING AT NOON
ENDING SUNDOWN,
STRONGEST LATTER
PART OF AFTERNOON.

COOLER AIR
ABOVE WATER

75°

STEADY BREEZE

LAND IS WARM

60°

ELS OR CHUTES MAY <u>DOUBLE</u> WIND SPEED.

~10MPH

40 MPH

FUNNEL

CANYON

30 MPH

FUNNEL

TYPICAL
SEA BREEZE

ATLANTIC
OCEAN

Royce 211

Basic weather patterns result from the sun, rotation of the earth, plus interaction of high & low pressure areas.

Wind direction is in a clockwise direction from a high or hill of air, flowing into the low pressure area in a counterclockwise direction. As the moist warm air reaches the center of the low pressure area, it rises, condenses, beings to precipitate, and a storm is born. So the low pressure area becomes a storm area, with the greater the difference between the low & high pressure areas, the more violent a storm it will produce.

Most U.S. weather or low pressure areas, flow across our continent from west to east, yet direction of the wind will vary according to the location of the high and low pressure areas. The relative pressure of these areas is measured by a BAROMETER as shown at right, then is reported in inches or *millibars. ISOBARS are lines of equal barometric pressure.

Note flow pattern of our weather on upper right of facing page. Westerlies due to earths rotation, generally move these lows about 500 miles every 24 hours during the summer, and about 700 miles, in the winter.

Suppose you do your boating in the New England area. Draw a 500 mile radius from your home, then note how a storm flowing through Illinois or down to the Carolinas, may funnel through your area the following day. New York weather however seldom flows to Chicago. Hurricanes coming from the Caribbean, make a slow turn to north & east, may also flow through the New England area.

Most storm clouds approach from, and may be seen in the SW, W, or NW quadrant anywhere from 15 minutes to several hours away.

Wind direction is reported as that in which the wind comes from. The term hurricane refers to a severe kind of a storm covering a large area. Hurricane strength winds also be found in a thunderstorm, pages 206 and 207.

212   * When buying a barometer, consider one with millibar markings, now the meterologists worldwide standard.

Barometer

basic storm paths

HIGH (air hill) 1040

storm cloud

LOW or depression

ISOBARS*

1006

clockwise rotation

HIGH 1040 1036

isobars*

isobars* 1033 1030

1027

1022 1019

1016 1011

1009

updraft

LOW 1006

counterclockwise rotation

millibars	inches
1050	31.0
1047	30.9
1044	30.8
1041	30.7
1038	30.6
1035	30.5
1032	
1029	30.4
1026	30.3
1023	30.2
1020	30.1
1017	30.0
1014	29.9
1011	29.8
1008	29.7
1005	29.6
1002	
999	29.5
996	29.4
993	29.3
990	29.2
987	
984	29.1
981	29.0
978	28.9
975	28.8
972	28.7
969	28.6
966	28.5
963	28.4
960	28.3
957	28.2
954	
951	28.1
948	28.0

*Isobars are lines of equal force.

Wind rotational direction reverses south of the equator.

10 11 12 1 2 3 4 5 6 7 8 9
high

10 11 12 1 2 3 4 5 6 7 8 9
low

high pressure

low pressure

1200
1100
1000
900
800
700
600
500
400
300
200
100
0

millibars

Since major U.S. marine weather forecast information is 213 given in millibars, the illustration shown uses millibars instead of inches.

Tide is the alternate vertical rise & fall of water, caused by gravitational pull of moon & sun. A month is required to go through the four tidal phases. Current is horizontal flow of water. When the tide causes a current that changes direction with change of tide, it is called a tidal current. A river current results only from the force of gravity.

Greatest normal tide range, is a spring tide that occurs twice a month when the sun & moon exert their greatest pull; the neap tides occur, when they nullify each other. Depths shown on our navigation charts are charted as being at Mean Low Tide on east coast, and Mean Lower Low Tide on the west coast.

In addition to these variables, is the elliptical course of the moon around the earth that results in Apogee and Perigee. During a hurricane, much greater highs & lower lows may be expect than found in spring tides, page 167.

The "tsunamis" or tidal wave may pass over the surface of the open ocean at jet plane speeds & be hardly noticed. As they approach the shore, the ocean may go out half a mile, then come in a similar distance above high tide. Shallow water may produce "tsunamis" waves 60-100' high.

Yearly tide & current table predictions are published by the U. S. Coast and Geodetic Survey. For Daylight Saving Time, be sure to ADD an hour.

The moon takes about 24 hours & 50 minutes in order to go around the earth. This corresponds to the two highs & lows in one area as illustrated on facing page showing a complete tidal day. This doesn't always apply near the equator, where tides follow different rhythms.

Continuous operation on the water provided us with a surprise. Potential collisions on the boat and on the highway seem to increase rapidly at periods of major tide ranges coinciding with the full moon, and reduce rapidly when periods of minimum tide ranges occur.

214 The "Sea Around Us" by Rachel Carson, is a must for every library, having excellent coverage of tide variables.

New Moon–Spring Tides

earth

moon

sun

First Quarter–
Neap Tides

Full Moon–
Spring Tides

Third Quarter–
Neap Tides

moon

Apogee

Perigee

spring tide range

mean tide range

neap tide range

Tide

moon   the tidal day------

HIGH
0.00 hours
ebb tide begins

LOW
6.12 hours
flood tide begins

HIGH
12.25 hours
ebb tide begins

LOW
18.37 hours
flood tide
begins

HIGH
0.50 hours on
the following day

One fathom
equals six feet

215

— wind →		
- current →		
lee tide	current wind	current
	windward tide	wind

When wind and current go same direction (1), wave action is minimum. When wind & current go against each other (2), a short stiff wave action develops. Combine strong opposing wind & current acting against seawall or jetty, & a wild stiff vertical chop (3), without pattern develops.

The river current is caused by gravity, a tidal current changes direction with change of tide. Between the two often exists a buffer zone that moves downstream during spring rains, and upstream during August to November.

Spend some time studying effects of current in your area so you can make them work for you. Our first boat was a "Folbot" (18' kayak) in which we spent many wonderful hours analyzing the treacherous New York harbor area tidal currents, afterwards shooting the Housatonic and Platte River rapids. This training proved most valuable for handling sailboats in tidal current areas.

The smoother more predictable current flow as example, is usually found in the middle and deeper part of a stream. For sailing against the current, it is necessary to work the shallower or fringe areas avoiding houses, trees & banks, that may cut off your wind.

Jetties should be given wide berth due to reverse eddies and disturbed current flow on the downstream side. For similar reason, plus the potentials of sudden downdrafts that may cause a sailboat to lose rudder control, avoid sailing close to large bridge supports. Sailing too close to a support of the George Washington Bridge one afternoon, caused a double knockdown from current eddies and from a sudden strong wind downdraft.

Drawbridges may open upon signal in some areas, while opening is only at scheduled times elsewhere. Signal for many drawbridges to open, is three long blasts.

Avoid cutting corners in a river bend as deep water is usually on the outer edge near the steep side of a river bank.

When going downstream past fixed objects, give considerable clearance so current won't set you upon them. Speed and strength of a current may often be judged by the size of eddies and current swirls on downstream side of piling, float, buoy, etc.

Greatest depth is found in center of V pointing downstream. For an upstream V, give it room since this usually indicates an underwater obstruction.

When powerboats meet in a current, the one going downstream has right-of-way (page 235) due to minimum rudder response. Situation with tug and tow is even more critical as discussed on page 240.

Sailboats generally make better headway toward destination if current can be kept on lee side called "lee bowing". During the spring, a sailor must keep a more critical lookout for floating debris due to spring rains and thaw. During late summer and fall with flow at minimum, more care should be given to shallower water that exposes sand bars, rocks, etc.

The sailor operating in a current situation should always have an anchor ready to go in case of upset. Boat otherwise may turn 180° and be dismasted and/or holed when drifting downstream across bars, etc.

wind

current

217

current

Fog signals must be given, Rule 15 (c). ". in fog, mist, falling snow, heavy rainstorms, or any other condition similarly restricts visibility, whether by day or night".

Fog signals must be given by all vessels underway, adrift or at anchor, and need to be started before a vessel enters a fog bank, see pages 220 and 221. Speed must be reduced and restricted by vessels ability to stop in half the distance of visibility, Rule 16(a). All vessels must carry a proper lookout with no other duties at the time, Rule & Art.29. These rules are unfortunately disregarded more times than a newcomer realizes.

Consider air as a large sponge on a warm day, that will soak up a lot of water vapor. On cold days it is a small sponge that can only soak up a small amount of vapor before saturation, dew point, or fog potentials are reached.

Previous editions discussed sling psychrometer to measure amount of moisture in the air. Theoretically it was a good idea yet was seldom used on small boats. We tested a RELATIVE HUMIDITY INDICATOR pg. 63, permanently mounted on the mast, which provided a very practical and liberal education for fog prediction.

We could tell for instance when a fog might be approaching up to five hours in advance . . . and the type of fog to be expected. A dense fog which still has sufficient visibility for operation, is indicated when relative humidity reaches 88 to 93%.

If the day or night was very clear with a relative humidity 100% or more, it indicated a pea souper moving in. This advance fog warning kept us out of trouble numerous times.

The inexpensive relative humidity indicator fog forecast accuracy has provided continual surprises to us and our students. We highly recommend you buy one such as is shown upper right, permanently mounted on your boat so it is easy to see and is protected from being hit. A word of caution, replace it before the humidity sensor begins to lose accuracy as nature is very hostile to this 218 sensitive instrument.   Sailing Illustrated

oisture particles in suspension

Humidity vs fog

uch is written about fogs.
hat is of major importance
s the ability to predict a
g...to keep you out of
ouble. We've had much luck
ith the indicator shown.

ir contains water in gaseous
rm, invisible below the
aturation point, dew point,
r maximum humidity that
s detailed below.

vy falling moisture particles

s humidity increases to
7-93% generally with temp-
rature drop, or inflow of
noist air...often indicated
everal hours ahead, a light
g moves in. It has sufficient
isibility for a boat to keep
nderway at displacement
peed.

uring two 14 month tests, the
ndicator shown was able to
redict all fogs encountered.

temperature

relative humidity

fog signals are often required

light to medium fog

Displacement speeds for daytime operation, avoid nighttime operation.

visibility 100 yards to a quarter mile

Fog is VISIBLE MOISTURE.

vy blanket of moisture particles

irst evidence of incoming
easoup fog, generally is a
lear sky with humidity 100%
105%. If a light fog exists
nd humidity climbs to 100%
r more, a peasouper may
e moving in.

he indicator predicted fogs
p to five hours ahead. When
he humidity drops during
g conditions, the fog often
fted four to five hours later.

fog signals are mandatory

heavy fog or 'peasouper'

Any boat movement may be hazardous.

DEW POINT is 100% humidity

visibility 100' or less

he temperature and humidity indicator
eeds to be permanently mounted outside
he cabin, since it takes several hours to
ully adjust to weather conditions.

hough designed for indoor use, we've
ad considerable luck with temperature/
umidity indicators made by —

Airguide Instrument Co.
221 Wabansia Ave.
Chicago, Ill 60647

protective shroud

eplace periodically, we replace it yearly!

The purpose of Admiralty Law is to prevent collisions with fog presenting a special set of circumstances.

A freon horn is most practical for your sailboat use as it makes a lot of noise when required. AVOID mouth blown horns as their signal is very weak.

International 72 COLREGS, Rule 35(c)-- ".. a sailing vessel .. shall .. sound at intervals (see left) of not more than 2 minutes, three blasts in succession, namely one prolonged followed by two short blasts".

The sailboat signal under International can as a result produce a complex situation as it is the same as vessels not under command, a vessel restricted in her ability to maneuver, a vessel constrained by her draft, a vessel engaged in fishing, and a vessel engaged in towing or pushing a vessel.

Inland Rules, Article 15(c). "A sailing vessel (see below) under way shall sound, at intervals of not more than one minute, when on the starboard tack, one blast; when on the port tack, two blasts in succession; and when with the wind abaft of the beam, three blasts in succession".

A sailboat under sail in Inland not only communicates its wind course, but it also can't be mistaken for a wide variety of vessels with the same signal, see facing page, such as a super tanker, tug with tow, etc.

wind

Fog Signals

International Rule 34 (b) "Any vessel may supplement the whistle signals... by light signals, repeated as appropriate"..

power vessel underway

INTERNATIONAL 72 COLREGS — R 35 (a) — 2 min. intervals

INLAND RULES — Art. 15 (a) — 1 minute interval

power vessel stopped

2 seconds pause — 2 min. intervals R 35 (b)

no special fog signal

Pilot vessel on pilot duty----

R 35 (i) Uses 35 (a) or (b) see above, plus 4 short blasts

(underway)

no special fog signal

also not under command

prolonged blast short blast R 35 (c) 1 sec. **restricted maneuverability** 2 min. intervals 4-6 sec. R 32 (b)(c) **fishing**

no special fog signal

no special fog signal

towing or pushing

towing or pushing — Art. 15 (e) 1 min. interval

ring for 5 sec. **bell ringing** 1 min. intervals

towing if manned

Art. 15 (e) vessel towed

bell ringing **plus three distinct strokes** 1 min. intervals R 35 (g)

aground

no special fog signal

ring for 5 sec. **bell ringing** 1 min. interval Rule 35 (f)

under 100 meters (under 300 feet)

1 min. interval Art. 15 (d)

Intervals of 1 min. ring bell for 5 sec. in forepart, then gong 5 sec. in after part R 35 (f) optional blasts every minute

over 100 meters (300')

no special Inland fog signal for large vessels

Your author has gone aground . . . and assisted more boats that have gone aground, than he cares to think about. Virtually all were caused by carelessness, or shoaling.

If you put a boat aground, think twice before asking for or taking assistance. In one grounding on a large boat, an overly eager navy tug wanted to assist. Since the tug crew was mainly trained to handle large vessels instead of yachts . . . our main problem was to keep the tug at a safe distance. As a puff moved in, the gennie and main were sheeted in hard, while a crew member swung out on the mizzen halyard. The boat heeled sufficiently to break it loose from the sticky mud. The only resulting damage . . . was to your authors pride.

Charts and tide tables provide a good basic knowledge of new areas, yet local knowledge is also useful where you may find shoaling. In addition, we recommend fathometers with alarms* that may be preset to go off at a desired depth, pg. 243, a useful warning for shallow water, also to locate schools of fish. We feel the need for fathometer alarms especially important for foggy weather.

Avoid taking deep keel vessels into shallow water on ebb tide, pg. 214. Take action right away if boat goes aground.

*Vexilar Eng., 1300 South First St., Minneapolis, Minn. 55404

NOTE: Maximum tide range periods increase chance of groundings . . . also affecting the thinking processes and judgment of boat operators, especially in heavy traffic. Worst offenders seem to be powerboats with LEFT hand controls, especially if they are located inside a cabin restricting the operators visibility.

THIS BOAT SHOULD DROP SAILS AND TRY TO TURN AROUND.

WHAT IS CURRENT, WIND DIRECTION, IS TIDE EBBING, USE WHICHEVER WILL BE ADVANTAGEOUS.

IF A KEEL BOAT IS STUCK WITH AN EBB TIDE, PROP IT UP. IF THIS ISN'T POSSIBLE LET IT FALL SO COCKPIT WILL NOT BE SWAMPED BEFORE RIGHTING, HAVE ANCHORS OUT.

THIS BOAT MIGHT BE POLED OFF. HAVE WEIGHT ON OTHER END, JUMPING MIGHT HELP TO ROCK THE BOAT LOOSE.

CENTERBOARD BOAT DROPS SAILS RAISES CENTERBOARD, MAYBE RUDDER, PADDLES OVER OBSTRUCTION OR CAN BACK OFF.

ROYCE

IF BOTTOM IS SANDY DON'T USE ENGINE AS IT MIGHT SUCK IN SAND. POWERBOAT WAKE MIGHT BREAK SAILBOAT LOOSE.

IF CENTERBOARD BOAT IS STILL STUCK, PUSH, POLE OR KEDGE OFF.

THIS BOAT IS KEDGING OFF AND WINCHING OUT.

223

For many years we've been outspoken over amateurish 'safety'standards faced by those on a vessel in distress, especially facing a long time survival situation.Suddenly we found our answers with a pilot/sailor . . George Sigler.

George was a navy fighter pilot with many hours combat duty,highly trained in the art of survival. After returning stateside,he & his wife Judy bought a .22' sailboat.He began researching ocean survival methods to find little of practical value. The deeper he probed, the worse it became.

George sold his sailboat to buy a 15' Mark III Zodiac outfitting it with survival equipment.He was soon joined by Charle Gore,a navy fighter pilot friend. Their inflatable 'Courageous' was towed 20 miles out past the Golden Gate Bridge and set adrift July 4, 1974, destination,Hawaii.

2700 miles and 56 days later the navy ordered them picked up, 65 miles from Oahu.The only water consumed came from solar stills changing salt water into fresh water.The food,three pounds of sugar and a few mouthfuls of mahi mahi speared 55 days out.After three days testing by service doctors,they left the hospital in good condition losing about 45 lbs. each in their self caused ordeal.

Charlie returned to the navy while George tested and began marketing a wide variety of items which may be needed for a long time survival situation in which individuals must rely on their own resources, as chance of organized rescue operations have been eliminated.

All equipment has to be simple AND reuseable.A good example is to eliminate weight and bulk of canned water which is only used once. A sealed solar still in a small container,may be inflated to supply the fresh water needs indefinitely for two adults under survival conditions.

We refer to Siglers operation as a 'one-stop center'for survival equipment.His specialty is preparing kits for all size craft including special medicines for those with medical problems,inflatable liferafts if desired,etc.

224

Photo of SIG II Kit shows equipment used by George and Charlie in their 56 day survival trip to Hawaii. It is the basis for increasing numbers of Sigler designed kits for cruising sailboats, powerboats, and fishing boats operating on the ocean and in coastal areas.

George stresses a survival inflatable needs some kind of maneuverability. 'Courageous' used a small square sail held up by a mop handle, providing maneuvering in a 90° downwind arc, the difference between drifting past an island again going out to sea, or hopefully making it ashore.

Many new and practical survival products are coming on the market directly or indirectly because of George Sigler who cared enough to risk his life to test survival products for ocean use .. to help YOU, a field unfortunately dominated for too many years with amateurism.

Whether you desire a solar still or a sealed kit for several persons including an inflatable liferaft, the man to contact for all your survival equipment needs is George Sigler, Survival & Safety Designs, 1 5th Ave., Oakland, CA 94606.

Approved cushion

traditional Approved vest

Approved Stearns vest

All boats must carry at least one USCG Approved preserver for every person aboard or the operator is subject to a stiff fine. While commendable in theory, it fell far short of its objective in the past... IF the goal was to save lives.

Little is known of the battles to have USCG Approve the variety of quality and practical life preserves we have today it calls PFD's. Up until around 1970 about all USCG would Approve was the cushion and AK 1 vest above.

After taking in sail at 2 a.m. in the 1958 Ensenada Race on a naked, plunging bowsprit in which I declined to wear a preserver feeling it would increase my chances of falling overboard, we began a systematic testing of many preservers... in the water.

This testing proved such a liberal education that we highly recommend you and your family or crew test the preservers carried on your boat in the water under protected conditions, swimming with them at least a half mile so if the need ever arises when you have to use one you will know its capabilities and limitations.

We found the Approved cushion a hazard in the water. Though new ones have excellent flotation, they are a poor swim aid as the victim in wave action has to waste most of his energy just to hold on to the darn thing... which wasn't even comfortable to sit on in a boat.

The most practical all-round preserver we found was the ski belt which we have tried to convince USCG of the need for its Approval since 1958 especially for small, open, high risk boats. While District 11 officers proved very interested in our findings, all we received from headquarters was silence... until 20 years later USCG finally Approved the first flotation belt preserver shown at right designed by a retired professional football player who designed it for his own use.

2'tow strap
8'tow line

Our testing of USCG AK 1 showed it awkward to put on and swim with. Being made of organic materials it is easily damaged by the elements, especially in an open boat subject to spray. The AK 1 is so clumsy and impractical for use on a tossing pitching boat of any size, it is seldom used...but it is supposed to hold an unconscious persons head out of water. In our research in sailboats and powerboats, I remember only one instance in which a person was knocked out when falling overboard.

When quality "Sterns" vest was introduced we put it through endless testing. It was practical for swimming, to wear under jacket in cool weather, comfortable to use in a summer storm as inner nylon mesh ventilates easily to reduce condensation found in vests without mesh. It was USCG Approved after endless testing (reluctantly we feel).

Flotation coats have been around for a decade, Approved ones, a few years. They are comfortable for cool weather operation, also walking around docks at night. They are excellent to float on back in water, yet may tend to float up around face and arms when victim is upright in the water.

Operators of small open boats, especially the high risk hunters and fishermen, faced a practical dilemma with preservers carried aboard their dinghies underway. Would it be the easily damaged impractical, Approved cushion, practical non-Approved flotation belt, or both, wasting precious storage space to satisfy an archaic law.

After probably the most thorough preserver testing in their history, the first flotation belt to receive USCG Approval is the Ettinger FLOTE-RITE,^{TM} Box 58, Lake City, TN 37769. It is an excellent swim aid that is comfortable to wear on hot days as a major heat source the heart is open, not covered as with jackets. We have been fighting for flotation belt Approval since 1960. If similar preservers were Approved just 10 years ago, how many more lives might have been saved?

227

We found the water world beneath our boat fascinating to discover with mask, snorkel, and fins. We found it just part of the story after installing a SEA TEMP* indicator. We can now find warm spots in the ocean for swimming and snorkeling, plus differences in fish activity with a 1° decrease, or 2° increase in water temperature, and when to anticipate hypothermia with water temp. below 70°.

Swimming is an excellent exercise, the perfect way to cool off on a hot day, and after a strenuous sail. But how far can you swim under normal conditions?

It is easy to fall overboard off most sailboats. If it is a nonswimmer, he panics immediately calling for help underwater. This is a hazardous type of rescue which must occur immediately...or it will be too late.

Our information indicates <u>3/4 of all drownings occur within 60' of shore.</u> If a person can swim just 100' in case of capsize or falling overboard, he will not usually panic, and be easy to rescue.

If you want to sail, can you swim 100' under normal conditions, and are you comfortable in the water? If not, take swimming lessons, though we wish pool instructors would reconsider the methods they use. We've had to teach a handful of persons they weren't able to teach.

We put flippers and ski belts on them for an hour or two swim a day for ten days or so in our bay. When the ski belt is suddenly removed they usually laugh as they now have honest confidence in their swimming ability which couldn't have been gained without such aids.

The main job is NOT to fall overboard. Have a couple of ski belts easy to reach, to throw to a victim in the water to secure around his waist, giving you ample time to prepare your boat for a pickup. Use a harness, pg. 194, to stay on your boat at night or in rough weather. More details are found pgs. 150-161, in "Trailer Boating Illus."

 *SEA TEMP Co., 19250 E. Colima Rd., La Puente, CA 91745

If you fall off your boat, can you come back aboard under your own power? We recommend you try to do this under ideal conditions, so you will know enough variables to help a person come aboard under adverse conditions . . . . or suppose the victim is you.

The bowline stirrup is the best method we've found for a person to come aboard a small sail or power boat by himself. This is an important consideration as an excited crew pulling a victim aboard, might pull him across sharp screw heads, a sharp cleat, or other object, causing unnecessary harm.

Our boat was less than a year old when we added a swim platform as we enjoy swimming and snorkeling, yet it was always ready to use if a student falls overboard, page 63.

"The EVER-READY" BOARDING LADDER[*] was recently introduced, an excellent boat ladder that fits a wide variety of transoms and boat sizes. It is light, made of stainless, and takes little room. This ladder can be installed with simple tools.

We've checked into a few simple, tragic, man overboard situations, when the victim couldn't climb back aboard, and those on the boat weren't able to help him.

After 15 to 20 minutes, especially in cold water, the victim falls into unconsciousness when the body heat is drained, soon followed by drowning in full sight of friends and loved ones. These drownings could have been avoided IF their owners had taken the time and effort to install a practical rigid boarding ladder. AVOID a rope ladder as it is next to impossible to climb aboard a boat of any size in even good conditions with a flexible ladder.

The sailor who uses reasonable preparation will have his share of excitement, yet the hazards will rank far below those we face daily, the auto and the bathtub.

[*]Stainless Rails, 46 Center Ave., At. Highlands, NJ 07716   229

Note how throat becomes a one-way valve while drowning
or suffocating with the back of the TONGUE pressing
against, and blocking upper air passageway. This must be
opened immediately by PULLING or PUSHING jaw into
jutting-out position so air can be inhaled into.... and
exhaled out from victim's lungs.

Third leading cause of accidental death in our country is
drownings ... with approximately 8000 victims a year. What
makes it worse, many victims considered beyond help in the
past due to long submergence and absence of life signs may
have been saved.

It is easy to understand and teach artificial respiration
methods. Most people avoid the thought, feeling they will
never have any use for it. Then with startling swiftness
someone elses life is in your hands ... or the situation
reversed and you the victim, with no one in your family
capable of administering artificial respiration.

Don't wait to pull drowning victim way up onto the beach,
then run to your car looking for a folder to show correct
mouth to mouth method as it may be too late. Try mouth to
mouth, or mouth to nose method soon as practical.

━━━━━━━━━ BEFORE YOU START ━━━━━━━━━

Clear victims mouth and air passages and begin mouth to
mouth breathing. Give victim FOUR quick breaths without
interruption ... then take a deep breath (twice normal), open
your mouth wide, place your mouth over victims mouth
and blow.

After artificial respiration method nas been started and it
is determined the heart has stopped, external heart massage
(CPR) should be started combined with artificial respiration.

Since a wide variety of accidents may happen in boating,
we recommend "First Aid Afloat" by Paul B. Sheldon, M.D.,
published by Yachting, 50 West 44th St., NY, NY 10036, for
your boat and camper, 116 pages, small practical size.

BREAKING AIR BLOCK

TILT HEAD so chin points 45° upward.

PUSH/PULL JAW into jutting-out position to lift tongue from back of throat.

BREATHING METHOD

Open your mouth and place it tightly over the victim's mouth. PINCH NOSE to make a tight seal on adult. BLOW FORCEFULLY to make the victim's chest rise.

Remove your mouth, turn your head to side and listen for OUTWARD RUSH of AIR indicating an air exchange.

For children and infants, cover BOTH mouth & nose with your mouth. Blow gently or use puffs.

BREATHING CYCLE

ADULT-once every 5 seconds (count 1000, 2000, 3000, 4000, 5000) or about 12 per minute. Blow forcefully and vigorously.

CHILD-once every 3 seconds, depending on size.

INFANTS-use short shallow puffs.

if OBSTRUCTION exists

Drowning victims swallow varying quantities of WATER, which with FOOD in stomach, could, if regurgitated obstruct air passage. If vomiting occurs, turn victim on side, wipe out mouth, reposition him and continue breathing.

If NO air EXCHANGE exists, check head & jaw. If still not successful –quickly turn victim on side. Hit several sharp blows between shoulder blades to dislodge obstruction, reposition, and continue breathing.

Occasionally sweep your fingers through victim's mouth to remove foreign matter.

RECOVERY

Continue cycle until victim breathes freely. Keep him quiet as possible until breathing regularly. Have him covered so body temperature doesn't go down. Treat for shock until doctor and/or transportation arrives.

NOTE: many drownings may be caused from ★ HEART ATTACKS. Doctors have been using this type respiration with coronary patients for a long time as emergency measure.

★ also sun strokes

pulling jaw

pinching nose

Is chest rising?

cover both mouth & nose

pushing jaw

Is chest rising?

Airways tube should only be used by professionals to avoid damage to throat.

Boating navigation rules are listed in Pamphlet CG-169, obtained from USCG, Wash., D.C. 20590. More thorough coverage will be found in, "The Rules of the Nautical Road", by Captain Farwell, and "A Mariner's Guide to the Rules of the Road", by William Tate. These and numerous other marine books may be purchased from the book order dept., US Naval Institute, Annapolis, MD 21402.

International Rules and Inland Articles are listed on the following pages. In some instances they are identical, in others, opposite. After Sept. '65, the upwind right-of-way was eliminated under International, becoming a port tack/ starboard tack, or windward/leeward situation. At time of writing, upwind right-of-way still applies under Inland.

After exposure to the rules, next step is application. A student challenged our statement that boating lights are violated to a considerable degree. The following night we observed 27 boats underway, with only 6 carrying correct International lights, displayed correctly. Another night we went through a large fishing fleet . . . with all of its vessels operating only on red and green running lights.

Consider larger lenses and brighter bulbs, carried higher and out on the pulpit where they cannot be blocked by crew nor sail to reduce collision potentials in calm and heavy weather operation. A masthead strobe, and a hand light will also prove useful. Choose lights for self-protection, avoid <u>minimum</u> USCG standards as they may not be adequate.

 Check cockpit visibility. Many sailboats carry jib tack on deck, blocking large arc of visibility. Jib tack on Pink Cloud, pg. 61, was raised 17" off deck to improve visibility. In light air it improved performance with steadier winds aloft. In heavy weather, waves broke aboard draining out under the jib. If tacked to the deck, the waves would break against or funnel into jib which could tear the sail, or break the sheets, pgs. 61, 67, 133, 147, 153.

poor visibility

good visibility

Rules and Articles are found in Pamphlet CG-169. Write to COHDT(GWLE) USCG, Wash., D. C., 20590 for your copy.

Sailboat Rules

...hen two sailing vessels are approaching one ...other so as to involve risk of collision, one ... them shall keep out of the way of the other, ... follows:—

RUNNING FREE and WIND AFT

WIND DIRECTION

PORT TACK

GREEN   RED

Rule 12(a)(i)

STARBOARD TACK

eliminated in International

EITHER TACK

☆ Rules (a) and (e) for Inland only.

★ (a) A vessel which is **RUNNING FREE** shall **KEEP OUT OF THE WAY** of a vessel which is close-hauled.

...) A vessel which is close-hauled on the ...ORT TACK shall KEEP OUT OF THE WAY ... a vessel which is close-hauled on the ...arboard tack,

★ (e) A vessel which has the **WIND AFT** shall **KEEP OUT OF THE WAY** of the other vessel.

PORT TACK

STARBOARD TACK

RED

GREEN

Rule 12(a)(i)

WINDWARD

LEEWARD

RED   GREEN

WINDWARD

LEEWARD

RED   GREEN

Rule 12(a)(ii)

...) When both are RUNNING ...REE, with the WIND ON ...FFERENT SIDES, the vessel ...hich has the wind on the ...ORT SIDE shall KEEP OUT ...F THE WAY of the other.

(d) When both are RUNNING FREE, with the WIND ON the SAME SIDE, the vessel which is to **WINDWARD** shall **KEEP OUT OF THE WAY** of the vessel which is to leeward.

...EETING, R. 18(a)(iv), Article 20, Sec. 80.8.

...hen a power-driven vessel and a sailing vessel ...e proceeding in such directions as to involve ...sk of collision, except as provided in Rules 13(a) ...VERTAKING) and 26 (VESSELS FISHING), the ...OWER-driven VESSEL shall KEEP OUT of WAY ... the SAILING VESSEL.

MEETING

OVERTAKING, Rule 13(b), Art. 24, Sec. 80.6.

Every VESSEL COMING UP with another vessel FROM any direction MORE THAN 2 POINTS (22 1/2 degrees) ABAFT HER BEAM-----shall be deemed to be an OVERTAKING VESSEL---until she is finally past and clear.

sailboat OR powerboat

OVERTAKING

135°

...ARGE VESSELS, Rule 9 (d). A vessel shall ...t cross a narrow channel or fairway if ...ch crossing IMPEDES the passage of a ...ssel which can safely navigate ONLY ...THIN SUCH CHANNEL or fairway.

OVERTAKING VESSELS, R. 13(a), A. 24, Sec. 80.6.

Notwithstanding anything contained in these Rules, every **VESSEL OVERTAKING** any other shall **KEEP OUT OF THE WAY** of the overtaken vessel.

Large vessels have right-of-way over sailing vessels and powerboats under Int'l Rule 20(b),"This Rule shall not give to a sailing vessel the right to hamper, in a narrow channel, the safe passage of a power-driven vessel which can navigate only inside such channel".Also Rule 25(c), "In a narrow channel a power-driven vessel of less than 65 feet in length shall not hamper the safe passage of a vessel which can navigate only inside such channel". The same rules are applied for Inland with Public Law 89-764.

These regulations provide for safe passage of deep draft tankers, freighter and passenger vessels inside narrow channels, in addition to handling and stopping limitations which they have, see pages 240 and 241.

In the meeting of sailboats and powerboats, a sailboat usually has right-of-way in meeting & crossing situations. IF a sailboat overtakes a power boat or meets a vessel using nets or trawls, the sailboat then becomes the vessel to give way. Rule 26 does not give to any vessel engaged in fishing, the right of obstructing a fairway used by vessels other than fishing vessels.

Meeting requirements of power boat to power boat, and aircraft to aircraft meeting at night, may be simplified if operator remembers . . . red-stop . . . green-go.

A vessel operating under sail and engine power in International Waters, is supposed to display a black conical signal. We haven't seen one used nor for sale since 1956.

I doubt if any Admiralty lawyer knows all of the endless duplicating, overlapping and confusing regulations which face the conscientious new boat owner on the federal, state, and local level . . . yet our legislators add new regulations continually. Only one set, the International Rules with a few simple additions, is really necessary.

R.34 (a) SIGNALS when vessels are in SIGHT, A.18-III, 80.01-.03, given when INTENT is IN DOUBT or collision RISK EXISTS.

Powerboat Rules

CROSSING

give-way
GREEN

RED
stand-on

DANGER ZONE exists from dead ahead to two points abaft the st'b'd beam; Rule 15, Article 19, Sec. 80.7.

RED GREEN

GREEN

DANGER ZONE

DANGER ZONE

Rule 17, stand-on vessel   give-way vessel, Rule 16

★ RULES refer to International, while ARTICLES & SECTIONS, refer to Inland Rules, CG-169

SHORT BLAST is 1 SECOND'S duration: Rule 32(b);

PROLONGED BLAST is 4 to 6 SECONDS, Rule 32(c): Article 15-2; Section 80.03:

LONG BLAST considered 8 to 10 SECONDS but isn't defined.

TOOT TOOT

GREEN

MEETING so as to involve risk of collision, each vessel shall alter course after giving passing signals. R. 14, Art. 18-I, & Sec. 80.4.

RED TOOT

TURN to RIGHT

GREEN

When meeting end on or nearly end on, vessels must pass PORT TO PORT after they have both signalled their passing intentions.

TOOT
RED

TOOT TOOT

★ Find rules in pamphlet CG-169; write COHDT(GWLE)USCG, Wash., D.C. 20590. Find legal decisions in Farwell's "Rules of the Nautical Road", 5th Edition, U.S. Naval Institute, Annapolis, MD 21402.

RIVERS and CHANNELS with CURRENTS— the DESCENDING POWERBOAT shall have the RIGHT-OF-WAY as listed below:

in CG-172, Rules for the GREAT LAKES, Rules 24, 25, and Section 90.5; also in CG-184, Rules for the WESTERN RIVERS, Rules Numbered 18(b), 19(a), Section 95.15.

Not listed in CG-169 Int'l or Inland Rules but applied in court decisions as Special Circumstances, R.2(a): A.27, 29; Sec. 80.11.

When LEAVING A DOCK or berth and other boats are liable to move toward it until fully in sight, same signal should be given as meeting at a bend, Article 18-V, also Pilot Rule Section 80.5.

TOOT

Power-driven vessel gives ONE PROLONGED BLAST 1/2 mile from BEND in CHANNEL, then round it with alertness & caution, Rule 34(e). Art. 18-V, & Sec. 80.5 are similar except signal is ONE LONG BLAST

In NARROW CHANNELS when it is safe and practicable, KEEP TO that side which lies on the STARBOARD SIDE of such vessel; Rule 9(a), Article 25, Sec. 80.5, & 80.10.

TOOT

TOOT TOOT

OVERTAKING SIGNALS— Art. 18-VIII, & Sec. 80.6.

TOOT

RED   GREEN

OVERTAKING vessel KEEP OUT of the WAY. Rules 13 a. b. c. d; Article 24; Sec. 80.6.

TOOT

TOOT TOOT

GREEN   RED

Engines going ASTERN, Rule 34(a).

Engines FULL SPEED ASTERN, Art. 28, & Sec. 80.03.

TOOT TOOT TOOT

TOOT TOOT TOOT TOOT TOOT

Rule 34(d) EITHER VESSEL IN DOUBT can give at least 5 SHORT RAPID BLASTS. Art. 18-III and Section 80.1; VESSEL IN DOUBT gives not less than 4 SHORT RAPID BLASTS. R.18(a)(iv); Art. 20, Sec. 80.8; Except when overtaken, POWER-driven VESSEL shall KEEP OUT of WAY of SAILBOAT when collision risk is involved.

Daytime, Int'l Rule 14-a vessel under power and sail carries a black conical signal, point downward, base not less than two foot dia.

Not required for power with sails down, or in Inland Waters.

32 point or 360° white masthead anchor light; also see note pg. 154.

engine light

Sailboat operating under power or sail and power at night, shows a 20 point or 225° white light in addition to its other navigation lights.

Pulpit mounted RED and GREEN running lights are more effective than hull mounted lights as they have less chance of being blanketed, and their visibility improves with height.

We would like to give thanks to Captain W. W. Barrow USCG, for his detailed help with these complex regulations.

A 360° circle is broken down into 32 units of 11 1/4° per unit. This system originated with older compasses which were marked in points instead of degrees commonly found today.

12 point or 135° white stern light is used to warn overtaking vessels.

RED 112 1/2° or 10 point light

GREEN 112 1/2° or 10 point light

Sailboat above carries lights with prescribed arcs used by sailing vessels on INTERNATIONAL WATERS. Since these lights are also acceptable for INLAND, WESTERN RIVERS and GREAT LAKES, it will simplify matters if all sailboats were rigged with the lights shown above according to regulations on the facing page.

We've had many uncomfortable moments when meeting a submarine at night underway on the ocean due to their inadequate running lights which are provided by law.

The new rotating AMBER light located above the masthead light now displayed on submarines, is a great improvement when used in addition to their standard navigation lights.

When you meet submarines, cruisers and destroyers on the ocean operating nearby at cruising speeds, prepare for a tremendous and possibly damaging wake.

INTERNATIONAL. Motorboat Act, Sec. 3(f)-'Any motorboat may carry and exhibit lights required by the (International) Regulations .. in lieu of lights required by this section.' This permits International Lights to also be used under INLAND, WESTERN RIVERS, and GREAT LAKES.

nautical miles		
	feet	
1.0	0.8	Visibility increases with height above the water's surface.
1.5	1.5	
2.0	3.0	
2.5	5.0	
3.0	7.5	
3.5	9.0	
4.0	12.0	
4.5	15.5	
5.0	19.0	

Small rowing boats under oars or sail -----

Use lantern or flashlight when overtaken. Rule 7(f).

VESSEL of less than 20 gross tons (under 40')

Sep. R & G, 10 point, 1 mile vis., Rule 7 (a)(ii).

OR fixed comb. R & G, 10 point, 1 mile vis., Rule 7 (a)(ii).

OR portable R & G lights ready to show in sufficient time to prevent collision.
Rule 6 (a)(b), 7 (d)

white, 12 point, 2 mile vis., Rules 5(a), 10(a)

VESSELS under 40 gross tons
(40 feet to 65 feet)

optional } Rule 5(b) — red — green

white 12 point, 2 mile vis. Rule 5(a) 10(a)

Sep. R & G or comb. R & G, 10 point, 1 mile visibility, Rule 7, 7a(ii)

under SAIL ALONE

jib should not blanket engine light

ENGINE light-
20 point white, 3 mile visibility.
Rule 7 (a)(i)

same   same

under POWER or SAIL & POWER

VESSELS over 40 gross tons
(65 feet and over)

optional } Rule 5(b) — red — green

same level

same

Sep. R & G, 10 point, Rule 5(a). 2 (a)(iv,v,vi)

under SAIL ALONE

jib should not blanket engine light

ENGINE light-
20 point white, 5 mile visibility.
Rule 2 (a)(i)

same   same

under POWER or SAIL & POWER

INLAND, WESTERN RIVERS and GREAT LAKES lights for motorboat classes A, 1, 2, 3 cannot be used on high seas (International Waters).

Sections listed are from 1940 Motorboat Act found in CG-169.

combination red and green sidelights are lower than the stern light

32 point, white, 2 mile vis.

comb. R & G. 20 point, 1 mile visibility

Sec. 3(a)(d)

Class A -under 16'

same as Class A

Class 1-16' or over & less than 26'

white 32 point 2 mile vis.

sep. R & G 10 pt. each. 1 mile visibility

white 20 point 2 mile visibility

Sec. 3(b,c,d)

Class 2-26' or over, less than 40'

same as Class 2

Class 3-40' or over, not over 65'

32 point white range light, Article 2(i)

15' minimum above fwd light

20 point white masthead light

towing lights *

RANGE LIGHTS------

They are shown on tug at left using Inland lights . . . while the large vessel below is operating under International Rules.

Rule 2(a)(i), masthead light, 20 point, white, 5 mile visibility.

Rule 2(a)(ii)(iii), range light, 20 point

range light

stern light, Rule 10(a) white, 12 pt. 2 mile visibility

towing lights

sep. R & G

15' min.

20' min.

green

INTERNATIONAL-vessel over 150' long displaying range lights.

*Tugs displaying TOWING LIGHTS only when towing, seagoing vessels don't
238 have to be equipped with towing lights except when actually engaged in towing.

INTERNATIONAL. Motorboat Act, Sec. 3(f)- 'Any motorboat may carry and exhibit lights required by the (International) Regulations . . . in lieu of lights required by this section'. This permits International Lights to also be used under INLAND, WESTERN RIVERS, and GREAT LAKES.

Fixed stern light preferred, otherwise lantern is shown in time to prevent collision, Rule 10(b).

Rule 7(c)-20 point white. Must be higher than red and green lights. . carry high as practical; it should not reflect in operators eyes.

(AVOID weak R & G flashlight battery powered lights as they are difficult to see.)

3' minimum

Combination OR separate R & G, 1 mile visibility, Rule 7(d).

Rule 10(a) white, 12 point. 2 mile vis., should be level with side lights if practical. (can be offset on outboards under 26', see Sec. 86.05-1)

Rule 7(c)--same as above. (20 point white light if located at same level as red and green lights, the white light will overpower the weaker red and green lights.)

3' minimum

Rule 7(d)--same as above.

Small power-driven vessel of less than 40 feet in length.

Rule 7(a)(i), white, 20 point, 3 mile vis., should be carried high as practical. It should be at least 9' above gunwale,

same as above

and at least 3' above R & G.

9' minimum

Rule 7(a)(ii), combination or separate R & G.

Power-driven vessel under 40 gross tons (40 feet to 65 feet).

Second white or RANGE LIGHT is required on vessels over 150'. It is optional on vessels less than 150', Rule 2(a)(ii)(iii). It may be less than 40' above hull of vessel.

same as above

Rule 2(a)(i,iii), 20 point white, 5 mile vis., at least 20' above the hull.

20'

Rule 2(a)(iv), separate 10 point GREEN; Rule 2(a)(v), separate 10 point RED; screens are required, Rule 2(a)(vi)

Power-driven vessel over 40 gross tons (over 65 feet).

We are given a new set of lights for International Waters, called 72 COLREGS, plus our own International variables, plus our endless redundant Inland light regulations.

The bulbs are a lot stronger, and the lights often installed higher to be able to meet the 1, 2, and 3 mile visibility standards. The lights are designed for earlier recognition to reduce collision potentials, with a larger battery draw.

Considerable debate ranged in the U.S. as to how far to apply these regulations. USCG was under a lot of pressure to find a practical application. If applied to its full extent this would have caused replacement of all sailboat and powerboat permanently installed navigation lights.

USCG finally decided not to have these regulations apply to powerboats and sailboats operating in U.S. waters to eliminate such an expensive refit, although it would be a good idea for owners to install them if they choose to.

A positive contribution for sailboats under 12 meters (39.4') for the cruising sailboat under sail only, is a tri-color masthead light with a single bulb having red, green, and white sectors. Visibility is excellent due to light intensity and height which cannot be blocked by waves. On the negative side is a climb to masthead to replace a bulb that has burned out, and two sets of running lights.

If your boat intends to go foreign after 7/78 for even short periods, it will be necessary under present law to refit your boat with the new light standards.

We often find 450 to 500 sailboats with accompanying powerboat escorts involved in the annual Newport Beach, California race to Ensenada, Mexico, plus a lot of other boats that tag along unofficially.

While the extra cost of the strong lights under the 72 COLREGS might help to reduce collisions for a short race out of the U.S., would it be worth the mandatory refit for all participants to be required to have these new lights installed before being able to enter this race?

Rule 25(d)(ii). Vessel under oars...show white light in...time to prevent collision.

Rule 23(c). Power driven vessel less than 7 meters (23') whose maximum speed doesn't exceed 7 knots may...exhibit an all-round white light...if practical, also exhibit sidelights.

Rule 22 (b)(c) with definition Rules 21 (a)(b)(c)

These Rules provide navigation light specifications for power driven vessels with maximum speed exceeding 7 knots.

Please note below the number of navigation lights used from sunset to sunrise are the same and their arc's, identical. The differences from a 15' outboard to the 163' powerboat are the distance visibility of the lights, and the height of masthead above R & G lights or gunwale.

	less than 12 meters (to 39.4 feet)	12 to 20 meters (to 65.7 feet)	less than 50 meters (to 164 feet)	
R/G 112.5° each	comb. or separate 1 mile vis.	comb. or separate 2 mile vis.	separate 3 miles vis.	Rule 21(b)
masthead 225°	2 miles vis. 3.3' above R/G	3 miles vis. 8.2' above gunwale	5 miles vis.	Rule 21(a)
stern light 135°	2 miles	2 miles	3 miles	Rule 21(c)

lookout on bridge

blind spot

suction area ahead

suction on side

Many conflicts have developed in recent years between commercial vessel and pleasure boat operators for the following reasons.

While underway at cruising speed, lookout on most vessels are stationed on the bridge. While the height gives tremendous visibility, the wide bow causes a considerable blind spot that may hide any small vessel in that area.

Large vessel must maintain 5 knot minimum to maintain steerageway in most conditions, even more when riding empty with beam wind or current condition. While even this slow speed makes a sizable WAKE, it is nothing compared to that left by destroyers, cruisers, subs, etc., operating at full speed. Tremendous damage may occur if you aren't prepared to compensate for the wake.

Prop SUCTION of large vessel operating at cruising speed, may extend vessel length ahead, to fill void developing at the stern. Closer a small vessel is to its bow, the greater the effect will be of large vessel suction.

Tremendous prop suction also may occur alongside a large vessel after it has stopped and picked up a pilot. During acceleration, the prop suction may pull smaller vessels close by, alongside the larger vessel and hold them prisoner. In shallow water this effect may be even more serious and pronounced.

Tug with tow has limited maneuverability, especially if going downstream. If tug suddenly has to use reverse, the tow would ride up and over the tugboats stern.

Other factors to consider are the considerable draft & stopping distance required of large vessel, see facing page.

242

Sailing Illustrated

C3 Freighter   T2 Tanker   Supertanker W. Alton Jones

(a) C3 Freighter, 492' loa, 69'6" beam, draft 33', 16.5 knots.
(b) T2 Tanker, 523'6" loa, 68' beam, 14 1/2 k. cruis. speed.
(c) The super tanker W. Alton Jones, 823.6" loa, 116 beam,
43' draft, 16 1/2 knot cruising speed.

The C3 freighter requires about 1800' to come to full stop
from cruising speed; 480' to make a 90° turn. The T2
tanker may require 4350' to come to a full stop, with
1880' for 90° turn. The supertanker may require to 6600'
for full stop from cruising speed, with 2200' for 90° turn.

Figures indicate size, draft, stopping distance of large
vessels with limited maneuverability... the flyweights.
New Bantry Bay Class is 1135' long, draft 81.5', 326,000
tons compared to T2 17,000 tons... read USCG Captain E.F.
Oliver's "Gargantuan Tankers", USN Proceedings, Sept. '70.

underway   at anchor

At left we see a large vessel underway, and at right,
docked or at anchor. Note how the ensign changes from
the mast to stern, black anchor ball is added, and crews
flag or Union Jack is carried on bow of military vessels.

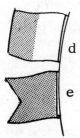

Two flags are flying from the bridge of the
vessel underway. The red and white flag at
right signifys that a pilot is aboard.

The second is a red flag that indicates
ammunition, flammable liquids, or explosives
are carried aboard vessel. It is also carried
on ammunition barges and on small harbor
work boats that deliver gasoline.

243

Our 1960 "Trailer Boating Illustrated" challenged inventors to produce a better hand propulsion method than oars and paddles, stern mounted, especially for planing hulls. We hoped it would need only one hand, the operator sitting in a comfortable position looking forward.

Several inventors seemed interested, without results, till a local inventor who spent many years in China, not knowing of our challenge, 13 years later produced POWR-OAR. He bought a Sabot after moving to the U.S. Not satisfied with normal operation he produced this new idea requiring a basic patent search almost as far back as Noah's Ark.

He had watched Chinese scull 20' to 30' junks for many years with long sweeps or oars, the start of the idea. It was combined with a fishes tail, providing much better underwater propulsion shape than the end of an oar.

Major sculling oar power loss motion occurs as the oar reaches end of arc. It must stop, be rotated, then reverse direction. A swivel motion was added to the blade so at the end of the arc it made efficient change of water pressure, instead of fighting itself and wasting power as with the sculling oar. The blade displaces water at stern pushing your boat forward, similar to the tail of a fish.

Still not being satisfied, it was also redesigned to work as a dinghy rudder for steering. A lanyard was released when it was changed to propulsion, the lanyard pulled in to again become a rudder . . . race committees, beware!

Dinghy space is at a premium. When disassembled it has short sections needing minimum stowage area, weight around 3 pounds. If parts fall overboard during a capsize, they will float. As the size of dinghy or rowboat increases, so must the size of the propulsion blade become larger. POWR-OAR seems to have an excellent future.

244 Moderncraft, 1306 W. Glenoaks Blvd., Glendale, Calif. 91201

335°M

to wedge

100' deep

| weak | strong | overpowered |

〜BR ᏒᏌᏁᏀᏀ〜

Our Newport jetty radiobeacon at left was ideal for new boat operator practice. Being low power it could be picked up about six miles out with the rdf set shown.

Steering on NULL, impulses began to show on sensitivity needle above. About 300 yards out with batteries in good condition, it would be overpowered on null. Fathometer meanwhile has been picking up the bottom, shallowing rapidly till preset alarm sounds at 100'.

A sharp right turn following 100' contour would take boat to entrance buoy. Hard left turn following compass course would take boat between jetties into harbor. A week before this page was written, we took our boat into the harbor with students aboard, in a peasoup fog. Accuracy was so good using this method, we almost hit the entrance buoy.

USCG insists rdf beacons only be used for cross bearings instead of homing. While ideal for freighter or 50' craft with more expensive equipment ... it is impractical for majority of smaller craft in pitching, rolling sea. For these, homing is ideal, yet practice is required in good weather to know capabilities & limitations of equipment.

After continuous practice with rdf through past years ... we feel many rdf limitation theories, seem based more on "Witch Doctor Tales", than actual use. Practice with your rdf, and make up your own mind as to its practical usage.

In late '64 USCG moved beacon 600 yards inshore of this position to wedge area known for spectacular body surfing wave action, a left turn putting boat on beach, a right turn into a rock jetty. It was an outstanding case of bad judgment till returned to original position in '74, ten years later.

The term boating safety covers the reduction of boating fatalities, injuries, and property damage. The major need is for more practical and useful boating instruction to be available nationwide . . . for the high risk portable boat.

Present research into boating safety is an outgrowth of the 1972 USCG push for boat operator licensing.

It became our job to prove to USCG the major high risk boating areas were fishermen and hunters using small, tippy, portable, or rental boats for transportation . . while the active boat owner was in a very low risk area.

Those in the high risk area were presently licensed for fishing and hunting. If they had to produce a certificate before license renewal they could swim 100' using any stroke, no time limit, it could eliminate many nonswimmer fatalities in tippy boats by people who can't swim, or convince them to take swimming lessons. We've researched several boating drownings in water so shallow they could have almost walked ashore, the reason behind our push for swim requirements. While we haven't found anyone with a better solution, no agency wanted to take over this responsibility . . . was it too practical of a solution?

It caused USCG to launch a 1973 and 1976 Nationwide Boating Survey by Chilton Research Services to find the missing statistics, proving the fishermen/hunter risk was much higher than any of us had anticipated.

The first National Boating Education Seminar sponsored by USCG and Am. Red Cross was held in 1976 in Maryland possibly as a result of this exposure. For the first time all boating education organization leaders met, agreeing a problem existed . . . the lack of sufficient boating education courses nationwide. No organization stepped forward to take over such national leadership with each satisfied with present goals and activities. The 1977 Oklahoma seminar furthered the idea, but the problem remained. After the rhetoric of the 1978 Southern California seminar theme, "How can we work together. ." had passed, the same 246 problem continued.   Sailing   Illustrated

An important finding developed in after hour discussions during the 1976 seminar,"The major key missing is the basic classroom text covering the well defined high risk world of the small portable powerboat and its trailer'!"

Our "TrailerBoating Illustrated" was underway. We were able to revise this book to what we hoped would provide the standards for this little known boating field defining a wide variety of problem areas, with a positive approach.

When we began the revision in 1972, seven major boating problem areas existed. The first answer was the 1972 DOT tire standards. A person could now choose the correct size tires for his trailer load range, and know the right inflation.

The Nationwide Boating Survey provided the first national picture of recreational boating (CG-B-003-78), available from Nat. Tech. Information Services, Springfield, VA 22161.

An unexpected contribution was made by George Sigler and Charlie Gore who sailed an inflatable Zodiac to Hawaii with water made in solar stills. They proved that man can survive for long periods on the ocean as castaways with practical basic equipment they tested (pgs. 224, 225), but not with much safety equipment available at the time.

In early 1978 USCG certified the first flotation belt preserver which we feel the most practical one for the high risk hunter/fisherman use (pgs. 226-227).

In late evening discussions at the second educational seminar we questioned whether passive lectures covering boating safety hazards were the best approach, or if the right text were available for study and analysis, would active classroom participation be a better approach?

"TrailerBoating Illustrated" is designed to fill these needs for classroom use and individual readers to keep operators out of trouble so they will enjoy boating and help others due to their exposure to endless variables in the world of portable boats. Since we had no precedent to follow, you may find it a considerably different boating book.

247

The U. S. Buoyage System is numbered proceeding from the sea. Two ways to remember correct side to pass buoys: (RRR)Red Right Returning, (BPOE)Black Port On Entering.

When buoys can be passed on either side with one being preferred, it is indicated by color of topmost band. The red & black combination buoys are also used for junctions & obstruction buoys. Mid channel vertically banded black and white buoys may be passed on either side.

Black and white horizontally banded buoys indicate fish traps; quarantine –yellow buoys; anchorage–white; dredging–white with green top; special purpose-orange & white bands. It is your authors feeling that another buoy just used for obstructions, is needed for our present system.

We have two traps that exist for the person entering new waters without advantage of a chart. In one is a conflict of parallel buoyage systems with underwater obstruction between; the other, when two systems meet and terminate together, such as found off City Island in the Long Island Sound. Many owners have tried to take a boat between the two, hitting a submerged rock called 'Big Tom .

After a storm, it is a good idea to bear close watch on floating buoys in exposed positions, that may have drifted off position, or the light is out. If such be the case, notify the closest USCG unit immediately.

Water depths on east coast are charted from Mean Low Water, west coast charts at Mean Lower Low Water. The latest correction date will be stamped on bottom of chart.

1 Buoy lights shown are; 1. flashing, 2. quick
2 flashing, 3. interrupted quick flashing, 4.
3 short long flashing, 5. occulting. 2 indicates
4 important turns, wrecks, etc., where special
5 caution is required; 3 indicates junction

lights or buoys and 4, mid channel buoys. As 5 requires shore current, its use is generally limited.

Buoyage System

N"8"

pass EITHER side

S"5"

S"6"

C"7"   N   EITHER side   N"6"

S

C

C"5"   preferred channel

N"4"

S"4"

S"3"

C"3"   preferred channel

N

S   S

junction   C   junction   N

S   S   this tone indicates shallow water

C   N

S"2"

S"1"

N"2"

C"1"   entering FROM seaward   this tone represents the color RED

Black Port On Entering   Red Right Returning

Horizontally banded buoy marks extremity of fish traps & nets.

249

Take a close look at a log burning in the fireplace. The wood must be first heated to the IGNITION POINT... so FLAMMABLE VAPORS begin to rise. Instead of the log, it is these vapors that burn ABOVE the logs surface.

The fire triangle is made of fuel, heat, and oxygen. Basic principle is to remove any one of these factors, and the fire ceases. Fires are usually divided into three classes:

A. Combustible material such a cloth, wood, paper, etc. To put out the fire, a deep penetrating COOLANT is required to reach the deep seated embers.

B. Flammable liquids, greases, paints, solvents, thinners, etc., cause a surface fire. A SMOTHERING effect such as baking soda or CO_2 is used to exclude the oxygen.

C. Electrical fires need HEAT source (current flow) broken. If all circuits are adequately fused, & the owner broke the circuits... or removed the battery lead when leaving his boat, most Class C fires would be eliminated.

It is a good idea to have pliers permanently mounted near the battery box to break circuit when required. Electrical fires may start Class A and Class B fires. Water should be avoided on electrical fires as it will act as a conductor.

7.6%

1.4%
Major cause of explosions and/or fires on boats are Class B gasoline fires. Note diagram at left of oxygen/fuel vapor ratio percentage that is explosive. The range is actually quite narrow; if mixture is too rich, gasoline won't explode.

Examine a 5 lb. dry chemical extinguisher... for its 8 BC rating. This is a UL rating in which this extinguisher must put out a 20 square feet gasoline spill fire. This rating is then reduced by 60% as a safety factor... or from 20 BC to 8 BC, or 8 square feet of Class B or C fire potential.

When part of a dry powder charge has been used, the remaining pressure may leak off in a day, a week, or a month, requiring a recharge right away. This type of extinguisher should be periodically shaken as pounding action of boats & autos tend to pack the baking soda.

In the first gasoline spill fire, a person normally moves in too close to the fire. He should stand almost erect to prevent a heat pocket forming under him, if he should bend over. If he stands 8' instead of 3' away from fire, the CONE of EFFECTIVENESS covers a greater area, so a larger fire can be put out in same amount of time. Use a quick swinging motion across fire area while you spray base of fire . . . or blanket above it to fall down and smother fire. Try both methods when possible.

●

Until a person has fought a fire, he tends to choose the least expensive extinguisher passing USCG requirements. He generally has little idea or interest whether it will work, or how it works.

Once he puts out a gasoline spill fire, he begins to think of self protection. He then buys the next larger size extinguisher, keeps it handy, checked, & in good condition.

●

If an LPG fire (Liquid Petroleum Gas-propane & butane) is put out by extinguisher, the LPG may continue to flow, then explode as it hits the red hot pipe area where fire was extinguished. Alternatives are to TURN OFF VALVE, or let an LPG fire burn itself out.

Alcohol fires may be smothered and put out with water spray. If bicarbonate of soda is used to put out alcohol fires, it will not harm the food . . . AVOID baking powder that may be explosive in an open flame. The best way to smother a cooking fire or one in a fuel container, is to put on the LID to exclude oxygen.

Pages 164-169 of "Trailer Boating Illustrated" cover more variables involved in fire fighting on and around boats.

251

United States Coast Guard ensign is flown from USCG vessels in commission. It has vertical orange and white stripes, with blue eagle and stars on a white background.

The United States Power Squadron ensign is flown from a members boat. It has blue and white vertical stripes, with white stars and anchor on red square background.

Coast Guard Auxiliary flag is flown from members boat after passing inspection. Color is dark blue with white diagonal stripe.

Red flag with white diagonal stripe indicates diver below, ir swimming to or from diving area. Flag may be on boat, float, or both.

For several years we've recommended a pennant be flown from bow of boat racing after five minute signal is given. It would be advantageous for jockeying in tight quarters with numerous classes in large regatta, also to avoid collisions with boats not racing.

racing
pennant

see pg. R 12

English and Canadians fly their ensigns from stern staff under sail, power, and at anchor, while traditional U.S. protocol is to fly it from leach of mainsail under sail.

Since the leach mounted ensign tangles with backstay when tacking or jibing, and hardly helps mainsail shape ... our U.S. sailing public is fortunately finding it more practical to carry it on the stern staff also under sail in increasing numbers each year finally adopted nationwide by U.S. in 1971.

Union Jack was crew flag for centuries indicating limited authority of professional crew at anchor or when docked. It is flown on anchored or docked military craft today; for reference see 'The Bluejackets' Manual'.

'Flag Etiquette'

Flag Etiquette originated from Navy usage. The New York Yacht Club then through precedent, established proper usage for the public, followed by NAYRU, CCA, etc.

An exception to this is the Ensign, which was formerly flown from a flag halyard going from outer end of boom to outer end of gaff, see below. Flag halyard was eliminated on marconi main leaving a large roach, with Ensign next sewn to leach or peak of main or mizzen.

Those in charge of U.S. sail etiquette finally realized impracticality and minimum use of roach mounted Ensign in 1971, agreeing to its stern mounted use under sail, power, and at anchor.

 National Ensign, the Yacht Ensign, USPS Ensign, CGA flag

 owner absent flag (blue), meal flag (white), guest flag (blue, white stripes)

 honoring a foreign ensign when in another country

yacht club burgee

officers flag or the owners private signal

Note: on a sloop the yacht club burgee is often given preference, instead of the officers flag or private signal from the masthead.

masthead

flag halyard — sail doesn't have roach

starboard spreader

Traditional Ensign location on flag halyard between boom & gaff.

starboard signal halyard

starboard shroud

Locations are shown above for vessels at anchor or under power, while below they are under sail.

owners flag to starboard

Jack Tars flag carried to port

after castle

fore castle

origin of Union Jack or Jack Tars Flag

black anchor ball Union Jack

When sailing near moored or anchored U.S. Navy or Coast Guard craft, watch the black anchor ball and Union Jack. If both are being lowered, keep clear as the vessel is raising anchor or leaving a dock, and needs room.

Commercial vessels usually follow the same procedure, without flying the Union Jack.

load waterline
sheer
curve of transverse area at load waterline
buttocks
waterlines
base line
buttocks
Sheer Plan (side)
sections
Body Plan (end)
diagonals
buttocks
waterlines
centerline
Half Breadth Plan (bottom)
diagonals
Table of Offsets

Shown above are drafting methods and terms used by naval architects to develop the lines of a boat, and to show hull form.

To understand these lines, it is necessary to know the sections, waterlines, buttocks, and diagonals shown in flat plan view above, and in perspective on the following pages.

Lines of a boat are shown with a side view called the SHEER PLAN, plus an end view or BODY PLAN comprised of a half view looking forward, & another half view looking aft. The HALF BREADTH PLAN or bottom view shows buttocks with waterlines on one side of the centerline & diagonals on the other. As the lines are symmetrical for port and starboard, it is only necessary to show one side.

These measurements are then enlarged to full size in the mold loft, using measurements given on the table of offsets. The sections or STATIONS shown in black on facing page, are the forms to which planking & bulkheads will fit, conform, or be shaped.

the Lines

SAILING SHIP HULLS WERE USUALLY
PLANNED WITH SCALE MODELS BEFORE
NAVAL ARCHITECTURE WAS FAR ENOUGH
ADVANCED. AFTER A MODEL HAD BEEN
APPROVED IT WAS OFTEN SAWN INTO SECTIONS
AND THEIR MEASUREMENTS ENLARGED
TO FULL SIZE.

BLACK AREAS ARE SECTIONS,
CROSS SECTIONS OR STATIONS
WHICH ARE ATHWARTSHIP
SECTIONS OF A HULL.

STA. 1
STA. 2
STA. 3
STA. 4
STA. 5
STA. 6
STA. 7
STA. 8
STA. 9
STA. 10
STA. 11

Royce

BEAM

L.W.L.
(LOAD WATERLINE)

255

WATERLINES ARE HORIZONTAL PLANES PARALLEL TO LOAD WATERLINE AND ARE OFTEN GIVEN IN INCHES.

BUTTOCK LINES REPRESENT VERTICAL PLANES SUCH AS SHOWN IN SHADED AREA AT REGULAR INTERVALS PARALLEL TO THE KEEL.

STA.1
STA.2
STA.3
STA.4
STA.5
STA.6
STA.7
STA.8
STA.9
STA.10
STA.11

WATERLINE C
WATERLINE B
WATERLINE A
WATERLINE 1
WATERLINE 2
WATERLINE 3
WATERLINE 1
WATERLINE C

BUTTOCK 3
BUTTOCK 2
BUTTOCK 1

LOAD WATERLINE

Royce

DIAGONALS ARE LINES USED TO DEVELOP A HULL FORM CROSSING THE FRAMES AS CLOSE TO RIGHT ANGLES AS POSSIBLE.

STA.1
STA.2
STA.3
STA.4
STA.5
STA.6
STA.7
STA.8
STA.9
STA.10
STA.11

RABBET

DIAGONAL 1
DIAGONAL 2
DIAGONAL 3
DIAGONAL 4
DIAGONAL 5

A RABBET IS A GROOVE THAT IS CUT INTO THE STEM, KEEL, STERN-POST, ETC, TO RECEIVE EDGES OR ENDS OF PLANKING.

257

One-design classes may race against each other using "Portsmouth Yardstick Book"-write Mr. Nolan Richards, 117 Kingswood dr., Florence, Alabama 35630;or by using Yachting's One-of-a-Kind Regatta method.

●

The Handicap Rating provides a method in which various kinds and sizes of sailboats are able to compete with each other on an equal basis.

In olden times, the longer boat was usually first one in, winning races due to a longer waterline speed factor, pg.14

To minimize the length advantage, the next step was to rate sailboats according to their LWL. Boat X with a 35.6 LWL had a 8 knot rated hull speed, and boat Y with an 80' LWL, had a 12 knot hull speed.

While an improvement, it was still not adequate due to variables in hull design and owner skill. The next step was to develop a boat rating, & a boat/owner rating.

Todays Ocean Racing Rating (ORR-boat only) is the result of the Cruising Club of America (CCA) formula.*It is quite complex, with many calculations having plus and minus values, formulated into a FEET rating. This includes the weight, displacement, overall length, sail area, height of mast, length of boom, size of battens, beam, freeboard heeling moment, and other factors.

Compilation of all factors equal OR Rating. If any hull or rigging changes are made, the boat must be remeasured at the time the change was made.

Let's take theoretical Ocean Racing Ratings & put them into practice with a ten mile race. One sailboat (A), will have a 20' rating, and the other (B), a 30' rating.

Boat B finishes the race in two hours. If boat A comes in 13 minutes and 46 seconds later, which of the two will win the race?

The foot rating must be converted into SECONDS per MILE, listed in the NAYRU Handbook (also Seawanhaka Yacht Club time table), shown on facing page.

258

boats	sec. per mi.	miles	seconds	corrected time
A (20'ORR)	306. 6	x 10 =	(3060 sec.)	or 51 min. 0. 0 sec.
B (30'ORR)	218. 0	x 10 =	(2180 sec.)	or 36 min. 20. 0 sec.

subtract the difference (880 sec.)   14 min. 40. 0 sec.

Hull B (30' ORR) would have to cross finish line more than 14 min. 40. 0 sec. ahead of the shorter boat to save her time. which she was unable to do. Sailboat A (20'ORR) was able to win the race by a minute.

Winning sailboats in such as the Honolulu, Acapulco, and Mazatlan races, often have little more than a ten minute spread on corrected time, even in such long distance races. This gives considerable proof as to the efficiency & equality of the Ocean Racing Ratings.

Next we have the boat and owner rating, covered by the Arbitrary Rating, Performance Rating (formerly PHRF), and others. This formula starts out with a rating similar to the previous one, but a lot more simple (listed in TIME such as "Malobi" K 40 rating of 130 seconds per mile, instead of a feet rating). The resultant rating is either raised or lowered according to the owners ability. If the boat and owner are consistant winners, the handicap rating will increase to make it more difficult to win next race. This rating goes with the boat when it is sold.

Miget Ocean Racing Fleet (MORF) was started for sailboats with a 25' LOA limit, original purpose being to improve quality of trailerable sailboats. MORF rating formula is comparable to CCA Rating Rule. According to local option, larger size boats may have an MORF Rating (in our local area, it covers sailboats up to 30').

Racing has many advantages. It improves the breed of boats as well as owner & crew competency, in order to consistently place or win.

*"Measurement Rule for Racing"; Cruising Club of America, 25 Broadway, New York, N. Y. 10004   259

The term SLOOP originated from the Dutch "sloep", the French "chaloup", and the English "shallop". In the beginning it was generally thought of as a large rowboat having a mast and sails that could be raised and used basically for harbor work.

The Dutch introduced the "sloep" to New York. In time a broad, shoal draft craft evolved using inboard ballast, being full in the bows, and carrying a tall mast. Later on it grew in size for commercial use up to 80' in the North River Sloop. Other uses of the term was a square-rigged Sloop of War (pg. 289), and today an English Navy gunboat.

Up to the turn of the century most large sailboats carried a bowsprit. They were called SLOOPS, while smaller ones without bowsprits were called KNOCKABOUTS. When better metals and improved engineering came along to make the taller masts practical, the term knockabout disappeared. The bowsprit is now limited to character boats, and to keep the anchor chain away from cruising hulls at anchor.

The MASTHEAD SLOOP rig has its jibstay going to the masthead. It is preferred for much of todays' ocean sailing boats from 24' where the wind is on the surface. Rigging is simple for cruising craft with a mast not designed for bending. All other factors equal, a masthead sloop will have a shorter mast than the standard sloop, making it able to carry a larger gennie to windward.

The STANDARD or FRACTIONAL sloop rig has jibstay or headstay going 3/4, 5/6, 7/8 or so, not all the way up to masthead. It is preferred for smaller one-design classes racing in protected areas where the wind may be several feet above the surface of the water.

The FRACTIONAL rig is preferred for all sizes of racing craft with mast bending being used to provide better sail trim starting with Snipe, Lightning, and Flying Dutchman ...all the way up to the highly complex 50' offshore racing dinghies. Many changes have taken place since 1956 when we were the first to question calling a sloop without a
260 bowsprit...a sloop. Sailing Illustrated

GAFF MAIN

Traditional sloop is shown at left, basic sloop terms below and page 7; Hudson River Sloop, page 275; Friendship Sloop, page 227; Sloop of War, pg. 288.

KNOCKABOUT—HAD NO BOWSPRIT.

CLUB FOOTED JIB

BOWSPRIT

MODERN SLOOP RIGS

LIDO 14' 14' LOA

TWIN HULL 'AIKANE' 46' LOA

12 METER 'COLUMBIA'-69.9' LOA

SMALL   TALLER MAST   LARGE

SHORTER MAST

3/4 JIB RIG

NOTE: Jumper strut is eliminated on most late racing rigs.

SIMPLER RIGGING

BOTH HULLS AND TOTAL SAIL AREA ARE IDENTICAL.

HEADSTAY

JIBSTAY

BACKSTAY

HEADSTAY

STANDARD OR CONVENTIONAL RIGGED SLOOP

MASTHEAD-RIGGED SLOOP

261

The sloop is permanently rigged for one headsail or jib, while the CUTTER is generally rigged to carry two. Since it requires more space forward for headsails, the mast is usually stepped further aft, carrying a smaller mainsail.

Another definition . . . the cutter has its mast stepped 2/5 or more of the waterline length aft. In some cases two headsails are used, while others under this rule such as the Calkins 50, only have provisions to carry one jib. Others under this rule such as the Owens Cutter may sail as a masthead sloop (cutter ?), or under the basic cutter definition with double headsails.

Americans tend toward light displacement, light weight, easy turning sloops for weekend racing and cruising. Reduce the amount of material required and the resulting boats weight, and it makes a price savings to the buyer. Because of this, long distance cruising merits of this type fiberglass hull are still not clear.

The cutter was developed for extended use in pilot boats off the English coast requiring the advantages of a sloop, yet being able to ride it out in rough weather under inner jib or forestaysail, when the sloop would have to run for cover under storm jib, or is down to bare poles.

Two decades ago many cruising sailboats carried two masts. A slow but steady change began to favor the heavy, long-keeled cutter up to 36' to about 1970. Blue-water cruising sailors then began choosing larger cutters up to 50' as self-tailing winches and improved reefing hardware began to appear. The cutter could usually point higher than ketches and schooners, had better storm riding ability, with less rigging.

Eric Hiscock is one of our favorite cruising authors. He has probably seen more miles cruising the world under cutter rig than any other cruising sailor. He catalogs his excellent experiences in books such as "Cruising Under Sail", "Beyond the West Horizon", "Around the World in Wanderer III", etc. They are very informative for the future generation of blue-water cruising sailors.

262

Sloop vs Cutter

JUMPER

(TALLER MAST)

RIGGED FOR ONE HEADSAIL

JIBSTAY

THE SLOOP

STAY

CUTTER IS PERMANENTLY RIGGED FOR TWO HEADSAILS, THE SLOOP ONLY FOR ONE.

HEADSTAY

(SHORTER MAST)

JIBSTAY

FORESTAY

RIGGED FOR TWO HEADSAILS STEPPING MAST FARTHER AFT.

FORE

JIB

THE CUTTER

STAYS'L

THE ORIGINAL CUTTER DESIGN

TOPS'L

THE TWO HEADSAILS ARE OFTEN CALLED THE OUTER JIB & THE INNER JIB.

OUTER JIB
INNER JIB

REMOVABLE BOWSPRIT

F. STAYS'L

JIB TOPS'L

JIB

FORE STAYS'L

BOWSPRIT

BOBSTAY

TOPPING LIFT

RUNNING BACKSTAY

ALL HEADSAILS SHOWN ARE LOOSEFOOTED.

Royce
263

Some larger sloops were yawl rigged and changed at a later date to sloop rig...and visa versa.This shows that many owners and designers are still in doubt as to which is the better sail rig for boats over 30'.

Some feel Carleton Mitchell has amply proved yawl rig superiority with his "Finisterre" detailed pages 67-69. Others feel prime factor in its outstanding racing record isn't the boat...but Mitchell. In recent years it has become much better known for its participation in books and magazine articles written by Carleton Mitchell for the National Geographic Society.

You may usually identify a yawl from a distance by size DIFFERENCE between the main and jigger. When it is closer you will be able to see the rudder post and tiller or wheel located BETWEEN the masts. While mizzen mast of ketch is located over engine or propeller shaft, jigger on a yawl is usually stepped aft of waterline, and often to either side on smaller yachts not to interfere with tiller.

In a light breeze while beating, the yawl will be carrying the gennie, main, and jigger. As the wind increases, the jigger acting as a steering trim tab will be eased, and finally dropped to minimize weather helm, page 135.Under storm conditions the yawl can reduce sail for balance similar to sloop and cutter methods.

A mizzen staysail, or a larger mizzen spinnaker may be carried while reaching or running downwind, for which the sloop has no provisions. For long distance cruising the jigger has another advantage distasteful to some sailors as it may be used as an outrigger for trolling. This may help to provide a continuous supply of fresh fish which reduces amount of canned goods otherwise carried aboard.

A single masted boat is usually preferred in the U.S. to boats with two masts under 30', as it will otherwise end up with too much rigging and not enough sail area. An exception to this occurs in the Hawaiian Islands where a common occurrence seems to be too much wind.

Yawls

YAWL WITH A
FULL COMPLEMENT
OF SAILS

SPINNAKER WITH
A HALF BRAU

TILLER

JIBBOOM

THROAT

BOOMKIN

LAZY JACKS

JACKSTRUT
(MUST ABSORB
TREMENDOUS THRUST)

JACKSTAY

TOPS'L

CLUB
FOOTED
JIB

CAT YAWL   Royce

EARLY YAWL, USUALLY SQUARE RIGGED   265

The ketch design under square sail dates to Colonial times. Coastwise commerce was their specialty later taken over by schooners. The extra speed of our early schooners more than made up for the larger crews that were required to operate them.

At the turn of the century, the ketch's popularity was revived for cruising boats with smaller crews and ease of handling, for owners not desiring extra speed of schooner.

The ketch has a larger combination of smaller sail areas that may be used without reefing, than the yawl. This is especially important in larger vessels as mainsail area is easier to reef, than on yawl of equal length.

It is difficult to generalize about todays ketch rig, without including hull form and sail design. Some have good pointing ability for weekend racing and cruising... while the poor design is limited to downwind racing, and a lot more of its hours spent under power with wind above the beam.

The MAIN TRYSAIL or WISHBONE RIG is classed as a ketch. The wishbone rig is raised and lowered with the sail. Advantages claimed are ease of handling, and no need to reef as sails are divided into many areas, any of which may be used for the desired combination.

The BACK STAYSAIL eliminates extra rigging normally required for second mast, with a permanent backstay going to stump mast. Resulting sail, is said to have a depressing effect on stern for downwind sailing. Most of these craft have been rerigged to other standards.

We treasure our autographed copy of "Sea Quest" given to us by author Charles A. Borden, who passed away just a couple of days later (Ballentine Books, Inc.).

Endless books and articles have tried to record experiences and philosophies of this blue water cruising field, yet it required Charles to provide the multi-faceted classic of this field. If you want a stimulating 'mental vacation' away from smog, politics, ecologists, and endless other 266 artifical pressures of everyday life ... try "Sea Quest".

Ketches

MIZZEN

MIZZEN STAYS'L

MAIN

JIB

F'ST'YS'L

TILLER

SPRING STAY

MIZZEN MAST

MAIN MAST

MAIN TRYSAIL

JIGGER

MIZZEN

MIZZEN STAYS'L

WISHBONE RIG

Royce

BACK STAYSAIL

EARLY KETCH

BACK STAYSAIL RIG

267

During the latter 1700's the schooners began taking the coastal trade away from the square riggers, as they required smaller crews & could sail higher to windward. Along the coasts a schooner could generally depend on a land/sea breeze for a steady beam reach.

Starting as two-masted sloop, the schooner kept growing in size until 1902 when the seven masted THOMAS W. LAWSON was launched. To simplify the sail names they finally named each after a day in the week. But the Lawson was hardly successful being under-canvassed & difficult to handle.

Schooner racing has a long tradition in the U.S. It began formerly when the "AMERICA" proved victorious over her English competitors in 1851.

For many years fishing schooners raced back from the Grand Banks . . . and to the winner went the highest price for his fish. Fishing soon became of second importance to the racing and betting. The day of the schooner was then in its prime as it produced huge racing machines flying acres of canvas.

Suppose a person has a conventional rigged schooner, and he wanted to use it for a long distance downwind cruise. It he rigged square sails on the forward mast, it would then become a TOPSAIL SCHOONER. If he had a STAYSAIL SCHOONER and rigged it with square sails on the forward mast, it would then become a half and half or HERMAPHRODITE BRIG, see page 282.

BLOCK ISLAND schooner was developed by fishermen on Block Island, to be launched from the beaches. For ballast on the way out, boulders were used. For return trip the rocks were dumped overboard with the fish being used for ballast.

Schooners

THOMAS W. LAWSON

SATURDAY PUSHER · FRIDAY DRIVER · THURSDAY JIGGER · WEDNESDAY SPANKER · TUESDAY MIZZEN · MONDAY MAIN · SUNDAY FORE

BLOCK ISLAND SCHOONER

NO STAYS · NO STAYS
LOOSEFOOTED MAIN · BOOMLESS FORE

THE 'AMERICA'

MAINS'L IS LACED TO BOOM · BOOMLESS FORE

GOODWILL AND PIONEER

SPRING STAY
MAIN TOPMAST STAY
TRIATIC STAY
MAIN TOPS'L
FORE TOPS'L
(TOPMASTED SCHOONER)

A TERN IS A SCHOONER WITH 3 OR MORE MASTS

BALDHEADED SCHOONER

SPRING STAY
GAFF VANG
MAINMAST
FOREMAST

CONVENTIONAL SCHOONER RIG

MARCONI MAIN
GAFF-HEADED FORES'L

DARK SAIL IS A GOLLYWOBBLER

STAYS'L SCHOONER

Royce
FISHERMAN
INNER JIB
OUTER JIB
STAYSAIL

269

The MOTOR SAILER is a compromise boat having a 50-50%, 40-60%, 30-70%, etc., ratio between sail and power. While some are questionable, there are many very able cruising boats in the motor sailer class. For the calms or narrow channels, the engine is used, if the wind comes up the sails are used. In some situations both engine and wind power are used. A good 85-15% compromise is the 40' Newporter.

On my first visit to the Puget Sound, many motorboats had small STEADYING SAILS shown. In a stiff wind the side to side roll of motorboats, combined with the fore and aft pitching can be most uncomfortable. If steadying sail is used for all courses except a following wind and sea, roll is minimized producing easier ride.

The LJUNGSTROM is one of the few original types of sailboats, as almost all others were outgrowths of a previous type. Mast has no stays and the sail is reefed or furled around a revolving mast. When sailing before the wind the sail area is doubled, vaguely resembling a spinnaker. The Ljungstrom is one of the very few fore and aft rigged boats without booms that doesn't have to worry about accidental jibe damage.

The CANEYE is a Chesapeake Bay rig resulting from combination of the bugeye and log canoe.

The SPRITSAIL was quite popular with the early Dutch when they first settled in New Amsterdam, or New York. This type rig is found today in a few sailboats all the way from the small OPTIMIST PRAM, to some of the THAMES BARGES to 70' long, still using wind propulsion.

The SLIDING GUNTHER is an adaptation of the gaff rig, with gaff locked into vertical position. It is the English version to have all spars and sails to fit inside a dinghy. The American version, is to have a two piece mast with upper half fitting into a sleeve secured to the bottom half of the mast, also providing stowage in dinghy.

Other Tykes

DOGHOUSE

MOTOR/SAILER

TWIN WING OR
LJUNGSTRÖM

STEADYING SAILS

CLUB FOOTED JIB

CANEYE

SLIDING GUNTHER

ROYCE

SPRIT SAIL

271

SHARPIES were numerous in the seventies and eighties, developing into a very popular sailboat on the eastern end of the Long Island Sound. It was an inexpensive, easy to build flat bottomed boat, some of which were up to sixty feet long. This peculiar rig sometimes carried a centerboard forward, and another aft. Sharpies were probably developed by oystermen that had previously used dugout canoes.

The SKIPJACK has a semi-V bottom with hard chines, straight frames, and is simple to build. The skipjack is sloop, yawl, or schooner rigged. The FLATTIE is an early sharpie with a mast having a small amount of rake aft.

The GLOUCESTER, ESSEX, or FRIENDSHIP SLOOP was developed by fishermen as an all-weather offshore boat. MUSCONGUS BAY SLOOPS were similar in appearance above the waterline but had a shallower draft. These were all New England built boats that were named after the fishing towns in which they were built, and from which they sailed.

The Chesapeake has its LOG CANOES to which early colonists added sails. It is hard to call the modern 30' to 40' sailboat that may carry up to eight sails with acres of sail a log canoe, but the name remains. As these shallow draft boats are very tender, it is common when beating to windward in a race, to have a crew member riding way out on the boomkin to raise the bow...and out on HIKING PLANKS that extend several feet over the weather side of boat. In the traditional design the masts aren't stayed.

Sailing Illustrated

Older Types

SHARPIE HULL

SHARPIE

SKIPJACK HULL

SKIPJACK

FRIENDSHIP SLOOP

CHESAPEAKE
LOG CANOE

Royce 273

It is believed our present day marconi or jib-headed rig was developed in Bermuda, and named by the British as the BERMUDIAN RIG.

Whether it started by the adaptation of a lateen sail to a mast instead of to a yard, or by eliminating the gaff on a gaff headed mainsail, is an unrecorded page of history. A BERMUDIAN SCHOONER of the 1830's is shown with an overlapping boomless foresail and a similar main. The mizzen was loosefooted yet bent to a boom.

The HUDSON or NORTH RIVER SLOOP was developed for shallow protected waters from New York to Albany. This type sailboat sometimes had to jibe all standing on the upper reaches of the Hudson, hence the origin of the HUDSON or NORTH RIVER JIBE. This type vessel carried a huge spread of canvas, and due to the area had to be close winded.

The inspiration for the CHESAPEAKE BUGEYE with two raking masts & a pointed stern is believed to come from the Bermudas, as it resembles the early Bermuda rig. The extreme rake of the mainmast is useful for loading & unloading cargo as the main halyard block is directly over the cargo hatch.

The SHARPSHOOTER is a Bermudian catboat with a loosefooted mainsail. This was developed by a yankee that combined the New England Cat with the early Bermudian rig. The boat is reputed to be difficult to handle if it is caught in irons.

A sailboat with a high pointed stern to lessen chance of its being pooped is called a PINK. As the name refers to the hull form instead of to the rig, it may be found in any type vessel from lateener, to sloop, to schooner.

Laugh and cry with Farley Mowat, articulate author of "The Boat Who Wouldn't Float", Little, Brown, & Co. Your sailboat problems will seem minor afterwards!

EARLY BERMUDIAN SCHOONER

HUDSON RIVER SLOOP

BUGEYE

SHARPSHOOTER

PINKS

Royce

275

The beginning of sail is obscured in the unrecorded pages of history.Many feel it started for downwind operation with a square sail.The yard was later tilted at an angle to sail a little higher into the wind, producing the lugger.

The challenge grew. Merchants could float their cargoes down the Nile,yet the vessels had to be rowed upstream on the return.The lugger yard was tried which kept growing to extend the sail high enough to make use of prevailing breezes over nearby hills . . . to eliminate rowing.

Lateeners became a favorite of Mediterraneal sailors, little changed from the days of early Phoenicians off the coast of Africa, the Red Sea, and the Indian Ocean . . . rapidly disappearing, read "Son of Sinbad", pg. 278.

A memory of the past, the LAKE GENEVA BARK, shows a 'goosewing' arrangement of lateen sails for downwind sailing. The NILE GYASSA is a large undecked sailing barge with shallow draft to avoid numerous mud shoals. It has a high bow,and extremely high lateen yard to catch light breezes high up,passing over nearby hills.

Changing tack on lateeners shown at right is complex. As sail is loosefooted, damage from accidental jibe is reduced as sail is loosefooted.

The Dutch used lateen sails on the Atlantic for vessels to outsail the Spanish blockading their ports . . . successful enough to be adopted by the British Navy,popular until the defeat of the Spanish Armada. By the 1700's the lateen sail was restricted to the mizzen, later replaced by a gaff-rigged spanker.

● PACIFIC SKIPPER,monthly,300 N. Newport Blvd.,Newport Beach, CA 92663. Excellent, varied, hard to find info for cruising enthusiasts.West Coast,Pacific Ocean oriented.

● CRUISING WORLD,monthly, 524 Thames St., Newport RI 03480. Excellent,the other side of the coin,east coast oriented.Serious cruising sailors need subscriptions to both publications for answers you can't find elsewhere.

Wearing Lateeners

SAILING WING & WING

A SWISS BARQUE

THE NILE GYASSA

INSTEAD OF COMING ABOUT WHEN ADVANCING TO WINDWARD A LATEENER MAY WEAR ABOUT.

STBD TACK

PORT TACK

WIND DIRECTION

SHROUDS NOW TO WINDWARD ARE SET UP TIGHT.

YARD IS SHEETED FORWARD ON OTHER SIDE OF MAST

YARD IS HAULED VERTICAL

SAIL IS COLLAPSED, SHROUDS WHICH WERE TO WINDWARD ARE CAST OFF.

Royce

277

In most places the internal combustion engine is replacing the sail for commercial use. One notable exception is the Arab that believes Allah will provide for the future. As a result he is carrying on sailing in his lateeners in the same manner he has done for hundreds of years.

As a result charts, barometers, logs, and insurance are unknown. Navigation is by eye, a makeshift leadline, Allah's will...and only recently the compass. As they don't pamper their customers, passengers usually carry & cook their own meals. In addition to the regular crew, is a full complement of insects and rodents.

Lateeners can't point as high as a fore and after. While maneuvering in tight harbors they are reputed to be clumsy. An Arab sailor told me that the lateeners usually have to wear about instead of coming about (see previous page). As this is a nuisance, long tacks are generally preferred. Lateen sails aren't designed for reefing. If a reduction in sail is indicated, the yard is lowered, a smaller sail bent on and raised. In port, the sails generally make very good awnings.

Lateen yards are often 80' to 150' long, and made of several tree trunks lashed together. As this type of yard doesn't permit rat lines or foot ropes, the crew has to scramble up the yard maintaining a precarious foothold to the lashings. Sometimes he must lash the back of his ankles together for a better foothold.

DHOW is used as general term to cover Arab lateeners that are SAMBUKS, ZAROOKS, BAGGALAS, and BOOMS, depending on size of hull.

Want to crew on a lateener? If you are interested, practice climbing 100' palm trees at midnight in a strong wind. It's a beginning.

Dhow information is scarce except for 'Sons of Sinbad', Charles Scribner's Sons, by Alan Villers of his interesting year sailing adventure on dhows deeply imbedded in a 278 culture, philosophy, and sailing methods foreign to us.

Lateeners

FELUCCA

XEBEC

ARK PROVENCALE

BAGGALA (DHOW)

Royce

SAMBUK (DHOW)

279

Luggers were ideal boats for slavers, pirates, smugglers and harbor work before the day of the gaff rig, as they could outdistance the square riggers by sailing closer to the wind.

Luggers weren't the easiest type boat to handle, as they need skilled crews, and were vicious if caught in irons.

The BALANCED LUG often had a boom at the foot of the sail, extended fore and aft. The sail was not lowered when changing tack.

The DIPPING LUG was common on the larger luggers. But the yard had to be dropped and hoisted again on the opposite side of the mast after changing tack. It is supposed to be better than standing lug for weatherlieness. Yet it is very dangerous and hard to handle if yard isn't dipped promptly, permitting sail to be caught in irons.

The STANDING LUG has the tack of sail made fast to lower portion of mast. It is not dipped when changing the tack.

The SPLIT LUG has a sail divided below the yard and at the line of the mast. The forward part acts as a jib with the tack made fast to bow, the clew shifted aft by sheets.

The Chinese have made practical use of their lug-rigged JUNKS for centuries. Needless to say they contributed many ideas of their own. The pole masts have neither shrouds nor stays, with sails often made of bamboo. The high stern and big rudder are troublesome in a rough sea. In addition the junks don't seem to be able to point too high to weather. Use of metals on imported junks is often much poorer quality than found on U.S. sailboats, or those imported from Europe.

Luggers such as the last one at right were quite large, some of them being up to eighty feet long.

"Posted Missing" by Alan Villers, pub. 1956 by Scribners, is a fascinating, educational book analyzing reasons why several vessels have vanished . . . including a battleship.

280

Luggers

LUGGER

BALANCED LUG

DIPPING LUG

STANDING LUG

SPLIT LUG

ROYCE

281

A vessel had to have three or more masts all carrying square sails to be SHIP RIGGED. The CLIPPERS could be square rigged or schooner rigged as term referred to narrow beam hulls with fine lines . . . rather than rigging. Previous hulls often seemed based on theory . . a CODFISH HEAD (wide blunt bows at waterline) and MACKEREL TAIL (slim stern at waterline). This theory was popular for several hundred years till advent of faster clipper hull.*

Square riggers were designed to sail BEFORE the wind, following the prevailing winds and currents around the world. When they neared a coastline, square riggers often had to fight adverse headwinds . . . or anchor to wait a wind shift, as they couldn't normally sail higher than 6 points of the wind, or 65-70° from eye of wind, if bottom was clean. Windward ability was decreased as bottom growth began to develop.

A compromise then began between them and the fore & aft rigged vessel which could point higher, and required half to third of crew on a similar size square rigger.

The HERMAPHRODITE BRIG is a half and half vessel while a BARKENTINE was more for coastal work, having two masts, fore and aft rigged. The BARK had three or more masts with only one being fore and aft rigged. A bark was made more for extended cruising than speed, an ideal combination for WHALERS.

BRIG & BRIGANTINE were two masted square riggers. If no provisions had been made to hang a mainsail, it was a brigantine. The SNOW had a close resemblence to the brigantine, except it had a third or trysail mast about a foot abaft the main or second mast.

For readers wanting to learn in depth the peak and decline of commercial square rig ships from 1890, we highly recommend "The Way of a Ship" by Alan Villers, Charles Scribner's Sons. It is THE classic of this much spoken of yet little understood era of square riggers.

FULL RIGGED SHIP, CLIPPER HULL

BRIG

HERMAPHRODITE BRIG

BRIGANTINE

BARKENTINE

BARK

BARK

Royce

283

Square rigger language is complex...as over 280,000 sailing vessels have been registered, each conforming to the owner, captain, or mates wishes. The only element remaining standard was location of lines coming to the same belaying pins on deck, whether American, Dutch, English, or Finnish square rigged vessels.

If we go to the 16-17th centuries we see bulky hulls, high poops, blunt bows, & oversized sails. As masts were taller on later ships it was necessary to divide some of the sails into two areas...upper & lower tops'ls, upper & lower "tugalants", as examples. This added to amount of lines, but simplified reefing in a storm when even small sails were dangerous and backbreaking to take in.

On facing page the upper & lower "tugalants" have been combined to show "moons'ls" that were quite small & only found on a few large sailing ships.

Again let us say sailing is a spoken instead of a written language so we find topgallant called "tugallant"; foresails, fors'ls; skysails, skys'ls; studding sails, stuns'ls; crossjack, crojik; etc. The slang usage simplified the pronounciation.

As square riggers grew in size the pole mast began to disappear, the trees no longer being tall enough. Trees had to be cut into sections & joined together between the HOUNDS & MAST CAP. Overlapping parts of these were called DOUBLINGS. The masts were solid & not long by themselves. Add three or four on top of one another, and it made a sizeable mast.

Deck terminology should be self explanatory except for the POOP DECK, which was sometimes a complete deck of its own. Other times it was the area directly behind the helmsman, though a part of the quarter deck. Note illustration of quarter deck on following page.

Want to know sailing in the 1819 "state of the art" as learned by seamen then? Their text "Lever's Young Sea Officer's Sheet Anchor", has been republished exactly as it was in 1819, by the Edward Sweetman Co. It is a 284 MUST for a knowledgeable sailor's library (pg. 184)!

Where is the CROW'S NEST? That was usually highest vantage point on a square rigger. On the whaler it was quite obvious, as there was a platform to stand on, plus two waist high iron hoops to encircle the lookouts.

The forward supports to the masts were STAYS; the aft, BACKSTAYS; while SHROUDS support mast on either side. BRACES control horizontal movement of yards that lead aft, except on after mast of a ship with three or more masts. In this case they lead forward on the mast that is the furthest aft.

The YARDS are hoisted by HALYARDS, and supported by LIFTS that lead thru blocks at masthead or fairleads, & then to the top, or below to the deck.

The CLEWS of squaresails are secured to yard beneath them, except for the foresail, mainsail, crojik, and jigger, that have SHEETS going aft, and TACKS going forward to hold the corners down.

Clewlines and buntlines are used for taking in or hauling up a sail. The BUNTLINE is on the forward side of sail, the CLEWLINE on the after side of sail.

REEF TACKLES go to leaches of squaresails. In reefing they are used to haul the leach up and out, giving slack for passing the earing & rousing cringle up into place.

BOWLINES lead forward from the BOWLINE BRIDLE. They were used on lowers and topsails to hold the leach well forward when sailing close hauled. Bowlines were supposed to be obsolete by the time of the clippers.

DOWNHAUL TACKLES are used to haul tops'l yards to just above the lower tops'l yards. The downhaul tackles also support the lower tops'l yard that usually had no lifts.

If you are interested in present day square rigger sailing methods read "Eagle Seamanship" for the USCG training ship Eagle, pub. by M. Evans & Co., Inc., New York.

Sailing Illustrated

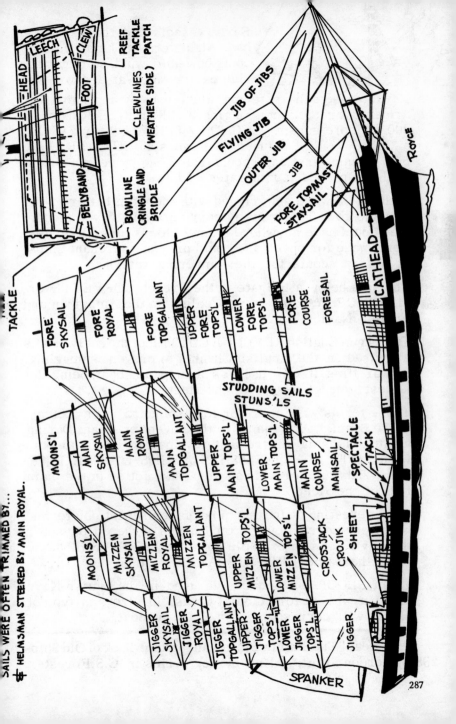

SAILS WERE OFTEN TRIMMED BY....
⚓ HELMSMAN STEERED BY MAIN ROYAL.

HEAD LEECH CLEW
FOOT
REEF TACKLE PATCH
BELLYBAND
CLEWLINES (WEATHER SIDE)
BOWLINE CRINGLE AND BRIDLE

TACKLE

JIB OF JIBS
FLYING JIB
OUTER JIB
JIB
FORE TOPMAST STAYSAIL

Royce

CATHEAD

FORE SKYSAIL
FORE ROYAL
FORE TOPGALLANT
UPPER FORE TOPS'L
LOWER FORE TOPS'L
FORE COURSE
FORESAIL

MOONS'L
MAIN SKYSAIL
MAIN ROYAL
MAIN TOPGALLANT
UPPER MAIN TOPS'L
LOWER MAIN TOPS'L
MAIN COURSE
MAINSAIL
SPECTACLE
TACK

STUDDING SAILS STUNS'LS

MOONS'L
MIZZEN SKYSAIL
MIZZEN ROYAL
MIZZEN TOPGALLANT
UPPER MIZZEN TOPS'L
LOWER MIZZEN TOPS'L
CROSSJACK
CROJIK
SHEET

JIGGER SKYSAIL
JIGGER ROYAL
JIGGER TOPGALLANT
UPPER JIGGER TOPS'L
LOWER JIGGER TOPS'L
JIGGER

SPANKER

287

Early vessels and todays' junks have high sterns to help weather-cock bow into wind, so they will ride easier when at anchor.

Naval vessels have terms which usually apply to their armament rather than rigging; a FIRST RATER carried 100 or more guns; a SECOND RATER, 90-99 guns; while a THIRD RATER carried 76-89 guns; a FOURTH RATER 54-75 guns. First and second rates had three gun decks while third and fourth rates had two.

FRIGATES were ship rigged with the main batteries in a single row. They usually carried 38 guns even though they could have anywhere from 24 to 50 guns. Frigates were made for speed and could prey on merchant ships, or act as scouts for the lumbering raters.

The size below a Frigate is the French CORVETTE or SLOOP OF WAR as it was called in the American and English Navies.

The 14 gun English REVENUE CUTTER of the early 1800's was used in the English Channel to prevent smuggling. In war time it was used as a dispatch boat, being the fastest type of vessel in the fleet.

These terms were more or less standard from defeat of the Spanish Armada up to the advent of steam. During a battle the smaller and faster ships ranged the flanks, while LINE-OF-BATTLE SHIPS or SHIPS-OF-THE-LINE (1st, 2nd, and 3rd raters) went into action in the main line of the fleet.

It is interesting to find that most of the present day terms have been carried over from canvas powered days of the navies. As an example the term BATTLESHIP came from the name LINE-OF-BATTLE SHIPS.

Term SLOOP for instance is used in the British Navy as a patrol boat for colonial areas. In size and type of use it will correspond to a U.S. gunboat.

Also read "The Ship" by Bjorn Landstrom; "Book of Old Ships" 288 by Gordon Grant; the Hornblower series by C.S. Forester.

Naval Sail Terms

REVENUE CUTTER
OF 1815

SLOOP OF WAR
OR CORVETTE

SQUARE
SPRITS'L

A FRIGATE
OF 1820

A FIRST RATER
OF 1750

HEAD

289

Royce

Our GLOSSARY is a dictionary of technical, obscure, and obsolete words. In it we provide coverage of tradition sailing terms in recent use, as well as obsolete sailing terms of the past frequently found in sea stories such as the Hornblower series... your authors and many of our readers favorite type of relaxation.

ABACK-set of ship's sails with wind on leeward side, in square rigger the sails would be pressed toward mast tending to force vessel astern, page 151.
ABAFT-comparison term of one object on shipboard being further aft than another; ABAFT the BEAM for example, is aft of the beam.
ABAFT the BEAM-bearing of object seen between beam and stern.
ABANDON-time to leave a sinking ship.
ABEAM-right angle from fore and aft centerline of boat, off the beam or on the side of a vessel, page 83.
ABLOCK-tackle taken in until both blocks come together.
ABOARD-in or on board a vessel.
ABOUT or ABOUT SHIP-to change tack, when bow of ship goes thru eye of wind, and pays off on other tack till sails again fill with wind, pages 108, 109.
ABOVE or ABOVEBOARD-above decks, straight forward or honest.
ABOX-square rigger maintaining position as waiting for pilot by bracing head and after yards on opposite sides or tacks, page 151.
ABREAST-side by side, alongside or abeam.
ABURTON-method of stowing casks athwartship and end to end.
ACCOMMODATION LADDER-ladder or portable steps to climb aboard ship.
A-COCK-BILL-position of anchor hanging from cathead; see 285 for location of cathead. Position of yards on square rigger topped up at angle with deck.
ACCOUNT, TO GO ON THE-a sailor turned pilot.
ADMIRALTY KNOT-6080 feet (Int'l Nautical Mile is 6076. 10').
ADRIFT-broken from the moorings or drifting.
ADVANCE-distance boat moves in original course after rudder is put over.
AFLOAT-boat or other buoyant object resting on surface of water.
AFORE-forward, opposite of abaft.
AFOUL-entangled or fouled in any way.
AFT-at, near, or toward the stern, page 82.
AFTER BODY-stern section of boat.
AFTER BOW SPRING-bow spring leading aft for docking, page 174.
AFTER BROW-an aft portable gangplank.
AFTER QUARTER SPRING-spring leading aft from boats bow, page 174.
AFTER WAIST SPRING-spring coming from amidship and going aft.
AFTER YARDS-yards abaft the foremast, page 285.
AFTER SAILS-sails bent to masts abaft the foremast.
AGROUND-keel or hull of boat resting on bottom, stranded, pages 222-225.
AHEAD-toward the bow or in front of, page 83.
AHOY-a greeting used in hailing a vessel or boat.
A-HULL-vessel hove to under bare poles, with helm alee.
AIR or FLOTATION TANK-sealed tank for buoyancy in capsize, pages 29, 31.
ALBATROSS-largest sea bird with wing span to 13', in Southern Hemisphere.
ALEE-to leeward side; helm away from wind, page 108.
ALIVE-wide awake.

G1

al ALL ABACK-when all sails are aback, see ABACK.

ALL-A-TAUNT-O-ship shape or all gear hauled in tight.

ALL HANDS-the entire crew.

ALL in the WIND-pointing too high, all sails shaking, pages 98, 104.

ALL NIGHT IN-maintaining no night watches.

ALL STANDING-'brought up standing' is be quickly brought to a stop;also, to turn in fully clothed, or be fully equipped.

ALOFT-up above;up the mast or in the rigging.

ALONGSIDE-side by side, by the side of a vessel or pier.

ALOW-below deck, or low in the rigging near the deck.

ALOW and ALOFT-all sails including studding sails are set, page 287.

ALTAR-steps of a drydock.   AMAIN-on the run, all at once.

AMBERGRIS-intestinal secretion of sperm whale used for blending ability in manufacture of perfume.

ANCHOR-device which digs into bottom preventing a boat from drifting, pg. 159.

ANCHORAGE-suitable place for anchoring.

ANCHOR AWEIGH-anchor broken out of bottom, or coming to surface.

ANCHOR HOY-lighter with derrick for handling heavy anchors.

ANCHOR LIGHTS-anchor riding lights carried on anchored vessels.

ANCHOR WATCH-deck detail to watch vessel anchored at night.

ANEMOMETER-wind velocity measuring instrument.

ANEROID BAROMETER-mechanical barometer without liquid.

ANGLE BAR-used to form inboard side of a waterway.

ANTI-CYCLONE-spiral eddy of wind that is flowing out.

ANVIL TOP-cirrus peak of thunderhead, pages 204-209.

APEAK-cable in vertical line with vessel over anchor. Also position of yards or oars when vertical or nearly so.

APORT-to the left or port side of a vessel when looking forward.

APPARENT WIND-wind direction felt on boat underway, pages 100. 102,131.

APRON-timber behind lower part of stem above fore end of keel.

ARC BOTTOM-see page 17.

ARDENT-sailing craft with excessive weather helm.

ARM-lower part of yachtsman and old fashioned anchor.

ARMING-cavity at bottom of lead line with tallow to bring up a bottom sample.

ARTIFICIAL RESPIRATION-see method on pages 230-231.

ASH BREEZE-calm requiring sailboat to use oars ... or iron spinnaker.

ASHORE-the same as aground.

ASTERN-in direction of stern;object bearing outside & behind vessel, pg. 83.

ATHWARTSHIP-across the keel of a vessel, page 82.

ATOLL-small circular coral island enclosing a lagoon.

ATRIP-position of anchor as it is raised above bottom.

A-TRY-vessel in gale without any sails set.

AUTO PILOT-mechanical helmsman set to compass heading.

AUXILIARY-engine used as secondary propulsion in sailboat.

AWEATHER-to windward, towards the weather side, 110.

AWEIGH-the same as ATRIP.

AWNING-tarp covering boat or deck for protection from sun or rain.

AYE-yes;reply than an officers orders are understood.

b BACK-to back sail is throw it ABACK;to BACK JIB is to hold it while coming about till wind catches its leeward side, pages 95, 108, 173.

BACKBOARD-vertical board rest used for helmsmans back.

BACKSTAY-mast support leading aft to deck or another mast, 35, 51-3, 63, 67, 79, 81.

RUNNING BACKSTAYS are temporary or shifting backstays, pages 68, 70, 109.

BACK STAYSAIL RIG-see page 267.

BACK WASH-churning water thrown aft by propeller.

BACKWATER-stop rowboat progress by reversing direction of the oars.

BACK WIND-sail back winds another by throwing wind on leeward side, 108,147.
BAG-a sail bags when leach is taut yet center of sail is slack.
BAGGY-WRINKLE-chafing gear made from old rope. 75.
BALANCING RING-ring fitted at balance point on shank for fishing older anchors.
BALANCED RUDDER-part of area is forward of rotation axis for powerboats.
BALDHEADED SCHOONER-schooner without topsails, page 268.
BALE-outer end of stock on old-fashioned anchor.
BALLAST-heavy material on bottom of sailboat to provide stability (in hold).
BALLAST TANKS-double bottom water tanks pumped out or flooded at will.
BALLOON STAYSAIL-used under spinnaker, pg. 69.
BANK-side of a river or shoal, page 216.
BAR-shoal or bank; CAPSTAN-BARS are heavy timbers that work the capstan.
BARE POLES-sailboat in gale with no sails set, page 137. 138.
BARE, SAILING-sailing with sheets too far in, page 104.
BARGE-ship's boat used by flag officers;THAMES BARGE is a flat bottomed
roomy boat for carrying cargo on the Thames River in England.
BARK (barque)-3 masted sailing vessel square rigged on fore & main, with the
mizzen fore and aft rigged, page 283.
BAR KEEL-a heavy steel or iron external keel.
BARKENTINE (barquentine)-3 masted sailing vessel square rigged on fore,
yet main and mizzen are fore and aft rigged, page 283.
BARNACLE-small shell fish that enjoys the bottom of your boat.
BARNEY POST-short post in cockpit with jam cleat for main sheet.
BAROMETER-instrument for registering atmosphere's pressure, page 212.
BARRATRY-shipmasters dishonest action such as unauthorized sale of ship.
BARRIER REEF-above-water reefs along a coast.
BATTEN-thin rigid strip fitted to pocked on after edge of sail to keep its shape,
page 91 ;metal strips fitted over hatch coamings to secure tarp.
BEACHCOMBER-unemployed derelict seaman found on waterfront.
BEACON-danger or recognition navigation mark placed on or near object.
BEAM-the greatest width of a vessel, pages 82, 83.
BEAM-ENDS-vessel listing or hove over till beam is almost vertical. Method
was used to scrape and repair boat bottoms before use of drydock.
BEAM SEA-wind at right angle to keel, BEAM REACH, BEAM WIND, page 99.
BEAR-object bears so & so when in direction a person is looking.
BEAR DOWN-to approach vessel from windward.
BEAR IN- to approach an object or shore.
BEARING-direction of object as to vessels heading or compass course, pg. 83.
BEAR OFF-steer away from wind, shore or object.
BEAR UP-steer up towards eye of wind, shore or object.
BEAT-advancing to windward on alternate tacks, pages 100, 101.
BECALMED-vessels sails hang limp & lifeless when becalmed.
BECKET-eye or loop made with fiber or wire rope.
BEE-BLOCK-chock taking standing part of reef pendant near aft end of boom.
BEES-pieces bolted to outer bowsprit end to reeve foretopmast stays thru.
BELAY- change order;make fast or secure rope to cleat or pin.
BELAYING PIN-iron or wooden pin fitted into railing to secure lines, page 73.
BELL BUOY-buoy with bell actuated by sea, page 249.
BELLY-fullness of sail when swelled out by wind.
BELLY STRAP-rope beneath boat for carrying out a kedge anchor.
BELOW-beneath or under the deck (seldom called 'downstairs').
BENCH HOOK-hook with swivel in cloth counteracting pull of sailors needle.
BEND-a knot by which one rope is made fast to another, page 189.
BEND a SAIL-make sail fast to spar or stay, 88-97. BEND a CABLE is make it
fast to anchor. BENDING SHACKLE connects chain cable to ring of anchor.
BENEAPED or NEAPED-boat aground at high tide, following tides cannot float,223.
BERMUDIAN RACING DINGHY-see page 48.

e BERMUDIAN SAIL-British term for marconi or jib-headed sail, pages 7, 274.

BERTH-dock or anchorage for boat, or place a person sleeps on board.

BERTH DECK-lower complete deck used for berthing near waterline.

BETWEEN DECKS-space between decks.

BIBBS-trestle-tree timber supports bolted to hounds of the mast.

BIGHT-bend in shore making cove, bay or inlet;bend in rope.

BILGE-curve of hull between gunwhale & keel, 16 ;largest dia. of cask.

BILGE BLOCKS-blocks in dry dock upon which ships bilge rests.

BILGED-when bilge is broken.

BILGE KEEL-keel at turn of bilge to reduce rolling of vessel.

BILGE STRINGERS- see STRINGERS, page 73.

BILGE WATER-water settled to bilge of boat, page 73.

BILGE WAYS-timbers bolted together & propped under keel for launching.

BILL-point at end of fluke on anchor.

BILL-BOARD-bed or plates for anchor to rest without marring deck.

BILL of HEALTH-port health certificate obtained as vessel clears port.

BILL of LADING-receipt from a vessel for cargo received.

BINNACLE-compass stand containing compensating magnets, 67, 75, 81.

BITE-to take hold.

BITTER END-last inboard link of an anchor chain or anchor line, 163, 186.

BITT-take turn around bitts with cable so it can be veered or held tight.

BITTS-posts in deck to secure mooring or towing lines, pages 61, 73.

BLACK GANG-engineering force when coal was principle fuel.

BLADE-back of anchor palm, flat part of oar or propeller.

BLANKET-leeward sailboat has wind taken out of sails by one to windward. A bridge, headland or building can also blanket sails.

BLOCK (pulley)-wood or metal container with pulley.

BLUFF-steep shore or full-bowed ship.

BOARD-tack or leg to windward when beating or closehauled, page 101.

BOAT BOOM-swings from boats side when at anchor to secure dinghy.

BOAT COVER-tarp or cover that protects a boat.   BOAT-see SHIP.

BOAT HOOK-pole with hook to pick up mooring buoy or ring.

BOS'N'S CHAIR-canvas or wood seat to raise man working aloft.

BOATSWAIN'S CHEST-deck chest for bos'n's gear.

BOATSWAIN, PETTY-officer in charge of rigging & calling crew to duty.

BOBSTAY-rod, chain or wire from stem to cutwater securing bowsprit, 71,285.

BOLLARD-vertical post on dock to which hawsers may be secured.

BOLSTERS-canvas covered wood for rigging eyes to rest on at trestle-trees.

BOLT-rolls of canvas.

BOLTS-round iron bars for securing;early bolts without threads were peened over to prevent their working loose.

BOLT ROPE-to which material is sewn going around sail, page 89.

BONE-spray at stem of vessel underway.

BONNET-extra canvas piece secured to foot of jib by lacings.

BOOBY HATCH-a small raised hatch.

BOOM-spar for extending foot of fore & aft or studding sail.

BOOM CRADLE (boom crutch)-support for boom when sail is furled, page 89.

BOOM HORSE-boom band metal fitting used as traveller for sheet block.

BOOM IRONS-rings on yards for studdingsail booms to be rigged out.

BOOMKIN-spar projecting from stern to secure backstay, page 71.

BOOT TOP-different color strip of paint at waterline, page 71.

BOTTOMRY-marine law term for mortgaging ships.

BOUND, WIND-adverse headwind keeping sailboat in port.

BOW-forward part of a hull-pages 82-3.

BOW BREAST-forward mooring line used in docking.

BOW BREAST MOORING-chain offshore permanent mooring using breast line.

BOWER-main anchor.   BEST BOWER-largest anchor.

BOW LINE-docking or moorling line led forward thru bow chock, pages 173-4.
BOW MOORING-same as BOW BREAST MOORING.
BOW PAINTER-line leading from boat to buoy or other boat, pages 95, 167.
BOWSE-to haul in and down on a tackle.
BOWSPRIT-spar extending forward from bow to secure headstays, pages 70-5,285.
BOWSPRITTING-sentence of sailor roped to bowsprit. He had choice of starving
to death as food & water allowance was small, or cutting the ropes & drowning.
BOX-HAULING-wearing a square rigger by backing the head sails.
BOXING OFF-boats head is paid off after missing stays.
BOXING the COMPASS-calling names of 32 compass points in order.
BRACE-line controlling horizontal movement of square sail yard, pages 285-6.
BRACKISH-mixture of fresh and salt water.
BRAIL-lines used to furl fore & aft sails vertically against the mast.
BREAKER-waves broken by shoals or ledges, small fresh water cask.
BREAK GROUND-to break loose anchor from bottom.
BREAK OFF-to stop.   BREAK OUT-to unstow.
BREAKS-a wave breaks when it curls forward into the surf.
BREAK SHEAR-vessel that is restless at anchor, see BULL ROPE.
BREAKWATER(splash board)-low bulkhead forward to prevent waves and spray
from coming into cockpit;a sea wall to break force of waves.
BREAST-meet the sea;docking line leading at right angles to vessels centerline.
BREAST BAND(breast rope)-canvas band across leadsmans chest lashed to chains.
BREAST FAST-line securing vessel broadside to wharf or other vessel.
BREAST HOOKS-knees in forward part of vessel, page 73.
BREAST OFF-shove out from dock or another vessel.
BRIDLE-rope span with ends secured for sheet block to ride on, pages 33, 35.
Boat moored to a bridle or span between two anchors.
BRIDLE-PORT-foremost port used for stowing anchors.
BRIG-ships jail;two masted square rigger, page 283.
BRIGANTINE-2 masted square rigger, square rigged on fore, fore & aft on the
main. The 'Yankee' was tops'l schooner by previous def.; now called brigantine.
BRIGHTWORK-varnished woodwork or polished brass that is not painted.
BRING -TO-stop sailing vessel by bring head to wind.
BROACH-TO-bow of vessel running before wind digs in & boat jibes.
BROADSIDE-side of vessel;firing salvo of all guns on one side of ship.
BROKEN BACK (hogged)vessel that droops at either end.
BROW-portable gang plank.
BROW LANDING-platform extending over ship's side to support gang plank.
BUCKLERS-plugs fitting into hawse pipe holes when at sea.
BUCKLING-bending or working.   BUGEYE-see page 275.
BUILDING SLIP-location of building ways.
BULB KEEL-racing keel with cigar shaped weight at bottom, page 21.
BULKHEAD-below deck partition separting one part of vessel from another.
BULL-sailors term for small one or two gallon keg.
BULL ROPE-shock cord leading from bowsprit end to mooring buoy to keep
buoy from bumping boat when wind & tide are opposed, page 174.
BULL the BUOY-a vessel that bumps a buoy with its side.
BULLSEYE-round wooden thimble used for changing lead of rope.
BULWARKS-railing around deck to prevent men & gear from going overboard.
BUMBOAT-boat alongside vessel in port with articles for sale.
BUMKIN(boomkin)-permanent stern spar providing backstay support, page 70.
BUMPKIN-support for main braceblocks from both quarters;timbers projecting
from vessel to secure the fore tack.
BUMPKIN SHROUDS-iron ropes securing bumpkin vertically to vessel's side.
BUNK-sleeping berth.
BUNT-middle of sail;loop of line or bagging portion of loosely hanging sail.
BUNTING-thin flag material or flags.
G5

BUNTLINES-lines used to haul up body of square sail, pages 286-287.
BURGEE-pointed or swallowtail flag indicating club boats owner belongs to, 253.
BURTON-special tackle often used to hoist heavy anchor aboard.
BUOY-floating marker for piloting, pg. 248; marker for permanent mooring,167.
BUOYANCY TANKS-airtight tanks for buoyancy in upset boat, page 32.
BUTT-where two planks or other members touch end to end. SCUTTLE BUTT
is gossip while drinking from water cask for crew kept on deck.
BUTTOCK-part of vessel between quarter & stern post, pages 254-256.
BY THE BOARD-overboard.   BY THE HEAD-bow lower than stern.
BY THE LEE-running with wind on same side as boom, page 123.
BY THE RUN-let go altogether.   BY THE STERN-stern lower than bow.
BY THE WIND-closehauled, page 99.

C CABIN-enclosed space of decked over boat, pages 52-4,63,67-75,79-81.
CABLE-large dia. rope, pg. 129; 200 yards or 1/10 nautical mile.
CABLE LENGTH-600 feet or 100 fathoms.
CABOOSE-deckhouse for cooking, usually called a galley in smaller boats.
CALL-bos'n's pipe.   CALM-wind under one knot, page 137.
CAMBER-athwartship curve of deck and cabin, page 73.
CAMEL-wooden float acting between dock and boat.
CAN BUOY-cylindrical black odd numbered buoy to port entering from seaward.
CANEYE-combination of Chesapeake log canoe and bugeye, page 271.
CANT-to turn a vessels head.   CANTED-inclined.
CAP-wooden block for holding spars.   CAPSIZE-to upset, page 145.
CAPSTAN-mechanical device for hoisting or heaving.
CAPSTAN-BAR-wooden or metal bar for heaving capstan around by hand.
CARDINAL POINTS-four main points of a compass.
CARLINE-timbers used as support for cabin or hatch, page 73.
CARRICK BEND-page 189.
CARRY AWAY-to part a rope, break a spar, to break or tear loose.
CARRY ON-carry all sails possible.
CARVEL-opposite of lapstrake, smooth planked.
CAST OFF-let go, pages 95, 172.
CAST, TO-sailboat bow pays off on tack it will use underway; to throw.
CAT-tackle used to heave anchor to cathead.
CATAMARAN-twin-hulled craft, pages 17, 18, 47, 79.
CATBOAT, CAT RIG-boat with one sail stepped well forward, page 5.
CATCH-ALL-see SAVE ALL.
CAT-HARPIN-iron leg to confine upper rigging to mast.
CATHEAD-timbers projecting from bow to secure anchor, page 287.
CATENARY(Br.)-sag or curve of anchor cable between boat & anchor, pg. 161.
CATSPAW-ruffled patch of water due to stronger wind puff at that spot, pg. 205.
CAT the ANCHOR-secure anchor for sea.
CAULK-fill boats seams with oakum or cotton to make them tight.
CAULKING OFF-sleeping.
CENTERBOARD-hinged plate lowered to reduce leeway sailing to windward, 19.
CENTERBOARD TRUNK-watertight housing for centerboard, page 19.
CENTER of EFFORT-center of sail area, page 133.
CENTER of LATERAL RESISTANCE-center of underwater profile, pages 133-5.
CHAFE-to damage by rubbing, anything used to prevent it is called CHAFING
GEAR. A CHAFING MAT is woven from rope strands.
CHAIN LOCKER-compartment for storing chain.
CHAIN PLATES-straps bolted to vessels side to secure shrouds, page 69.
CHAINS-station for leadsman under bowsprit.
CHAIN STOPPER-short length of chain for quick release of anchor for anchoring.
CHANNEL BUOY-buoy marker showing extreme limits of channel, page 249.
CHARLEY NOBLE-galley smokestack named after meticulous Br. Admiral, 75.

CHANNELS-ledges bolted lengthwise & built out to increase spread of shroud, 285.
CHECK-ease off gradually to ease cable from parting.
CHEEKS-side of block;projections trestle trees rest on each side of mast.
CHINE-intersection of boats side and bottom, page 17.
CHINES-drive oakum into seams of boat.
CHIP LOG-early device to measure boat speed, see Laing's 'Clipper Ship Men'.
CHIPS-ships carpenter.
CHOCK-wedges a dinghy is secure to when hoisted aboard ship.
CHOCK-A-BLOCK(two blocked)-upper & lower blocks of tackle run together.
CHRONOMETER-accurate clock used for navigation.
CHOW-food.   CIRRUS-high frozen clouds, 205-9.
CLAMP DOWN-swab down a deck.
CLAMPS-thick planks supporting end of beams on inside of a vessel.
CLAP ON-add more sail or haul away on a rope.
CLAPPER-moveable wooden piece to prevent jaws of gaff from jamming.
CLAW OFF-trying to clear a lee shore sailing closehauled.
CLEAN-boat with smooth lines.
CLEAR-work clear of bar or shoal;untangle lines, gear, or rigging;land is
cleared as vessel sails away;leaving port with all formalities transacted.
CLEAR for RUNNING-ready to run without fouling.
CLEARING PAPERS-they indicate all regulations met & approved by the port
authorities before leaving.
CLEAT-varied fittings to secure rope without making a hitch, pages 22-81, 144, 19
CLEW-lower aft corner of fore & aft sail, pg. 5, 7, 33, 89; for spinnaker, the side
to which sheet is secured, pages 126-9;for square sail see page 287.
CLEWLINE-hauls up clew of square sail, page 287.
CLINCH-half-hitch which is stopped to its own part.
CLINKER(clinker built)-overlapping planks, opp. of smooth planking, page 16.
CLINOMETER-instrument measuring heel or degree of roll, page 134, 145.
CLIPPER BOW(schooner bow)-stem with forward curve and flaring sides.
CLOSE-HAULED-sailing close to wind as efficiency permits, pages 99, 104.
CLOSING-a vessel closes with the shore or another vessel.
CLOUD FORMATIONS-see pages 205-209.
CLOVE-HITCH-two half hitches around rope or spar, page 191.
CLUB-spar on bottom of staysail or topsail, page 71.
CLUBBING-using anchor to use current going downstream or around a point.
CLUB TOPSAIL-topsail with foot laced to club, luff laced to a sprit.
CLUMP BLOCK-small oval block with rounded shell.
COAMING-railing around cockpit, hatches, etc., page 72.
COCKBILL-see A-COCK-BILL.
COCKPIT-opening aft for feet or passengers.
CODLINE-eighteen thread line.
COFFERDAM-partitions separating tanks in the hull of a ship.
COIL-to lay a rope in a circle.
COIR-weak buoyant rope made from coconut fibers, often found on lateeners.
COLD WALL-current flowing southward of cold water, inside Gulf Stream.
COLLAR-eye to go over masthead, found on end of shroud or stay.
COLLIER-a ship that carries coal.
COME HOME-anchor broken loose and being pulled in.
COME UP-slack away so gear may be belayed after hauling.
COMING ABOUT-changing course so bow swings thru eye of wind to pay off on
other tack, pages 101, 109.
COMMISSIONING PENNANT-ship of war pennant flown at the main truck.
COMPANION-wooden covering over staircase to a cabin.
COMPANIONWAY-staircase to cabin or below, page 67.
COMPASS (mariner's, magnetic)-magnetized needles floating on compass card,
that tends to point to the magnetic north and south poles, pg. 244-245.

CO COMPASS CARD-calibrated card having points of the compass.
COMPASS POINT -11 1/4° or 1/32 part of a full circle.
COMPASS ROSE-graduated circle printed on chart with points of the compass.
COMPENSATE-correcting compass from local attractions on boat.
COMPOSITE, COMPOSITE BUILT-vessel with wooden skin & metal frame.
CONE-signal displayed on sailboat under power & sail, page 236;racing,page R2.
CONNING-direction helmsman is steering a vessel.
CONTROLLING DEPTH-minimum depth of anchorage or channel.
CORDAGE-term for all kinds of rope.
CORINTHIAN-:-amateur interested in a sport without thought of compensation.
CORVETTE-page 289.
COSTON SIGNALS-colored fireworks sometimes used for signalling.
COUNTER-the side of a vessels quarter.
COURSE-angle sailboat is sailing into or away from the wind, page 99; it can
also be the compass heading of a boat, 244-247.
COURSES-sails set to lower yards-fore course & main course, page 287.
COW HITCH-page 191.
COWL-vent opening, often bell shaped, page 73.
COW'S TAIL(fag, irish pennant)-untidy frayed end of rope.
COXSWAIN-person in charge of steering a boat.
CRADLE-frame vessel rests on when hauled out of the water.
CRAFT-general term for small vessels.
CRANK(cranky, tender)-top heavy sailing vessel that heels too easily.
CRANSE IRON-metal cap or ring at end of bowsprit to secure stays.
CREEPER-metal device with claws for dragging bottoms.
CRINGLE-rope eye formed around metal thimble, spliced into the bolt rope
of a sail, pages 5, 287.   CROJIK-same as cross jack, page 287.
CROJIK YARD(cross-jack yard)-lower yard on mizzen mast, page 287.
CROSS PAWL-timbers bracing boat frames during construction.
CROSS PIECE-timber connecting two bitts.
CROSS SPALES-timbers securing frames together until knees are bolted.
CROSS TREES-cross pieces near top of mast, spreading shrouds so they
can make a greater angle to the mast, page 285.
CROWD ON-use all sail possible.
CROWFOOT-several small ropes used to suspend an awning.
CROWN-camber of deck, page 73;for anchor, see page 158.
CROW'S NEST-lookout platform or area up mast, see page 286.
CRUTCH-support for boom when sails are furled, page 89.
CUDDY-small shelter cabin.
CUT OF THE JIB-general appearance of a vessel or a person.
CUTTER-single masted sailboat with mast stepped 2/5 or more of the
waterline length from the bow, pages 9, 263.
CUTWATER-foremost part of bow or stem, page 73.
CYCLONE-circular wind storm of strong intensity.

d DAGGERBOARD-plate raised/lowered vertically to reduce leeway, 18,25,33,46,79.
DAN BUOY-used to mark fishing nets, or navy buoy markers in foreign waters.
DANFORTH ANCHOR-see pages 158, 159, 162.
DANGER BUOY-buoy marking danger spot or area.
DASH-long period of sound or light in Morse Code.
DASHER BLOCK-small signal halyard secured to end of spanker gaff.
DAVIT-pair of posts with curved arms for raising & lowering a dinghy. Spar
with sheave at its end for fishing an anchor is called a FISH DAVIT.
DAVY JONES-spirit of the sea.   DAVY JONES LOCKER-bottom of sea.
DAY'S DUTY-24 hour tour of duty aboard ship.
DAY'S WORK-noon to noon navigation work to determine a ship's position.
DEAD AHEAD-directly ahead of vessels course, page 83.
DEADEYE-wooden block thru which lanyards are rove to set up rigging.

DEAD LIGHT-ports placed in cabin windows.
DEAD MEN (Irish pennants, cow's tail)sloppy loose end of a rope.
DEAD RECKONING-time & distance record of a vessels course.
DEADRISE-vertical distance between turn of bilge and keel.
DEAD-RISING (rising-line)-where floor timbers terminate on lower futtock.
DEAD ROPE-line not led thru a block or sheave.
DEAD WATER-water pulled along with a vessel underway.
DEADWOOD-strengthening members securing keel to stern and stem, pg. 72.
DECK-planked floor of a ship or boat, page 72.
DECK BEAM-athwartship support for deck, page 73.
DECK CHEST-chest for deck gear secured topsides.
DECKHEAD-under surface of the deck.
DECK HORSE-athwartship rod for sheet block traveller.
DECK LIGHT-piece of glass fitted flush to deck.
DECK STOPPER-stopper with lanyard for lashing cable,fitted with stopper knot.
DECK TACKLE-heavy double purchase used above deck.
DECLINATION-angle measured from earths center thru a celestial body.
DEEPS-fathom of a lead line which is not marked.
DEEP SEA LEAD-50 lb. lead used in 120 fathoms or more.
DEEP SIX-throw it overboard.
DEGREE-1/360 th part of a circumference.
DEPARTURE-bearing of coast object from which vessel commences dead rec'ning.
DERELICT-abandoned ship at sea.
DEVIATION-compass error due to objects on boat that varies with heading, 245.
DEW POINT-air saturation point, page 219.
DHOW-general term for lateeners, page 279.
DIAGONAL-see pages 254, 257.   DIAMOND KNOT-ornamental knot.
DINGHY-small open boat, pages 22-27, 75.
DIP-dipping an ensign, is to lower & rehoist it as a salute, 253.
DISMANTLE-strip a vessel of spars, masts, and rigging.
DISMAST-carry away the masts of a vessel.
DISPLACEMENT-weight of water displaced by a vessel.
DOG-metal fitting used to close hatches, covers, etc.
DOG'S EAR-small bight of sails leach when reefed.
DOGHOUSE-enclosure or shelter built over companionway, page 75.
DOG VANE-small wind vane usually made of bunting.
DOG WATCH-half watches from 4 to 6 and 6 to 8 p.m.
DOLDRUMS-belts of little wind on either sides of Equator.
DOLPHIN-spar mooring buoy;strap around mast secures puddening at slings
of lower yard.
DOLPHIN-STRIKER (martingale boom)-spar projecting below bowsprit to
counteract strain of head stays, page 285.
DORY-flat-bottomed boat with narrow stern and flaring sides.
DOT-short period of sound or light in the Morse Code.
DOUBLE BLOCK-block with two sheaves.
DOUBLE ENDER-boat with pointed bow and stern, see Int'l 110, page 41.
DOUBLE SHEET BEND-page 189.
DOUBLING-sailing around point of land;overlapping parts of two masts, pg. 284.
DOUSE (dowse)-lower & take in sail;put out light; cover with water.
DOWNDRAFT- wind flow with vertical angle, page 123, 206-207.
DOWNHAUL-line used to pull down tack of sail, pages 88-91, 119, 121.
DOWNHAUL TACKLE-page 286.
DOWN HELM-bring boat up into wind.   DOWN THE MAST-no wind.
DRAFT-water depth required to float a vessel, page 222;sail airfoil 10, 102-5.
DRAG-anchor failing to hold vessel;storm anchor used to keep vessels head or
stern to wind in heavy weather, pages 156-7;machine for dragging bottom;area
of turbulence behind or to leeward of sail, page 103.

dr DRAW-sail filled with wind (draft); a boat draws enough water to float it.
DREDGE-vessel used for digging out a channel.
DRIFT-vessels leeway, pages 106-7; amount of current; distance between the blocks of a tackle, or spare end of a rope.
DRIFT LEAD-lead weight over anchored vessels side indicates dragging anchor.
DRIFT, TO-to move with the tide or current.
DRIVE-drifting in a current or scudding before a gale.
DRIVER-6th mast of 7 masted schooner. DROGUE-storm anchor, page 157.
DROP-distance from head to foot of a square sail.
DRUM-HEAD-top of the capstan.
DRY SAILING-boat kept on trailer when not being used.
DUB-reduce end of a timber.   DUCK-light canvas.
DRY BULB THERMOMETER-measures air temperature.
DRY DOCK-basin for repairing vessels that can be pumped dry.
DUFF-flour and water.   DUMB COMPASS-pelorus.
DUNNAGE-sailors personal effects; loose material stowed in boat.
DUTCH COURAGE-artificial courage caused by drinking.

e EARING (earring)-short lines securing reefed sail to boom, page 149.
EASE-to slacken; put helm alee and luff sailboat head to wind.
EASE IN-to slowly work up to a dock, mooring or slip.
EASE OFF-to slack off.   EASE OUT-to slack out.
EASING-OUT LINE-line for easing out. EASE RUDDER-bring it more amidship.
EASE UP-to slowly let up or work out.   EASY-slowly, carefully.
EBB TIDE-tide passing from high to low point, with tidal current ebbing out to sea, pages 214, 216.
EDDY-circular or confused air or water currents, page 217.
EDGE AWAY-slowly pay off from course, dock, or berth.
ELBOW-2 crosses in a hawse.   EMBARK-go on board or to begin.
END LINK-open link next abaft end shackle.   END ON-head on, 235.
END SEIZING-round seizing at the two ends of a rope.
END TO END-reversing position of object such as rope.
ENLARGED LINK-wider link connecting common link to swivel or short or a long-end link.
ENSIGN-national or organizational flag carried aboard a vessel 252, 253; a navy officer equivalent to a army second lieutenant.
ENTRANCE-a vessels bow just above the waterline.
EQUINOX-date that the sun crosses the equator during spring and fall.
EUPHROE (euvrou)-wooden piece helping to extend an awning.
EVEN KEEL-floating level.
EYE-closed loop of rope.
EYE BOLT-bolt or iron bar to secure a tackle.
EYELET HOLES-holes in a sail for reef points or cringle.
EYE of the WIND-into center of the wind, pages 98-104.
EYE SPLICE-spliced loop in end of rope, page 196-201.
EYES of a VESSEL-forward portion of weather deck or ships bow.

f FAG (fagged)-untwisted or frayed end of rope; Irish pennant or cow's tail.
FAIRBODY-line formed by outside bottom edge of plank touching keel; rabbet,
FAIRLEADS (fair leader)-fitting to change direction of rope lead, 7, 12, 31-5, 43, 47.
FAIR TIDE-current running with vessel. FAIRWAY-a navigation channel, pg.249.
FAIR WIND-favorable wind.   FAKE-single turn of rope in a coil.
FAKE (flake) DOWN-each coil of rope overlaps the one inside of it.
FALL-hauling part of rope, also part of tackle which force is applied.
FALLING GLASS-lowering barometer pressure, page 212.
FALLING HOME (tumble home)-side of boat inclining inboard above waterline.
FALL OFF (falling off)-paying off to leeward or from the wind.
FALSE KEEL-protective wood strip bolted outside main keel, page 72.

FANCY LINE-downhaul for gaff;line used to cross haul lee topping-lift.
FANNING-sailboat with little headway in light airs.
FASHION BOARD-panel to prevent water entering companionway.
FAST-to make fast is to secure, also docking lines.
FATHOM-one fathom equals six feet, a depth measurement of water, 215.
FATHOMETER-electronic instrument for sounding water depth, page 222,243.
FAVOR-reduce load as in a weak spar or old sail.
FEATHER-sailboat class;turning oar blade at end of stroke to reduce splashing.
FELUCCA-lateener that can also be rowed, page 279.
FENDER-cushions to prevent chafing on a boats side.
FENDERBOARD-board used with two or more fenders to give hull protection.
FENDER SPAR-floating spar fender secured alongside a boat.
TO FETCH-sailboat able to make windward mark without changing tack, 106.
FIBERGLASS HULL-boat hulls made of fiberglass cloth & resin.
FIBER ROPE-rope made of organic instead of synthetic or metal materials.
FID-pointed pin or stick for working rope, page 202. Short bar passing thru
hole in heel of bowsprit or topmast resting on trestle-trees,
FIDDLE-bar with sheaves for leads with light running gear.
FIDDLE HEAD-ornamental timber substitute for figure head.
FIDDLES-strips around tables to prevent dishes from sliding off.
FIDDLEY-framework of deck hatch around a ladder going below.
FIELD DAY-one for general ship cleaning.
FIFE-RAIL (pin-rail)-wooden railing around mast for belaying pins, pg. 73.
FIGURE EIGHT KNOT-page 184.
FIGUREHEAD-ornamental head, bust, or figure carried under bowsprit.
FILL AWAY-sails filling & boat gathering headway after changing tack, pg.109.
FIN KEEL-straight or bulb section on bottom of keel, page 20.
FISH-strengthen spar with lashing or splints;heaving anchor flukes on gunwale.
FISH BLOCK (fish-davit, fish-hook, fish-davit)-parts used for fishing an anchor.
FISHERMANS KNOT-page 189.
FIT OUT-overhauling period before trip, or before boat goes into the water.
FIX-finding vessels position by land or celestial observations.
FLAKE-see FAKE DOWN.
FLARE-upward outward curve of bow or side, opposite of tumble home.
FLARE-UP-a signal light designed to flare up.
FLAT-a sail empty without wind pressure.
FLAT ABACK-wind on wrong side of sails of a square rigger.
FLAT BOTTOM-page 17.   FLAT CALM-no wind pressure.
FLAT SPINNAKER-page 125.   FLATTEN IN-haul in on sheets.
FLAW (catspaw)-a gust of wind, 205.
FLEET-haul blocks of purchase apart;shifting position of fall or block.
FLEMISH DOWN-coil rope flat on deck with each roll outside of another.
FLEMISH HORSE-additional foot rope at ends of topsail yards.
FLOAT-raft moored alongside or pier making access to a boat easier, pg. 169.
FLOOD-incoming tidal current, page 215.
FLOOR-bottom of boat on each side of keelson, page 72.
FLOTATION TANK-air tank to prevent swamped boat from sinking, 26-31.
FLOTSAM-floating wreckage, driftwood, etc.
FLOW-spilling the wind by easing the sheets also called luffing.
FLOWING SHEETS-sailboat running before the wind with sheets eased.
FLUKE-wind irregularities;digging ends of an anchor.
FLY-horizontal length of a flag.
FLYING MOOR-sailboat dropping anchor underway, then sails, and finally a
second anchor. Vessel then drops to midway point between the anchors.
FOGHORN-pages 220-221.   FOOT -lower edge of sail, 5,7,89,287.
FOOT ROPE-support under bowsprit for reefing or lowering sail.
FORE-opposite to aft, forward part of a boat.

fo FORE AND AFT-lengthwise, parallel to the keel, pages 6, 82.
FO 'C 'SLE (forecastle) -square rigger crews quarter forward, pages 253, 285.
FOREFOOT-timber between keel and stem, page 73.
FORE MAST-foremost mast of schooner or square rigger, pages 269, 282-289.
FORE PEAK-extreme bow space foreward on smaller vessels, page 63.
FORE REACH-movement of sailboat passing through eye of wind.
FORESAIL (fore staysail)-pages 269, 287. FORE TOPMAST STAYSAIL-pg. 287.
FORGE AHEAD-shoot ahead when going in stays or coming to anchor.
FORWARD-in front of, page 82.
FORWARD PLATFORM-mounted forward of foremast in eyes of a boat.
FOTHER (fodder)-draw a sail under vessels bottom filled with oakum to stop leaks.
FOUL-jammed, stuck, not clean.
FOULED ANCHOR-caught or twisted up in its own anchor line, page 161.
FOUL HAWSE-twisted or crossed anchor lines.   FOUND-equipped.
FOUNDER-a boat filled with water and sinking.
FRAME-ribs of a boat, page 73.
FRAP-pass ropes around sail or awning to keep it from blowing loose.
FREE-sailing with wind aft, pg.99.; after water is pumped out of boat.
FREEBOARD-vertical distance of boat above waters surface.
FRIENDSHIP SLOOP-page 272.   FRESH BREEZE(fresh gale)-pg. 137.
FRESHEN-an increasing wind.
FRESHEN THE NIP-shift a stay or portion of anchor line to reduce chafe, 156.
FRIGATE-page 289.
FULL AND BY (full and bye)-close hauled square rigger term, page 99.
FULL SPREAD-all sails set.
FURL-to roll sail snugly on top of boom, 86, 87, or under a yard.
FUTTOCK PLATES-corresponds to platform of a top.
FUTTOCK STAFF-short spar serving as topmast rigging shear-pole.
FUTTOCK TIMBERS-part of a frame.

g GADGET-term used only by a landlubber.
GAFF-spar for head of a gaff sail, pages 5, 260-269; scandalizing, page 148.
GAFF JAWS-inboard end fitting of gaff around a mast, page 5.
GAFF SAIL-quadrilateral sail fitted with gaff, page 5.
GAFF TOPSAIL-sail above & with foot spread by gaff, pages 70, 265.
GAFF VANG-line going to gaff peak used to steady the gaff, page 269.
GAGE-position of vessel in regards to wind, sun, or another vessel.
GAIN the WIND-to work to windward of another sailboat.
GALE-force 7-10, page 137, 139.   GALLEY-floating kitchen, page 74.
GALLOWS-permanent frame to rest end of boom after sail is lowered.
GALLOWS-BITTS-strong frame amidships for spare spars, etc.
GAMMONING-fastenings of bowsprit on vertical stem.
GANG PLANK-board used as walkway from ship to dock.
GANGWAY-step aside, get out of the way; ladder or passageway aboard a ship.
GANTLINE (girthline)-line secured aloft & rove through a single block.
GARBOARD STRAKE-planks on both sides of keel, page 73.
GARLAND-strap or rope lashed to spar when hoisting it aboard.
GARNET-purchase for hoisting on the mainstay.
GASKET-canvas strip for furling a sail, pages 86, 87.
GATHER WAY-pick up momentum.   GEAR-general term for rigging.
GENOA JIB (gennie)-largest size jib, pages 12-15.
GHOSTING-sailboat making little way in light breeze.
GIMBALS-bearing rings & pivots to keep compass card level on boat.
GIMLET-turn anything around on its end, turning anchor around by its stock.
GINGERLY-with caution.
GIRT-boat with tight mooring line that does not swing to tide or wind.
GIRTHLINE-see gantline.   GIRTHBAND-page 287.

GIRT the SAIL-line leading across lee side of sail making a hard ridge.
GLASS-trad. barometer term, pg. 212.   GLORY HOLE-lazarette.
GOB-LINE (gaub-line)-a martingale support or guy.
GO ABOUT-change tack over bow, 99; 109. GO ADRIFT-break loose.
GO FREE-running, page 99.   GO LARGE-same as running.
GOLLYWOBBLER-large sail peculiar to schooner, pages 15, 269.
GOOD FULL-course between close reach & close hauled.
GOOSENECK-fitting that secures boom to mast, pages 23,27,35,46,59,89.
GOOSE WING-same as sailing wing and wing, pages 99, 105, 111, 123, 277.
GOOSE WING JIBE-only bottom part of sail jibes, page 123.
GORES-sail cloths cut at angle to give sail desired shape.
GORING CLOTHS-sail material cut obliquely adding to depth of sail.
GRAFTING-weaving yarns together to cover a rope.
GRAPNEL (grappling iron)-small anchor with several claws, page 159.
GRATING-framework made of wood or metal to let in air or light.
GREAVE-cleaning ships bottom by burning.   GREAT GUNS-a violent wind.
GREEN SEA-large amount of water taken aboard that isn't foamy.
GRIP-an anchor when it bites and holds, page 160-162.
GRIPES-sailboat with excessive weather helm, page
GROMMET-rope ring, an eye sewn on edge of sail (cringle), page 5.
GROUNDING-running ashore, page 223.
GROUND SWELL-large wave or waves crossing shoal or bar.
GROUND TACKLE-general term for anchor & anchor gear, pages 158-163.
GUDGEON-eye supports for rudder pintles, page 7,23,24,29.
GUNKHOLING-shallow water sailing.
GUN-TACK PURCHASE-purchase made with two single blocks.
GUNTER (sliding gunther)-a vertical gaff in small dinghy, so mast, boom, and
gaff can be stored in boat when not in use, page 271.
GUNWALE-boat or cockpit railing, 26.   GUSSET-a brace.
GUST-sudden wind puff.   GUY-steadying line, pages 125-130.
GYASSA-pages 276-277.   GYBE-British for jibe.
HAIL-call to men in different part of ship or another vessel.
HALF MAST-a flag hoisted half way.
HALF RATER-small sailboat with jib & main, no bowsprit, see knockabout.
HALF SEAS OVER-quite drunk.
HALYARD   (halliard, haliard)-lines used to raise sails, flags, gaffs, 5, 7, 88-96.
HAND-crew member.   HANDICAP RATING-pages 2, 258-259.
HAND, TO-to furl a sail or haul in a patent log.
HAND LEAD-small sounding lead.   HAND RAIL-steadying rail on ladder.
HANDSOMELY-opposite of hasty; smoothly, moderately.
HANDSPIKE-wooden bar used for heaving at a windlass.
HAND TIGHT-tight as can usually be pulled by hand.
HANDY BILLY-see watch tackle.
HANKED ON-sail secured to stay by hanks, page 93.
HANKS-hooks or rings which secure jibs or staysails to their stays.
HARD-A-LEE-command to come about, page 109.
HARD-A-WEATHER -put helm up to sail further away from the wind, 111.
HARD DOWN (hard-a-lee)-shove tiller far to leeward as possible.
HARDEN IN-haul in on a sheet to flatten a sail.
HARD OVER -same has hard down or hard-a-lee, also helms alee.
HARD UP-order to shove tiller rapidly to eye of wind.
HATCH-opening in a deck with a cover, pages 61, 68-81.
HAUL YOUR WIND-sail closer to wind; HAUL is a clockwise wind shift.
HAULING LINE-line from aloft used to haul up gear.
HAULING PART-part of tackle upon which power is applied.
HAUL TO WINDWARD (hauling her wind)-change from run to reach.

ha HAWSE-space forward from vessel to directly over anchor.

HAWSE BLOCK-wooden plug fitting into hawse hole in vessel at sea.

HAWSER-heavy line used for warping, springs, etc.

HAWSER-LAID ROPE-3 strand left-handed lay rope.

HEAD-toilet compartment aboard a vessel;originally small lower deck forward with most privacy, well defined on vessels such as Santa Maria, Mayflower, etc. In later days it was the forward part of a vessel on schooners, etc., pg. 61,139,289.

HEADBOARD-page 7.

HEAD of SAIL-upper corner of a sail, pages 7, 287.

HEADSAILS-originally, all staysails set forward of foremast, pages 12-15.

HEAD SHEETS-sheets secured to headsails or staysails.

HEAD STAY-forward stay, pages 24-81.

HEAD to WIND-position of sailboat in eye of the wind, pages 98, 108.

HEADS UP-warning to watch out or look up.

HEADWAY-moving ahead.

HEAVE AWAY, order to heave around a capstan or to haul away.

HEAVE DOWN-to pull vessel over to repair or inspect bottom when dry docks and ordinary docking facilities are absent.

HEAVE IN-to haul in.

HEAVER-short wooden bar used as purchase and tapering at either end.

HEAVE SHORT-to heave in till boat is riding almost over its anchor.

HEAVE-TAUT-to haul in till a line has a strain upon it.

HEAVE TO-bring boats head to wind by sail or engine and holding it there,151.

HEAVE, TO-to haul, to throw;a boat rising and falling in a seaway.

HEAVING LINE-small line used for heaving, pg. 194;ANCHOR heaving, pg. 162.

HEEL-lower end of spar or after end of keel.

HEELING(heel, to heel)-to list or lay over, pages 100, 132-134.

HELM-tiller or wheel,22-81, 108-110.   HERMAPHRODITE BRIG—page 283.

HIGH and DRY-boat aground above high water mark, page 223.

HIKE-climbing to windward to prevent excessive heeling.

HIKING STICK- pages 23-63.   HITCH-page 191.

HELM DOWN(helms alee) -tiller pushed away from wind, page 109 to come about;opposite of HELM AWEATHER for jibing, page 111.

HOGGED(hog backed)-vessel drooping at either end due to shrouds turned down too tight(reverse sheer pg. 60, is designed with ends lower than midship).

HOGGING MOMENT-position of vessel with wave under middle.

HOIST-vertical edge of a sail or flag.   HOIST, TO-to haul aloft.

HOLD-below decks space for cargo, stores or ballast.

HOLD, TO-anchor digging in so that it will not move.

HOLYSTONE-large porous flat stone used to clean & whiten deck or woodwork.

HOME-sheets slacked far as possible;anchor broken out of bottom.

HORNS-jaws of gaff or boom;arms of cleat.   HORN TIMBERS-page 72.

HORSE, DECK HORSE(traveller)-athwartship rail or bar for sheet block.

HOUNDS-wood shoulders bolted to mast to support trestle-trees, page 284.

HOUSE-to secure or stow in a safe place.

HOUSE FLAG-special flag on mainmast of merchant ship denoting company.

HOUSING-inboard part of bowsprit;part of mast below upper deck.

HOVE DOWN-sailboat heeling excessively or to have bottom scraped.

HOVE TO(heave to)-page 151.   HUDSON RIVER SLOOP-page 274.

HUG-to keep close.   HULK-stripped & worn out vessel.

HULL-body of vessel without mast or gear.

HULL DOWN-sailing vessel with only spars visible due to distance.

HULL SPEED-speed limit of displacement vessel, pages 140-143.

HURRICANE-wind force above 65 knots, 137-9.   Named after Caribbean natives with similar name that originally called it a 'big wind'.

•

i IN-a person is said to be in a vessel, not on her.
INBOARD-towards fore and aft centerline of vessel.
IN BOWS-order to boat oars & stand by with boat hooks for landing.
INHAUL-opposite of outhaul.
IN IRONS-sailing vessel head to wind, bow won't pay off on either tack, 99, 104.
INITIAL STABILITY-resistance of sailing vessel to heel, page 17.
INNER JIB-headsail forward of fore staysail on vessel with two or more headsails.
INNER KEEL-the keelson.   IN SAIL-order to take in sail.
INSHORE-in the direction of the shore.
IN STAYS (in irons)-head to wind, all sails shaking, pages 99, 104.
IN the WIND-pointing too high or pinching, page 104.
INWALE-strip of wood at sheer line, page 27.

j JETTY-dike at mouth of a river, pier or wharf, page 217.
JEWEL BLOCKS-single leads for stuns'l halyards at the yardarms.
JEW'S HARP-shackle connecting cable to anchor.
JIB-modern usage is sails secured to stay or stays forward of mast. Also
called headsails and staysails, pages 7, 13, 15, 93.
JIB BOOM-spar extension beyond bowsprit for add'l headsails, page 285.
JIBE (B r.—gybe)-changing wind or tack over stern of sailboat, page 111.
JIB HEADED-same as marconi and bermudian, first called leg-of-mutton, pg. 3.
JIB TOPSAIL-headsail forward of mast tacked higher than jib, page 70, 263.
JIB-purchase which is on a halyards bight.
JIGGER (mizzen) -aft sail on yawl or ketch, pg. 265;after mast of a four masted
ship carrying spanker, page 285 ;handy small tackle for general use aloft.
JIMMY LEGS-master at arms.
JIMMY SQUAREFOOT (Davy Jones)-mythical ocean bottom character.
JOE DECOSTE-sail piece acting as lee for lookout in the weather rigging.
JOGGLE-SHACKLE-long jawed shackle used for cable work.
JOLLY BOAT-work boat or dink carried on stern of coastal sailing vessel.
JOLLY ROGER-pirate flag displaying skull and crossbones.
JUMBO-fore staysail on fore and aft rigged sailing vessel, page 14.
JUMP-a short, quick, choppy sea.
JUMPER-stay on outer end of whiskers to martingale preventing spar from
jumping up, page 285 ;chain stays from outer end of jib-boom to lower end of
martingale boom or dolphine striker.
JUMPER STAY-extra stay going from rail to masthead, 7,113-4,119,121,261
JUMP SHIP-leaving without authorized permission.
JUNK-lateen or lug rigged Chinese or Japanese sailing vessel with sails of
woven matting, page 281 ;term for old rope.
JURY-makeshift or temporary rig to take damaged vessel back to port.
JUTE ROPE-rope that comes from fiber of jute plant.

k KAPOK-buoyant vegetable fiber used in cushions, jackets, etc.
KECKLING-chafing stuff made of old rope that is wound around cables.
KEDGE-small anchor for warping a ship ahead, or kedging off bar.
KEDGING (to kedge)-move vessel by hauling on kedge anchor. Drifting with
anchor just touching bottom is called DREDGING or CLUBBING.
KEEL-fore and aft backbone of ship, pages 20-21, 72.
KEEL BLOCK-line of blocks to take a vessels keel in a dry dock.
KEELEK-small kedge anchor.
KEEL HAUL-ancient sailors punishment where main is hauled under keel of
ship and up other side by ropes or whips from yardarms.
KEELSON-timber connecting floors to keel that are running fore and aft.
KEEP AWAY-change course from wind, or far enough to avoid danger.
KEEP HER FULL-order to keep the sails filled.
KEEP HER OFF-order to keep sailing vessel further from the wind.
KEEP HER SO-an order of steady on her course.

ke KEEP YOUR LUFF-sail close hauled without flutter in sails luff.
KELLET or SENTINEL-page 161.   KELP-seaweed.
KENTLEDGE-shaped pieces of pig iron ballast.
KETCH-two masted sailboat having after mast forward of rudder post, 266-7.
KETTLE-BOTTOMED-vessel with a flat bottom.
KEVEL(cavil)-variation of cleat.
KICK-distance vessels stern is thrown away from direction of turn.
KILLOCK(killick)-page 159.   KINK-twist in a rope.
KING PLANK-main deck plank which others feed into, page 73.
KING POST-short mast to support a boom such as loading cargo, pg. 240.
KING SPOKE-marked upper spoke of wheel when rudder is amidships.
KNEE-timber with two arms connecting vessels beams to frames, page 73.
KNIGHTHEADS-vertical timbers on either side of bowsprit.
KNOCKABOUT-obsolete term of sloop without a bowsprit, page 260.
KNOCKED DOWN-sailboat heeled so far it doesn't recover, page 144.
KNOT-one nautical mile per hour, or 6076 to 6080', one min. of latitude.

l LABOR-a vessel labors when it rolls or pitches heavily in a seaway.
LACING-lines used to secure sail to spar or mast, page 5.
LAID UP-dry docked, such as a boat thru the winter months.
LAND BREEZE-night breeze from land to sea, page 211.
LAND FALL-when land is first sighted. A good landfall is the intended one.
LAND HO!-the hail when land has first been sighted.
LANDLOCKED-entirely surrounded by land.
LANDLUBBER-sailors term for person that doesn't go to sea.
LANDMARK-a distinct object on shore.
LANDS-overlapping part of plank in clinker built boat.
LANYARD-a lashing;ropes for setting up rigging, rove thru deadeyes.
LARBOARD-term formerly used for port or left side of vessel, page 82.
LARGE-see page 99.   LASH-secure or bind with rope.
LATCHINGS-loops on head rope of bonnet by which it is laced to foot of sail.
LATEEN-triangular fore & aft rigged sails secured to long yard and hoisted
obliquely to mast, page 55,49,279.
LATITUDE-distance north or south of equator measured in degrees.
LAUNCH-the long boat.   LAUNCH, TO-to set afloat.
LAY(laid)-direction strands of rope or hawser are twisted, page 184;to come
or go such as LAY FORWARD, LAY AFT, LAY ALOFT.
LAY OFF-to rule off a course.
LAY, TO-same as fetch;sailboat lays mark if it doesn't have to change tack.
LAYUP-hauling out a boat for the winter season.
LAZARETTE-below deck space aft where provisions, parts,etc., are kept.
LAZY GUY(preventer)-rigging to steady boom to prevent jibe in rough sea.
LAZYJACKS(jacks)-lines used to gather sail for raising or lowering, page 5.
LAZYLIFTS-lazyjacks which also combine use of topping lift.
LEACH(leech)-after edge of fore & aft rigged sail, 5,7, 11;square sail, 287.
LEACH LINE-line in leach used to tighten leach of a sail.
LEAD-shaped piece of lead with line secured to upper end, and hole on bottom
to get sample of bottom formation;obsoleted by fathometer to record depth.
LEADEN-when skies are a dull leaden hue.
LEADER-line with eye in upper end free to slide on topmast, used to keep a
topsails luff close to the mast.
LEADING EDGE-forward part of a sail.
LEADING WIND-a beam or quarter wind.
LEAD LINE-line secured to lead, marked at regular intervals to test depth.
LEADSMAN-sailor detailed to chains under bowsprit for heaving the lead.
LEAGUE-distance memasurement of three nautical miles.
LEAK-accidental crack or opening allowing water to enter boat.

LEAVE-permission granting leave period from station or ship.
LEE-wind blows onto lee shore, wind flows from the windward to the leeward side of a vessel, and from windward rigging to rigging on leeward side.
LEEBOARD-pivoted board secured to side of sailboat, pages 18, 23.
LEECH-see leach.
LEE HELM-sailboat out of balance that will turn to beam reach if rudder is suddenly released, pages 132-5.
LEE HELMSMAN-assistant helmsman on lee side of steering wheel.
BY THE LEE (running on the lee)-running with wind on same side, page 123.
LEE-OH!-helm has been put down for sailboat to come about.
LEE TIDE-tidal current running with the wind, page 216.
LEE, UNDER THE-object or another boat between you and the wind.
LEEWARD-direction which is away from the wind.
LEG-length of tack or board, page 101; brace to keep stranded boat upright, 223.
LEG of MUTTON-original term for marconi, bermudian & jib headed sail.
LET DRAW-fill sail on desired tack.   LET FLY-drop the sheets.
LET HER OFF-order to head farther from the wind.
LET HER RIDE-sailboat is on course.
LET HER UP-order to head up or point higher into the wind.
LET GO-drop an anchor.
LIE TO-square rigger slowing down by reducing sail to make little or no progress, or by counter bracing yards;also heave to, page 151.
LIFEBOAT-ships boat for emergency use.
LIFE BUOY-ring buoy for life saving.
LIFELINE-stout line around deck to prevent crew being washed overboard. A sailor can also have lifeline secured to his waist, pages 194, 228.
LIFE PRESERVER-buoyant aid to keep a person afloat, pages 226-9.
LIFE RAFT-float made of cork, canvas, or rubber.
LIFT-line such as topping lift to take weight of a spar, pages 75,96. On square riggers it could be tackle going from yardarms to masthead, purpose being to support & move yard, 285;clearing in fog; wind may lift or raise sail slightly.
LIGHT-lift along;to light out is move out;lighten up is to slack away.
LIGHT AIRS-page 137.   LIGHT BREEZE-page 137.
LIGHTER-harbor craft for loading & unloading ships, or to carry merchandise.
LIGHTNING-sailboat class,pgs. 34-7;damage prevention, page 206.
LIGNUM VITAE-hard wood with own lubricant, used for blocks (pulleys).
LIMBERHOLE (limbers)-drain holes cut into frames next to keel, page 73.
LINE-rope becomes line when used in operation of a vessel,see rope definition.
LINES-drawings of a hulls contours, page 254.
LINES, HEAVING-light line with weight on end for heaving, pg. 194.
LIPPER-small sea coming over the rail.
LIST-vessel inclination due to excess weight on side or either end.
LIZARD-line leader for running rigging fitted with a thimble or thimbles.
LJUNGSTROM-sailboat eliminating danger of accidental jibe, pages 270-271.
L. O. A. (length over all)-extreme length of a hull, page 254.
LOCK-canal compartment used to bring vessel to different water level.
LOCKER-chest,box,or clothes wardrobe to stow items away.
BOATSWAIN'S LOCKER-where rigging & small stuff are stowed.
CHAIN LOCKER-compartment where chain cables are kept.
LOFTY-high, towering, such as masts or clouds.
LOG-device to estimate vessels speed, see CHIP LOG.
LOG BOOK-boats diary containing daily record of course, distance, weather, ships activities and other items of importance.
LOG CANOE, CHESAPEAKE-page 273.   LOG LINE-line secured to log.
LOG SHIP-marked line & float used to determine a vessels speed.
LONG BOARD-long tack, page 101.   LONG BOAT-largest ships boat.

lo LONG in the JAW-a rope that has stretched.

LONGITUDE-distance in degrees east or west of Greenwich, England, meridian.

LONGITUDINAL-fore and aft strengthening member of vessels structure.

LONG LEGGED-deep draft vessel.

LONGSHOREMAN-laborer who loads and unloads cargo.

LONG SPLICE-joining two ropes so dia. is not increased at splice.

LOOF-part of vessel where planks begin to bend as they approach stern.

LOOKOUT-observer on vessel to report objects seen, pages 154, 240.

LOOK UP-order to point closer due to favorable wind shift.

LOOM-illusion at sea; part of an oar.   LOOSE-to unfurl a sail.

LOOSE-FOOTED-fore and aft sail not secured along full length of boom, 23-25.

LOUVRE-wire mesh cap covering end of a ventilator pipe.

LOW-area of low pressure, pg. 212.   LUBBER-a beginner.

LOWER AWAY-order to lower down object such as a lifeboat, or sail.

LUBBER LINE (lubbers point)-mark on compass stand indicating it is on the fore and aft centerline of a vessel, or one that is parallel.

LUFF-bring sailboat higher into wind, or without changing course to slack off on the sheet, both procedures being to break sails airfoil, pgs. 104, 168; the luff is the forward edge of fore and aft sails, pgs. 5, 7.

LUFF EARING-short line to secure luff reef cringle to boom while reefing, 149.

LUFF HER-order to bring sailboat into wind to break sail airfoil.

LUG (lugger)-pages 280-1.   LULL-period of calm.

LURCH-sudden rolling of a vessel to one side.

L. W. L. (load waterline)-waterline reached with boat trimmed to float to the designers specifications, pages 254.

m MACKEREL SKY-page 204.   MADE-put together, not one piece.

MAGAZINE-space provided in a ship to store explosives.

MAIN DECK-highest full length deck of a ship, page 285.

MAINMAST-the taller of the masts on ketches, yawls, and two masted schooners; usually second mast from bow on square riggers, pages 264-285.

MAINSAIL-fore & aft sail set to after side of mainmast, pages 7, 11, 26-91, 264-284 ; it is hung from main yard on a square rigger, page 287.

MAKE SAIL-to set sail.   MAKE FAST-secure or belay a rope.

MAKE STERNBOARD-caught in irons & going astern under sail.

MAKE WATER-to leak.   MALLET-serving or caulking mallet.

MAKE LAND-a landfall.   MANILA-see page 185.

MANGER-space aft of hawse pipes in square rigger having low coaming to keep out water.

MAN ROPE-steadying ropes used in going up & down vessels side or ladder.

MAN the BOAT-order to climb into a rowboat.

MARCONI RIG-triangular sail with luff secured to vertical or nearly so mast. Other names are jib-headed and Bermudian, pages 6, 275.

MARES TAILS-pages 205-209.   MARITIME-pertaining to the sea.

MARINA-facility offering docking & other facilities to boat owners.

MARK-lead line markings to record water depth visually or by feel.

MARL-take frequent turns, each being half hitched, at frequent intervals on line.

MARLINE-small two stranded twine used for marling.

MARLINESPIKE (marlinspike, marlingspike)-pointed wood or steel wedge used to open strands of rope and wire for splicing, 202.

MAROON-abandon a person by putting him ashore.

MARRY-sewing rope ends together to thread one thru block; joining ropes by worming over both in order to haul equally on both.

MARTINGALE (dolphin striker)-short perpendicular spar extending from bowsprit, used for counteracting pull of headstays, page 285.

MAST-vertical spar to support rigging, yards and sails, pages 5, 7.

MAST CAP, page 284.   MASTER-captain of a vessel.

MASTHEAD LIGHT-white running light carried fwd by power vessel underway pages 236-241;light carried by anchored vessels in undesignated anchorages.
MASTHEAD SPINNAKER-pages 124-5.   MAST HEEL(step)-pgs. 23,73.
MAST HOLE-deck opening for mast.
MAST HOOP-wooden mast hoops found on traditional gaff rig, pages 5, 71.
MAST STEP-frame or slot to secure lower end of mast, pages 23, 73.
MAT-used to prevent chafing, made of old rope strands.
MATE-officer ranking next to the captain . . . or his wife.
MATTHEW WALKER-stopper knot used on standing end of lanyard.
MEAL PENNANT-white rectangular flag flown on pleasure craft, page 253.
MEND-refurl improperly furled sail;rebend sail to boom.
MERIDIAN-true north and south line.
MESSENGER-light line used to haul over heavier line or cable,172, 194, 203.
METEOROLOGICAL-pertaining to the weather.
MID-CHANNEL BUOY-buoy to be passed on either side, page 249.
MIDSHIPMAN-usually naval cadet.
MIDSHIPS, AMIDSHIPS-widest part of vessel;order to center rudder.
MILDEW-fungus activity on organic product, see 'TrailerBoating Illustrated'.
MILE-nautical mile is 6080'(Int' Naut. Mile,6076.10'), one min. of latitude.
MIRAGE-seeing an object not there.
MISS STAYS, TO-sailboat failing to change tack, page 99.
MITCHBOARD-boom crutch on rail to support boom when sail is lowered.
MITER(Br. -mitre)-type of sail cut, pages 11, 13.
MIZZENMAST-after mast in 2 & 3 masted sailing vessels, 264-269, 284.
MIZZENSAIL -sail set from mizzenmast.
MIZZEN STAYSAIL-staysail set from mizzen masthead, pages 69, 124, 266.
MODERATE BREEZE-page 137.   MODERATE GALE-page 137.
MOLE-breakwater used for loading pier.
MONKEY FIST- knot worked in end of heaving line.
MONKEY BLOCK-small single block which swivels.
MONKEY GAFF-small gaff on after masthead to display colors underway.
MONSOON-wind periodically blowing one direction for several months, then the other direction for the rest of year.
MOONSAIL-rare small sail above skysail carried in light winds, page 287.
MOORING-permanent anchorage or dock space for a boat, pages 165-7, 175.
MOTHER CAREY'S CHICKEN-the stormy petrel.
MOTORBOAT ACT-regulations are given in CG-169, pages 232-235.
MOULD LOFT-large room for preparing full size boatbuilding templates.
MOULDS-patterns of which frames of a boat are worked out.
MOTOR SAILER-vessel combining features of sail & power boat, 270-271.
MOUSE-turn small stuff around hook to prevent jerking out of its hold.
MUFFLE-oars muffled by canvas around looms in the rowlocks.
MULE-questionable sail, page 14.
MUSHROOM-heavy permanent mooring anchor, pages 159, 167.

n NAUTICAL-pertaining to ships, navigation or seamen.
NAVEL PIPE-pipe thru which anchor chain passes to chain locker(Br. term).
NAVIGABLE-sufficient water depth to permit passage of vessels.
NAVIGATION-skill of conducting vessel from port to port.
NEAPED-boat gone ashore at height of spring tide and following tides fail to float her. NEAP TIDE occurs between full & new moon, having a smaller range than a spring tide, page 215.
NEAR-close to wind.   NEPTUNE-mythical god of sea.
NESTING-stowing one boat inside of another, or mooring several together.
NETTING-rope net work   NIGGER HEAD-drum or winch head.
NIMBUS-storm clouds, page 204.
NIP- twist in line passing through fairlead;part of anchor line in chock.
G19

no NOCK -upper forward end of sail without a boom.
NO HIGHER -order for sailboat to point no higher into wind.
NORMAN -pin to prevent hawsers from slipping off a bollard.
NORTH RIVER SLOOP -page 275.   NOSE -cutwater of vessel.
NOTHING OFF -order for sailboat not to pay further from the wind.
NOT UNDER CONTROL (or command) -disabled vessel out of control.
NUN BUOY -red navigation buoy tapered at top found on starboard side of a
channel when entering from seaward, page 249.
NUT -projections to secure anchor stock located on anchors shank.

O OAKUM -yarn strands of old rope used for caulking, etc.
OAR -wooden pole with blade on one end used for rowing.
OARLOCK -guide fitted to boat acting as pivot for oars.
OFF AND ON -stand toward land & off again on different tacks.
OFFING -to seaward but a safe distance from shore.
OFFSHORE WIND -wind blowing from the shore, page 211.
OFFSETS -naval architect measurements used to lay out boats lines, page 254.
OFF the WIND -sailing downwind in fore and after, page 99;all courses but the
beam reach and closehauled for a square rigger.
OIL BAG -oil filled bag container used to calm rough seas, page 157, 163.
OILSKINS -waterproof clothing.
OLD FASHIONED ANCHOR -similar to yachtsman, with permanent stock, 159.
OLD MAN -the captain.   ON -wind blowing on the lee shore.
ON A WIND -close hauled, page 99.   ON THE BEAM -abeam, 82-3, 99.
ON THE BOW -object bearing from forward to abeam, page 82.
ON THE QUARTER -object bearing between beam and stern.
ON THE WIND (on a wind) -racing sailors term for closehauled.
ONE DESIGN -sailboats built to same specifications. See page 2.
OPEN -unprotected anchorage, away from shelter, a boat without decking.
OPEN HAWSE -riding to two anchors without swivel or crossing each other.
OPEN UP -boat leaking as seams start to open up, or planks shrink.
ORLOP DECK -lower partial deck on old sailing vessels, on or above the
protective deck and below the berth deck.
OUTBOARD -beyond a vessels side;portable propulsion unit -page 181.
OUT FOOT -one vessel sailing faster than another.
OUTHAUL -line use to haul OUT the clew, pages 7,23-79.
OUTLYING -objects at a distance from shore.
OUT OF TRIM -improperly ballasted, page 115.
OUT POINT -sail closer to wind than another sailboat, page 98.
OUT RIGGER -spar spreading standing or running rigging;spar extending from
side of canoe to prevent upset, pages 17, 49, 81.
OUTSAIL -sailboat that can sail faster and outpoint another.
OVER ALL (L. O. A.) -extreme fore & aft vessel measurement, page 254.
OVERBOARD -over the side.   OVERCAST -cloud covered sky.
OVERFALL -tide rip, shoal, seas breaking due to currents over a shallow area.
OVERHAND KNOT and LOOP -page 184.
OVERHANG -part of vessel extending beyond waterline at bow & stern, page 152.
OVERHATTED -sailing vessel which is oversparred.
OVERHAUL, TO -gain on another boat;slacken rope;examine rigging & make
ready;lengthen fall by separating blocks of a tackle.
OVERLAP -in racing a sailboat within 2 overall lengths of boat to windward.
OVER RIGGED -heavier sailing gear than necessary.
OVER SPARRED -vessel with heavier spars than necessary.
OVERTAKEN -sailboat being overtaken by another, pages 233, 235.
OWNERS FLAG -private signal carrying boatowners own design, page 253.

PACKET-mail boat with a regular schedule.
PAD-metal eye permanently secured to deck or bulkhead.
PAINTER-short piece of rope secured to bow of boat, pages 95. 167.
PALM-leather fitting over hand to thust needle through sailcloth.
the flat part of an anchors fluke or blade on old fashioned anchors.
PARA-ANCHOR-parachute surface anchor for deep water, page 155-6,161.
PARACHUTE SPINNAKER- pages 124-5.
PARBUCKLE-raising cylindrical object upwards or over side by bight of two
ropes, hauling in on one rope while making the other fast.
PARCEL-wrap canvas strips tightly around a rope with its lay.
PARREL- rollers to slide gaff jaws up & down a mast.
PART-to break;hauling, standing or running part of a rope.
PARTNERS-framework where mast goes thru the deck, pages   23, 24, 27, 73.
PASS, TO-take securing turns with a lashing or rope.
PASSAGE SAILS & PASSAGE WINDS-downwind sails used to follow the steady
trade wind routes of square riggers, page 131.
PASS A LINE-reeve & secure a line.   PASS A STOPPER-reeve & secure stopper.
PATENT ANCHOR-originally Navy anchor or stockless, term now obsolete.
PATENT LOG-distance recording device on vessel, see CHIP LOG.
PATENT BLOCK or SHEAVE-sheave with roller bearings.
PAUNCH MAT-thick mat often placed at slings of a yard.
PAWLS-short iron bars to prevent capstan barrel from turning backwards.
PAY, TO-to fill a boats seams after it has been caulked.
PAY OFF-turn bow of sailboat away from the wind.
PAY OUT-to slacken out on a cable, rope, or line.
PAZAREE-line used for guying clews out when running before wind. Line is
attached to clew of fores'l, rove thru block on a swinging boom(also passaree).
PEA-point of hook or anchor.
PEA COAT-sailors dark blue winter jacket.
PEAK-upper after corner of a gaff sail-pages 5. 148.
PEAK HALYARD-hoists peak of gaff sail, pages 5, 70, 148.
PELORUS-sighting vane over compass card to take bearings and azimuths.
PENDANT-wire or rope attachment between parts for mooring, jib luff, etc.
PENGUIN-sailboat class, page 24.
PENNANT-long narrow three cornered flag, page 253; bunting streamer for
commission, homeward bound, etc.;often substituted for pendant, page 63.
PENNANT, REEF-line to secure clew earing of reefed sail to boom, page 149.
PERMANENT BACKSTAY-one that clears boom, 35,37,45,51-3,63,67,75,79,81.
PIER-HEADED LEAP-wild jump deserter makes as ship approaches the dock.
PIG-cast piece of metal ballast.
PILE-spar projecting above water with lower end driven firmly into bottom.
FENDER PILES are those at the corner of a dock.
PILLOW-block supporting inner end of a bowsprit.
PILOT BOAT-stationed at harbor entrance carrying pilots that are transferred
to large vessels coming into a harbor.
PILOT'S LUFF-making a weather mark by pinching a boat.
PILOT RULES-see CG-169, page 233.
PIN-axle of sheave in block;short wood or iron rod for belaying ropes.
PINCH (pinch her)-pointing too high to windward, page 104.
PINK STERN-sailboat with high, narrow, pointed stern, page 275.
PINRAIL-railing with holes for belaying pins, page   73.
PINNACE-loosely, a boat or vessel that can be sailed or rowed.
PINTLE-metal pin used as swinging support for rudder, pages 23, 24, 28.
PITCH-fore & aft plunging & rising of vessel, 152, 270—271 ;pine tree product
used to fill seams of a wooden vessel.
PITCH POLE- boat or catamaran turning end over end (cartwheeling).
PIVOTING POINT-point in a vessel about which it turns. CLR, pg. 133.

PLAIN SAIL-regular working sails, page   9.
PLAT-braiding, used only with small stuff.
PLATFORM DECK-partial deck below lowest complete deck.
PLIMSOLL MARK-marking of allowed loading depths on merchant ship side.
PLOW-English anchor resembling a plow, page 159.
PLUG-drain plug in a boat.
POINT-11 1/4° or 1/32 part of circumference;work end of rope with knittles.
POINTING-sailing closehauled. One sailboat may point higher than another.
POINTS, CARDINAL-North, South, East, West.
POINTS, REEF-cords going thru reinforcements on sails foot while it is
being reefed, pages 5, 7, 149.
POLE MAST-one piece mast;highest mast on ship such as sky-sail pole.
POOP-partial deck aft above main deck. If wheel is on main deck, it is the deck
portion aft of the helmsman, page 284. A sailboat is POOPED when running before
the wind, a heavy sea breaks aboard over stern;a worn out feeling.
POPPETS-timbers on fore & aft part of bilgeways when launching.
PORCUPINE-fraying of wire rope.
PORT, PORTHOLE-opening on vessels side, page 72.
PORT CAPTAIN-official in charge of harbor berthing, activities, etc.
PORT (also see larboard)-left side of boat when looking forward, pages 82, 83.
PORT TACK-wind coming over port bow, beam, or stern, pages 98, 101, 111, 233.
PORTOISE-gunwale of a boat.
PORTUGUESE MAN OF WAR-jellyfish with vertical sail like fin.
POUNDING-flat hull surface rising, falling & hitting the waters surface hard.
PRAM-rectangular dinghy. . . see the Naples Sabot, page 23.
PRATIQUE-limited quarantine;permit stating vessel free of contagious diseases.
PRAYER BOOK-small flat holystone.
PREFORMED ROPE-wire rope resisting being unlaid.
PRESS OF SAIL-all sail a vessel can carry.
PREVENTER-line running forward from boom to prevent a jibe, pages 120-3.
PRICKER-small marlinspike.
PRIDE OF THE MORNING-early morning mist before a lovely day.
PRIVILEGED VESSEL-it has right-of-way & must maintain course, 232-235.
PROFILE-side view silhouette of a vessel.
PROLONGED BLAST-one of 4 to 6 seconds duration, page 235.
PROW-part of bow above water.
PUCKER STRING (leach line)-line used to tighten leach of a sail.
PUDDEN (puddin)-fender to protect vessels side.
PUDDENING-oakum,matting,or yarns used to prevent chafing.
PUNT-rectangular flat bottom boat or dinghy.
PURCHASE-rope & block arrangements to increase hauling power.
PUT TO SEA-to leave port.

q QUADRANT-navigation instrument;metal fitting on rudder to secure steering ropes.
QUADRILATERAL SPINNAKER-obscure European spinnaker, see shadow.
QUANT-(Br.)-long punting pole.
QUARANTINE-period of time before a ship is cleared by port doctor as having
no evidence of contagious diseases.
QUARANTINE BUOY-yellow buoy quarantine anchorage, page 248.
QUARTER-vessels side aft of beam & forward of stern, pages 83, 98.
QUARTER DECK-part of upper deck abaft mainmast,officers territory, 285.
QUARTER MASTER-petty officer attending to helm, binnacle, signals, etc.
QUARTERING SEA-wind & waves on a ships quarter, page 99.
QUAY-wharf used to discharge cargo.
QUICK WORK-part of ship's side above gunwales and decks.
QUILTING-woven rope covering on outside of container.
QUOIN-wood wedge which the breach of a gun rests on.

RABBET-groove cut in keel, sternpost, stem, etc., for end or edge of plank, pg. 257.

RACE-water disturbed due to confusing currents.

RACK-seizing two ropes together with cross turns of spun yarn.

RACK BLOCK-set of blocks for fairlead made from single piece of wood.

RAFFEE-triangular sail set above square sail, page 131.

RAIL-top of bulwarks on edge of a deck, page 73.

RAISE-bringing an object on the horizon into view.

RAKE-inclination of mast from the vertical, pages 26-7, 32, 91, 114-121.

RANGE-difference between fall & rise of tide, page 215; two objects in line used as aid to steer a course.

RANGE ALONGSIDE-come close abeam of another boat.

RANGE LIGHTS-vertical white lights indicating vessels direction, page 238.

RANGE OF CABLE-lay qunatity of cable on deck ready to use.

RAPT FULL-all sails full.   RATER-Naval term, pages 288, 289.

RATLINE-horizontal rope ladders up the shrouds to go aloft, pages 75, 285.

RAT TAIL-bolt rope worked down to a small point,

RATTLING DOWN-rigging ratlines.

RAZEE-vessel of war with one deck cut down.

REACH-all courses between running free and close hauled, page 99.

REACHING JIB-page 13.

READY ABOUT-preparatory order to coming about, page 109.

REEF-to shorten sail, pages 133, 146-149.

REEF BAND-reenforcing band on sail with reef points & earrings, 5, 287.

REEF, SPANISH-tie a knot in the material of a headsail.

REEF CRINGLE (reef earing)-metal eye in sail for reefing, page 149.

REEF POINTS-short lengths of rope through reefband to secure foot of sail when it is reefed, pages 5, 7, 149.

REEF TACKLE-tackle used to haul out foot of sail; in a square sail, to haul in the middle of each leach for reefing, page 70.

REEVE, TO-to pass end of rope thru a lead, hole, or block.

REGISTRY-ships certificate showing nationality and ownership.

RELIEVING TACKLE-emergency tackle.

RENDER-rope slides or runs freely through a block.

RHUMB LINE-a straight line is the shortest distance between two points.

RIB-frame of vessel, pages 72-73.   RIDE-to lie at anchor, pg. 288.

RIDE OUT-weather a storm safely underway or at anchor.

RIDERS-upper layer of barrels stowed in a hold.

RIDING CHOCKS-deck chock thru which anchor line rides.

RIDING DOWN the RIGGING-sliding down rigging in a boatswains chair.

RIDING LIGHT-white anchor light displayed in fore part of anchored vessel.

RIG-arrangement of a boats sails, masts, and rigging.

RIGGING-standing rigging is permanent including shrouds and stays, while running rigging consists of halyards, braces and sheets which raise, trim and control the sails, page 67.

RIGHT-sailboat returning to upright position after heeling.

RIGHT-HANDED-rope is usually twisted from right to left, page 184.

RIGHT THE HELM-put it amidships.

RING-ring at upper end of anchor to which cable is bent, page 159.

RINGBOLT-eyebolt used for leading running rigging.

RINGBUOY-circular preserver.

RINGTAIL-small sail set abaft spanker in light winds, see page 48.

RIP, TIDE-water disturbance caused by confliciting currents or winds.

RISING (riser)-fore & aft stringers to support thwarts on a small boat.

RISING GLASS-rising barometer.

ROACH-outward upward curve of leach, pages 5, 7.

ROADSTEAD (road)-open anchorage at a distance from shore.

ROCKER-upward curve of boats bottom, see 'TrailerBoating Illustrated'.

RO RODE-small boats anchor line.

ROGUE'S YARN-colored yarn in center of rope for identification.

ROLL-side to side motion of a vessel, see pg. 162.

ROLL CLOUD-pages 205 -207.

ROLLER REEFING-sail is rolled around revolving boom for reefing, 149.

ROLLING TACKLE-used to steady square rigger yards in heavy seas.

ROPE- strands of fiber or wire braided or twisted together, pages 184, 185.
Ropes used in operation of a sailboat became lines. Ropes which remained
ropes on square riggers were;foot ropes, yard ropes, bell ropes, bucket ropes,
bolt ropes, back ropes, top ropes & man ropes.

ROUND TREE-unfinished spar.   ROUND BOTTOM-page 16.

ROUND DOWN-overhauling tackle so lower block will come down.

ROUND IN-haul in.   ROUNDLY-quickly, steadily.

ROUNDS-Jacob's ladder rungs.

ROUND TO(round up)-change course heading from run to reach, pg. 108.

ROUND TURN- a full turn around any object.

ROUSE IN-to haul in by manpower.

ROWLOCK (oarlock)-pivoting point on boats side for oars.

BOWSER CHOCK-chock which is closed.

ROYAL-sail above topgallant in a square rigger, pages 285-287.

ROYAL YARD-yard to which the royal sail is set, pages 285-287.

RUBBING STRAKE-additional planking outside & below gunwale to reduce
damage of chafe to a vessels side.

RUDDER-flat plate hinged to stern used to steer a vessel,pages 5-7, 23-53.

RUFFLE-drum roll used when rendering honors.

RULES OF THE ROAD-found in CG-169, pages 232-239.

RUN-after underwater narrowing part of a vessel.

RUNNING(to run)-sailing before the wind, pages 99, 105, 111, 120-123, 131.

RUN AWAY-desert;seize a line and to haul it on the run.

RUN DOWN-sail along a coast;overtake & collide with another vessel;run
down the trades;sail north or south at a given parallel of latitude.

RUNG HEADS-upper ends of floor timbers.

RUNNER-purchase used for tightening a backstay, pages 45, 70-71, 109.

RUNNING BACKSTAYS-a temporary backstay set up to windward as a boat
comes about, and the leeward one slacked off, pages 45, 70, 71, 109.

RUNNING BY THE LEE-sailing with wind over same quarter as boom, pg. 123.

RUNNING LARGE-page 99.

RUNNING LIGHTS-carried by vessels underway from dusk to dawn, 236-239.

RUNNING RIGGING-see rigging;used to raise, set, trim sails, pg. 67.

RUN OUT-to send out such as to run out a towing hawser.

S SADDLES-wood brackets secured to lower part of mast for boom to rest on.

SAG-drift to leeward;waist of ship settling below level of bow & stern.

SAIL BAG-pages 86-96.   SAIL COVER-protects furled sails.

SAILING FREE (running)-sailing with the wind aft, page 98.

SAIL HO! cry used when a sail was sighted at sea.

SAILING THWART-midship plank to support mast on boat that can be rowed.

SAILING TRIM-most efficient trim of sails, pages 104-105, 114-135.

SAILS-flexible vertical airfoils using wind pressure to propel a sailboat.

SALTINGS (marshes)-flat land flooded at high tide.

SALVAGE-pay for saving cargo or ship from danger.

SAMPSON POST (samson post)-strong post in bow or stern to secure dock
lines, anchor lines, or tow lines, pgs. 61 and 73, also called mooring bitt.

SAND BAGGERS-see page 48.

SAVE ALL(catch all) small sail set under foot of lower sails.

SCALE-to climb up;rust formation on metal plating.

SCANDALIZING-dropping peak halyard on a gaff rigger, page 148.

SCANTLINGS-standardized part dimensions used in ship building.
SCARF (scarphing)-join timber ends by tapering and overlapping them.
SCEND-boat lifting to a swell or seaway.
SCHOOL-large body of fish.
SCHOONER-see pages 5, 268, 269.   SCHOONER BOW-fiddle or clipper bow.
SCOPE-length of mooring or anchor line let out, page 161.
SCORF-groove in dead eye or block to take wire or rope strap.
SCOTCHMAN-grommet at luff of tops'l, at end of mitre gore for purchase;to
secure pole or haul leading edge of sail towards mast and down, page 70.
SCOW-rectangular sailboat hull, pg 45;barge for hauling sand, gravel, refuse,etc.
SCRAPER-small hand tool used for scraping sides, decks, masts, etc.
SCREEN-sidelight boards limiting horizontal arc of red & green sidelights,236-9.
SCREENED LIGHT-box limiting arc of light in horizontal arc, pages 236-239.
SCREW STOPPER-chain stopper fitted with turnbuckle.
SCROWL-timber substitute for a figurehead.
SCUD-low lying mist clouds usually moving quite fast.
SCUDDING-driving before a gale with steadying sails or no sails.
SCULL-short oar;to propel small boat with single oar by working it from side
to side over the stern, action resembles movement of a fishes tail.
SCULLERY-compartment used for stowing and washing dishes.
SCUPPERS-overboard drainholes on deck, page 69, 72.
SCUPPER LIP-protrusion to prevent water coming aboard thru scuppers.
SCUTTLE-deliberately sink a vessel;small hatch or trunk for air & light.
SCUTTLE BUTT-crews fresh water drinking cask;crew meeting place also.
SEA-waves or swells.
SEA ANCHOR—anchor getting purchase from waters surface.STORM ANCHORS
pg.157, only become effective in strong winds. The PARA-ANCHOR pgs. 155, 156,
161, gives maximum purchase in light and strong winds.
SEA BOAT-seaworthy vessel with ability to weather storms, page 154.
SEA BREEZE-cooling breeze blowing from large body of water, page 211.
SEA BUOY(farewell buoy)-last large buoy of channel to seaward.
SEA CHEST-intake between sea valve & ships side; sailors trunk.
SEACOCK-a drain;vessel may be flooded if seacocks are opened, page 154.
SEA DOG-an old seasoned sailor.
SEA GOING-a vessel capable of going to sea.
SEA KINDLY-vessel riding comfortably in rough weather, page 152.
SEA LADDER-portable ladder to climb up or down side of a ship.
SEA LAWYER-belligerant seaman enjoying arguments against authority.
SEAM-space between planks;stitching holding two cloths together.
SEA ROOM-enough distance from land permitting unrestricted maneuvers.
SEAWAY-area with rough or moderate sea running.
SEAWORTHY-vessel able to meet usual sea conditions, page 154.
SECOND DECK-first complete deck below main deck.
SECTION-vessel shape at right angle to keel, pages 254-255.
SECURE-to make fast.
SECURE FOR SEA-order for extra lashings on all movable objects.
SEIZE-binding together ropes with small stuff.
SEIZINGS-small stuff for binding.   SELVAGE-yarn marled together.
SENNIT (sinnit)-braided rope yarn.   SENTINEL (kellet)-page 161.
SERVE (serving)-bindings against rope lay to prevent chafing.
SERVING BOARD-small flat board with handle used for serving small rope.
SERVING MALLET-mallet having groove cut lengthwise in head to serve rope.
SET-direction of tide, current, or leeway course of a sailboat.
SET A COURSE-to steer.
SET FLYING-sail filling before it is in place, see spinnaker, page 126, 127.
SET TAUT-preparatory order to heave in, to take in slack.
SETTLE-ship slowly sinking, lower a sail slowly.

ROYCE'S
sailing
illustrated

the best of ALL sailing worlds

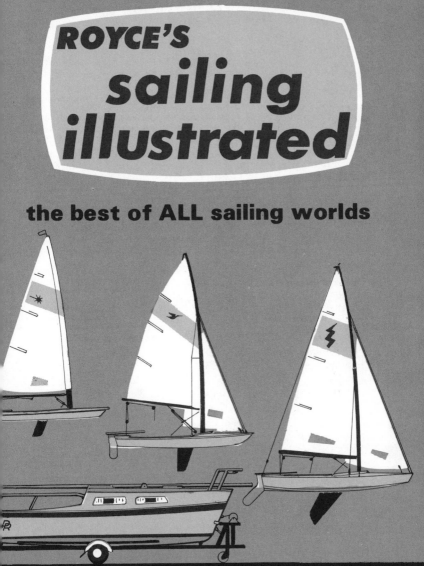

the most recommended sailing reference ashore and afloat

the SAILOR'S BIBLE since '56

REVISED AND ENLARGED FOR EASIER READING

TRAILERBOATING ILLUSTRATED
Series 1, 6"x9", 192 pages,
$5.95, each, fully illustrated

Explore THE trailerboating classic by th
author who first introduced the term i
1960 with his first edition of this book. P₂
is a pioneer in this field with his boo
helping to formulate the standards of th
highly complex, specialized world all of i
own.

This book has distilled the basics and sifte
them into their sequence so you can grasp
good foundation in the trailerable outboar
and outdrive fields, plus propellers, rop
handling, trailers, and an excellent chapt
on seamanship in this specialized boating world you can readily apply
found in no other publication.

● *"Seldom is a boating book offered in this price range which contai*
so much information about so many things. . .The author draws fro
many years of practical experience and does not hesitate
recommend or turn thumbs down on equipment or seamansh
techniques. A book that should be in every boating enthusias
library." Dix Brow, SEA MAGAZINE.

● *"The book covers just about everything a person needs to know*
efficiently operate and enjoy a trailerable powerboat. . .The book
written in easy to understand language and illustrated with hundre
of illustrations. . .it's convenient to thumb through and take aboa
your boat." . . .Nancy Wolff, ARIZONA WATERWAYS.

● *"The smaller the boat and higher its performance, the more fun it*
when things are going right. When it is out of tune, things start to
wrong very fast. By exposure to these ideas we hope to keep t
reader out of trouble". . .CASTOFF.

● *"If you study this book before buying a boat, it may save you a l*
of money. If you have a new boat, read every page before launc
time for that memorable (or castastrophic) event.

"If you are an old timer in this field, you will find many ideas yc
have forgotten about your boat and trailer plus short cuts and ne
ways to do things more easily. Norman Phillips — TRAILERBOAT
MAGAZINE.

● *". . .Royce is a commercial artist as well as a lifetime boater, and*
man of extraordinary humor that surfaces in his sketches and wor
He distinguishes himself by covering all of the basics in a succule
style, and in addition incorporates hundreds of tips and techniques
value to the trailerboater.

●

"Unlike most trailerboating manuals, Royc
handbook covers survival at sea". .
F.M. Paulson — FIELD & STREAN

SAILING ILLUSTRATED...352 pages, with 137 full page illustrations — $7.95 each

Follow the present and future trends of sailing with the "Sailor's Bible" first published in 1956, when wooden hulls, canvas sails, and manila rope were the standards. It is now in the 16th revision to bring you up to today's sailing standards.

Probably the most noticeable change is our book being printed to a larger size making it easier to study the large number of sailboats detailed which often take a month or more each to complete to the authors satisfaction, plus larger type from stem to stern for easier reading.

Chances are you will find at least one well thumbed copy handy when sailors gather at an inland yacht club, a clambake, or when deep water sailors meet in a foreign port to splice the main brace while they try to justify their "almost true" sea stories.

MARINER'S CATALOG (Intl. Marine Pub. Co.)..."our favorite how-to-sail manual; Royce understands beginners. He knows what they are up against and makes every effort — without an ounce of patronization — to make things clear, simple, and concise."

WEBB CHILES, author of "Storm Passage" sailed around the world in 279 days..."This book is by far the best of its kind"...

"Sailors have been waiting for more than three centuries for this book...once you see it you have no choice but to make it yours."
SEA MAGAZINE, Skip Warren, editor to 1957.

SAILING ILLUSTRATED has worldwide acceptance with orders coming direct from almost every country (even Timbuktu) but Russia, even orders a day apart from the North and South Poles.

Many sailors buy three copies, one for their boat, the second for their home library, and a third for that special sailing friend.

SAILING ILLUSTRATED WORKBOOK
36 pages plus cover, $2.95 each

This sail course workbook was developed by the author for use in his full day sailing lessons on the water, time permitting, since '62. It has been fully tested under the best and WORST conditions.

This is the best answer for classroom use as well as those learning to sail by themselves. Both sailing and racing courses are in a programmed sequence, the best way to learn the new language, the most difficult part of sailing.

Order Form

•1980 PACIFIC BOATING ALMANACS
_____ Southern California, Arizona, Baja edition / 6.95
_____ Northern California & Nevada edition / 6.95
_____ Pacific Northwest edition / 6.95

•ROYCE PUBLICATIONS
_____ Sailing Illustrated / 7.95
_____ Sailing Illustrated Workbook / 2.95
_____ Trailerboating Illustrated-1: Planing Hulls-
        Trailers-Seamanship / 5.95

•CLYMER BOATING MAINTENANCE HANDBOOKS
_____ Sailboat Maintenance / 9.00
_____ Powerboat Maintenance / 9.00
_____ British Seagull Outboards / 8.00
_____ Chrysler Outboards (3.5 to 20 HP) / 8.00
_____ Chrysler Outboards (25 to 135 HP) / 8.00
_____ Evinrude Outboards (1.5 to 35 HP) / 8.00
_____ Evinrude Outboards (40 to 140 HP) / 8.00
_____ Johnson Outboards (1.5 to 35 HP) / 8.00
_____ Johnson Outboards (40 to 140 HP) / 8.00
_____ Mercury Outboards (4 to 40 HP) / 8.00
_____ Mercury Outboards (50 to 175 HP) / 8.00
_____ Stern Drive Service / 9.00

•OTHER SELECT MARINE BOOKS
_____ Complete Book of Inflatable Boats / 7.95
_____ Cruising Guide to Channel Islands / 16.95
_____ Exploring the Coast by Boat - B.C. & Wash. / 8.95
_____ Exploring the Seashore - B.C., Wash. & Oregon / 9.95
_____ Landfalls of Paradise - Guide to Pac. Islands / 24.95
_____ Northwest Passages-I / 8.95
_____ 141 Dives in Protected Waters of Wash. & B.C. / 9.95
_____ Pac. Coast Inshore Fishes / 10.95
_____ Pac. Coast Nudibranchs / 14.95
_____ Pac. Coast Subtidal Marine Invertebrates / 9.50
_____ VHF Radio Procedures Guide (Laminated) / 2.95
_____ Southeastern Alaska / 5.95
_____ 1980 Spyglass / 5.95

•TIDAL CURRENT CHARTS (Laminated)
_____ Puget Sound, Southern Part / 5.95
_____ Puget Sound, Northern Part / 5.95
_____ San Francisco Bay / 5.95

Send order to your neighborhood bookstore, marine store, or
Western Marine Enterprises, Inc., Box Q, Ventura, CA 93002

[ ] Rush the books checked above.
    Check or money order is enclosed.

_____ Sub total

$1.25 _____ Shipping charge per order

_____ California Residents add 6% sales tax

_____
Ship to: (Name and complete address)

_____

_____

_____ Zip_____

● **Money Back Guarantee**
If not completely satisfied,
return your order within 10
days for a full refund.

Note: Prices listed here are in
effect June 1980 and are sub-
ject to change without notice.
In Canada, order from Gordon
Soules, 525-355 Burrard St.,
Vancouver, B.C. V6C 2G8.
Prices in Canada are generally
higher than U.S. prices.

se SET the COURSE-give helmsman course to be steered.

SET the WATCH-dividing ships crew into watches.

SETTEE-long, sharp bowed lateen rigged sailing ship.

SET UP, TO-to tighten rigging or to flatten the sails.

SEXTANT-navigation instrument that determines altitude of sun and stars.

SHACKLE-shaped metal fitting with pin or bolt; 15 fathoms of chain.

SHADOW-obsolete quadrilateral spinnaker with short gaff.

SHAKE-sails shake when boat is pointing too high or sail is luffing, page 99.

SHAKEDOWN CRUISE-first cruise of newly commissioned vessel.

SHAKE OUT-let out a reef;hoist the sails.

SHAKINGS-rope,waste canvas,small stuff.   SHANK-arm of anchor,page 158.

SHANK PAINTER-line securing fluke of anchor to billboard.

SHAPE-cone or ball used in distance signals.

SHAPE a COURSE-plot proper course to reach specific port or point.

SHARK'S MOUTH-opening thru awning around a mast.

SHARPIE-page 273.   SHARPSHOOTER-page 275.

SHARP UP-yards braced as near fore and aft as possible.

SHEARS-two or more spars raised at angles & lashed together for hoisting or lowering heavy objects.

SHEAR HULK-old vessel used to put in or take out spars on other sailing vessels.

SHEATHING (sheathed)-copper plates covering ships bottoms.

SHEAVE-wheel of a block.

SHEEPSHANK-bend or hitch temporarily used to shorten a rope.

SHEER-sudden course change; side view of boat, page 62;sheer plan, page 254.

SHEER ABOUT-boat that is restless on mooring or when anchored.

SHEER OFF-bear away.   SHEER PLAN-side view, page 254.

SHEERPOLE-rod across foot of shrouds for spreader to prevent untwisting.

SHEER STRAKE-topmost plank in ships side,page 73.

SHEER, TO-to move across.

SHEET-trimming line secured to sails boom or clew,pages 5-95.

SHEET ANCHOR-loosely used term for various kinds of anchors.

SHEET BEND-page 189.   SHELL-outer casing of a block.

SHIFT-change sails clothes, etc.

SHIFTING BACKSTAY-another term for running backstay, page 70-71, 109.

SHIP-(trad.)sailing vessel square rigged on 3 or more masts,page 282. Today it usually refers to a power driven vessel over 75' long, that is capable of taking passengers and/or cargo for long seagoing voyages.

SHIP, TO-a boat is shipping water when water comes aboard.

SHIPPING ARTICLES-agreement between Navy & recruit, or ships officers and crew with agents or owners.

SHIPSHAPE-everything in place.

SHIPS PAPERS-documents carried on ship required by various authorities.

SHIVER (shake)-sail airfoil broken by pointing too high into wind, pages 99, 104.

SHOAL-shallow.

SHOD-anchor won't bite as it is caked with mud or clay.

SHOE-false keel to give vessel more draft;lower rudder support, see skeg, 72.

SHOOT-momentum or distance a sailboat will keep going when pointing head to wind, for going through a crowded mooring area, page 165.

SHORE (shore up)-to prop up or buttress an object.

SHORT BOARD-short tack;LONG BOARD is a long tack, page 101.

SHORT HANDED-not enough crew members.

SHORTEN-reducing sail area by reefing or dropping sail, page 146-149.

SHORT STAY-scope of anchor line almost vertical.

SHOT-15 fathoms of chain.

SHOULDER of MUTTON-quad. sail with short gaff or club, often boomless, pg. 3.

SHOVE OFF-push bow of boat away from dock while getting underway.

SHOW A LEG-make haste.

SHROUD LAID-four strand right handed rope.
SHROUDS-a mast is secured fore and aft by stays, and shrouds going to either side, also called sidestays, pages 24-81, 112.
SIDE BOYS-crew manning side of ship in honor of visiting officers or officials.
SIDE LIGHTS-red & green running lights, see pages 236-239.
SIGHT the ANCHOR-raise anchor to see if it is clear, and let it go again.
SILL-horizontal timbers between frames to form and secure openings.
SILT-sediment, mud.   SINGLE STICKER-one masted vessel.
SING OUT-call out.   SISTER SHIPS-built to same design.
SKEG-after keel timbers or extension supporting a rudder, pages 20-23, 72.
SKIFF-small light pulling boat.
SKIN-outer surface of furled sail;outer planking of a vessel.
SKIPJACK-page 273.   SKIPPER-the captain.
SKYSAIL (skysail yard)-next above royal, page 287.
SKY SCRAPER-triangular skysail.   SKY PILOT-chaplain.
SKYLIGHT-hatch covering admitting air and light.
SLABLINE-small line used to haul up foot of course, page 287.
SLACK-ease off, part of sail or rope that hangs limp.
SLACK CLOTHS-baggy sail.
SLACK IN STAYS-sailboat that has long keel changes tack slowly.
SLACK WATER-period of tide change when there is no current.
SLANT OF WIND-favorable wind change.
SLEEPER-partially submerged log;knees connecting aft timbers to transom.
SLEW (slough) - swampy river inlet area where fresh & salt water mingle.
SLICK-smooth water on lee side of drifting vessel; an oil slick, page 157.
SLIDING GUNTHER-small sailboat with sliding topmast or vertical gaff.
Purpose is to permit all spars capable of being stowed in dinghy, page 271.
SLING-a tackle to hoist or lower.
SLINGS-ropes securing center of yard to mast.
SLIP-dock or pole mooring area.   SLIPPERY HITCH-page 191.
SLIP THE MOORING-cast off from the mooring, page 95.
SLOOP-one masted sailboat. Traditional term now obsolete required sailboat to have a bowsprit. SLOOP vs CUTTER difference was considerable during last century, pages 262-3.
SLOOP OF WAR-vessel mounting 18-32 guns, no particular rig, page 289.
SLUSH-grease used for making a mast slippery.
SMACK-small sloop or cutter rigged fishing boat.
SMALL STUFF-smallest rope, marline, or yarn.
SMART-seamanlike, snappy, an efficient ship.
SMITING LINE-used to break light sail sent up in stops.
SNAKE-wrapping rope with small stuff, similar to worming.
SNIED-crooked.   SNIPE-j page 33.
SNORTER (snotter)-rope sending down royal & topgallant yards, etc.
SNUB-check a rope suddenly.
SNUG DOWN-reduce sail, close hatches, secure loose objects before a blow.
SNUGGED DOWN-under small but comfortable sail area.
SNY-small toggle on a flag.
SNYING-curved plank used to work in vessels bow.
SO-order to stop hauling as object is now in correct position.
SOFT EYE-eye at end of rope that does not contain a metal thimble.
SOLDIERS WIND-fair wind.
SOLE-(Br.) cabin or saloon floor;timber extension on bottom of rudder.
SOUND-measuring depth of water.   SOUNDINGS-charted depths.
SOU'WESTER-oilskin hat having a broad rear brim.
SPAN-rope or chain with both ends made fast to same object so purchase can be hooked into its bight for lifting.
SPANKER-aft mast & sail of full rigged ship or bark, pages 283-287.

sp SPANKING BREEZE-good wind coming over stern or quarter.
SPAR-general term for yards, booms, gaffs, masts, etc.
SPAR BUOY-pole spar for piloting used in buoyage system, page 249.
SPEAK-communicating with vessel in sight.   SPECTACLE-page 287.
SPELL-interval or period of time given to any job.
SPELL, TO-to relieve another.
SPENCER-small boomless sail set from gaff and hoisted from a small 'spencer'
mast that is abaft the fore and main masts.
SPIDER HOOP(or band)-metal band around mast to contain belaying pins.
SPILE-pile.   SPILL-to empty wind out of sail.
SPILLING LINE-used in bad weather to spill wind out of a sail.
SPINNAKER-large triangular racing sail set from mast & boom, 124-130.
SPITFIRE JIB-small heavy weather jib, page 14. The spinnaker staysail or
ballooner has been recently nicknamed spitfire, pages 68, 69.
SPLICE-weaving strands of two ropes together-pages 195-201.
SPLICE THE MAIN BRACE-have a drink.
SPLINE-thin wooden strip fitted to seam instead of stopping.
SPOKE-handle of a steering wheel.
SPONSOR-person christening a ship when it is launched.
SPOON DRIFT-spray swept from top of wave in bad weather covering area.
SPRAY-particles of water blown from top of waves, page 137.
SPREADER-horizontal strut used to support the mast to spread shrouds, 7, 68.
SPRING-pivot line used for docking, undocking, or preventing boat from moving
ahead or astern while at dock, pages 174, 175.
SPRING STAY-horizontal stay between lower mastheads.
SPRING TIDE-occurs at maximum range between new & full moon, that takes
place · twice monthly instead of during the spring, page 215.
SPRIT (sprit sail)-quadrilateral sail with peak extended by spar called sprit
that goes from peak to tack, page 271, later version. The original had the
sprits'l yard with quadilateral square sail under bowsprit shown on page
289, common from Columbus' Santa Maria'to the 1800's.
SPRUNG-mast, spar, or hull that is warped or strained.
SPUDS-vertical timbers used in holding a dredge in place.
SPUN YARN-rough stuff used for seizings, etc.
SPURLING LINE-wire or chain between telltail and tiller.
SPURS-half beams to support deck where full length beams cannot be used.
Timbers bolted to vessels side above water fixed to bilgeways.
SPURSHORE-spar used to hold a vessel clear of a dock.
SPY GLASS-small hand telescope.
SQUALL-sudden violent gust of wind;a local storm, page 206-7.
SQUARE A YARD-bring it square with the braces.
SQUARED-yards squared by lifts on horizontal plane, and at right angles to the
keel by braces.
SQUARESAIL-quad. sail set from yard on square riggers that is most efficient
for sailing downwind or following trade winds around the world, 131, 282-289.
STAFF-a mast or pole used to hoist flags upon.
STABILITY-vessel steady, firm and stable.
STAYSAIL SCHOONER-page 269.   STAR-page 21, 42-3.
SQUARE MARK-running rigging marked to indicate correct setting.
STAGGER-overcanvassed vessel that does not ride well.
STANCHIONS-upright support posts-page 66-81.
STAND-period when tide is rising or falling that has intervals between, without
apparent vertical motion.
STAND BY-preparatory order.   STANDING LUG-page 281.
STANDING OFF & ON-sail towards and away while waiting instead of anchoring.
STAND ON-maintain ones course and speed.
STANDING PART-part of line or fall made fast & not hauled upon. pg. 184.

STANDING RIGGING-permanently secured rigging, see page 67.
STARBOARD-right side of vessel looking forward, pages 82, 83.
STARBOARD TACK-sailing with wind over st'b'd bow, beam or stern, 98, 233.
START, TO-to slack off, to loosen.
STATION BILL-posted list with crews instructions.
STAUNCH-able, stiff, steady, seaworthy. STAVE IN-to crush in.
STAY-support for mast, pages 67-81.
STAYS, IN- caught in irons, page 99.
STAYSAIL-fore & aft triangular sail set upon a stay, pgs. 13-15; schooner, 269.
STAY TACKLE-used to hoist cargo, made fast to stay.
STEADY-order to maintain present course.
STEADYING LINE-one used for steadying purposes.
STEERAGE-portion of vessel occupied by passengers paying lowest fare.
STEEVE-bowsprit's angle with the horizon.
STEM-forward vertical timber of keel supporting the bow planks, page 73.
STEM THE TIDE-sailing against current yet still making some headway.
STEP-block for stepping mast, pages 23-24, 73.
STERN-after end of a boat or ship, page 82.
STERNBOARD-sailboat in irons going backwards.
STERN LIGHT-12 pt. white stern light on vessel, pages 236-239.
STERNPOST-after end of a vessel.
STERNSHEETS-part of open boat abaft rowers for passengers.
STEVEDORE-worker loading & unloading cargo.
STIFF-sailboat with minimum heel, opposite of crank.
STIRRUPS-rope supports for yard footropes. BOWLINE or FABRIC STIRRUP is
used as foot pivot to take person aboard boat, page 192.
STOCK-crosspiece on anchor, page 158. STOCKS-frame for building a ship.
STOOLS-short channels for the backstay deadeyes.
STOPPER-short stout rope used for various purposes.
STOPPER KNOT-terminal knot on rope to stop it running thru block, etc.
STOPS-weak yarns to temporarily secure spinnaker or balloon jib, pg. 127.
STOPWATER-small wooden plug driven into hole bored across a joint, that
can hardly be caulked to prevent leakage, page 72 ; also called treenail.
STORM SAILS-small heavy weather sails pg. 15 ; steadying sails, 150, 271.
STORM WARNINGS -pages 136-139.
STOVE IN-broken in.   STOW-to place.
STOWAWAY-person illegally aboard.   STRAKE-a side plank, page 73.
STRAND-number of yarns woven together, page 184.
STRANDED-vessel driven ashore, 223. STRAP-binding around a block.
STRATOCUMULUS-page 205.   STRATUS-flat cloud, page 205.
STREAM ANCHOR-medium sized anchor.
STREAM, TO- let out a sea anchor or log.
STRETCHER-oarsman footbrace.   STRIKE-to lower.
STRINGER-fore & aft strip on inner side of timbers or frames, page 73.
STROP-rope or metal band.
STUDS-metal fittings across chain links to prevent kinking.
STUDDINGSAILS (stuns'ls)-sails extending beyond square sail yards, pg. 287.
SUN OVER THE FOREYARD-first drink time expression.
SUPERSTRUCTURE DECK-partial deck above f'c'sle, upper, main or poop deck
which does not extend full width of vessel.
SUPPORTERS-knee timbers under the catheads.
SURF-swell of a wave as it breaks as it goes into the shore.
SURGE-effect of large wave on boat; to slack suddenly.
SWAB-rope mop.   SWALLOW-groove in block for sheave.
SWAMP-boat full of water in sinking condition.
SWAY (sway aloft)-to hoist aloft.   SWEDISH JIB-original genoa jib, pg. 125.
SWEEP-long oars.   SWELL-long easy waves not breaking.
G29

SW SWIFT (swifter in)-bring stays or shrouds together by turns of rope.
SWIFTER-foremost shrouds;ropes confining capstan bars.
SWIG, TO (swig off)-hauling on rope & taking in slack.
SWING SHIP, TO-swinging ship thru all points of compass to record deviation.
SWING, TO-wind or tide changes anchored/moored vessels heading.
SWIVEL-two fitted links turning upon an axis between, rather than than kinking.
SYPHERING-overlapping plank edges for a bulkhead.

t TABERNACLE (Eng.)-housing that permits sailboat mast to be lowered and raised again after vessel has gone under a bridge, or for trailering, 56,57,63.
TABLING-broad hem sewn around a sail, page 11.
TACK-sailing course,page 98;sails forward lower corner, pages 5, 7, 126-130.
TACK, CHANGE-change wind or boom to other side of boat, pages 109, 111.
TACKLE-combination of blocks to form a purchase.
TACKLINE-signal halyards;line to haul down tack of gaff topsail.
TAFFRAIL-railing around or across the stern, pg. 75.
TAFFRAIL LOG-device to determine vessels speed.
TAIL-short rope spliced to block so it can be secured to an object.
TAIL ON-pull on a rope.   TAKE IN-lower or stow a sail.
TAKE OFF-remove sail;decreasing tide velocity & range,changing to neap tide.
TAKE UP-tighten or shorten rigging;planks swelling & no longer leaking.
TANG-fitting on spar or mast to secure rigging to.
TAN, TO-treat organic material sails to prevent mildew.
TAR-sailor; preservative for standing rigging.
TARP (tarpaulin)-heavy canvas covering.   TAUNT-tall sparred vessel.
TAUT-stretched tight, snug.   TEETH-into the wind.
TELL-TAIL (or tale)-flexible wind indicator, 7, 12, 13, 29, 100, 101, 119.
TEND-taking care of anchored boat especially at tide change.
TENDER-dinghy; sailboat with insufficient stability or too much sail area.
TENON-mast heel fitted to go into a step.
TEREDO-sea worm that eats into unprotected wood surfaces.
THAT'S HIGH-order to stop hoisting.   THIMBLE-metal ring.
THOLE PINS-rowlock pins.   THREE SHEETS in the WIND-very drunk.
THROAT-forward upper corner of gaff or spritsail, and the end of a boom or gaff nearest the mast, page 5.
THRUM-yarn made for chafing gear or a collision mat.
THRUST-page 107.   THUMB CLEATS-jam cleats.
THWARTS-athwart seats on a small vessel, pages 23, 24, 26, 29, 38.
TIDE-alternate rise and fall of ocean water, page 215.
TIDE RACE (tide rip)-tidal current eddies caused by uneven bottom shoal waters.
TIDE RODE-moored boat riding to tide & not wind;opp. of WIND RODE.
TIDEWAY-part of channel where current is strongest.
TIE ROD-page 72.
TIER-stow cable in chain locker;short rope or strip of canvas to secure a sail.
TIER, CABLE-between decks area or hold where cable is stowed.
TIGHT-a boat that does not leak.
TILLER-steering handle fitted to head of rudder, pages 23-53.
TIMBER-large pieces of wood used in boat building often bent to shape.
TIMBERHEADS-frames coming thru deck for belaying ropes or hawser.
TOGGLE-pin thru eye or bight of rope used as a quick release.
TO LEEWARD-away from the wind, page 110.
TOMPION (pron. tompkin)-plug in cannon to keep out dampness.
TONGUE-wooden block between gaff jaws which travels on a mast.
TONNAGE-vessel cargo capacity measured in tons.
TOP-mast platforms used to spread rigging above, page 285.
TOP A YARD-raise up one end of a boom or yard.
TOPGALLANT (pron. tu-gallant)-3 rd mast and sail above the deck, page 285.

TOP HAMPER-rigging and spars above deck.
TOP HEAVY-vessel too heavy aloft.   TOP LIGHT-signal light carried to top.
TOP LINING-lining to prevent chafe against top rim on after part of sail.
TOPMAST-second mast above deck, page 285.
TOPPING LIFT-line taking booms weight while sail is being raised, 63, 67, 75, 96.
TOPPING LIFT BRIDLE-bridle thru which topping lift is rove.
TOP ROPE-used for raising and lowering topmasts.
TOPSAIL-triangular sail set above a gaff, page 269.
TOPSAIL SCHOONER-schooner square rigged on her foremast, page 269.
TOPSIDES-above deck.
TOUCH-luffing a sailboat until the leach is also luffing.
TOW-pulling a vessel thru the water.   TOWING LIGHT-see page 238.
TRACK-course of a vessel.
TRADES-steady tropic winds blowing NE or SE near equator, page 131.
TRAIN TACKLE-used to run guns in and out.
TRANSOM-stern planking of a square sterned boat, pages 23-81.
TRAVELLER-track with slide or car to adjust mainsheet. ROD with ring or
roller slide is also used, 23-63,116-121BRIDLE is a flexible traveller, 23-51,116.
TREENAILS (trunnels)-wooden pegs before metal nails. Their history and use
is very interestingly described in 'Clipper Ship Men' by Laing, pg. 286.
TREND—basically the general direction.
TRESTLE TREES-timbers supporting cross trees & heel of mast above, 285.
TRIATIC STAY-stay connecting mainmast and foremast, pg. 269.
TRICE-haul up.   TRICK-time period at wheel.
TRIM-fore & aft balance of vessel;trim sails more efficiently.
TRIPPING LINE-used to capsize sea and storm anchor, pages 156, 161, 152.
TROUGH-hollow between the crests of two waves.
TROCHOIDAL WAVE-made by wind in deep water, the stronger the wind the
greater the distance will be between wave crests, page 140.
TRUCK-wooden cap at masthead;wheels of a gun carriage.
TRUE WIND-direction it blows on dock differing from apparent wind underway.
TRUNK-vertical shaft;centerboard trunk, 17-19 ;rudder trunk, page 72.
TRUNNION-cannon axis on which it rests, is elevated and depressed.
TRUSS-line keeping center of yard in towards the mast.
TRYSAIL-loosefooted storm sail, page 15.
TUCK, TO-splice or weave rope.
TUMBLE HOME (falling home)-inward curve of vessels side above waterline,
common on vessels to 1800's making it difficult for pirate ships to board.
TURKS HEAD-ornamental knot.   TURN-loop in a rope.
TURNBUCKLE-threaded link to pull two eyes together for setting up standing
rigging, pages 69, 112.   TURN IN-go to sleep.
TURNING BUOY-marks channel turn.   TURN TURTLE-upset.
TO TURN-tack to windward steering a zigzag course, page 101.
TURN, TAKE A-pass a rope once or twice around an object.
TURN UP, TO-make fast or belay a rope on a pin or cleat.
TYE-rope or chain connected to bunt of square yard, on which tackle is
attached for hoisting.
TYPHOON-hurricane in the Eastern seas often occurring at change of the
monsoon, a seasonal wind.   TWIN SPINNAKERS-page 131.

U UNA RIG-English catboat named after 'Una', first U.S. catboat sent to England.
UNBEND-to cast off;undo;remove sails from spars.
UNDER BARE POLES-vessel with no sails set in storm, page 137.
UNBITT-cast turn of a cable off the bitts.
UNDER FOOT-anchor directly under hawse hole.
UNDER HACK-confinement as punishment for an officer.
UNDER MANNED-short handed, not enough crew members.

UN UNDER the LEE-to leeward of a sailboat, building, or headland.
UNDERTOW-off shore current noticeable in the surf.
UNDERWAY-vessel not aground, at anchor, made fast to shore or dock.
UNFURL-unfold a sail.
UNION-upper inner corner of a flag, the rest is called the fly.
UNION JACK-crews flag with 50 (?) stars flown from f'c'stle on docked or moored vessel, indicating crews limited authority, page 252.
UNMOOR-leave one anchor down and heave up on the other.
UNREEVE-hauling a line out of a block.
UNSHIP, TO-to remove or take apart.   UP ANCHOR-order to weigh anchor.
UP and DOWN-anchor cable vertical, further hauling will break anchor out.
UPPER DECK-partial deck over main deck amidships.
UPPER TOPSAIL-page 287.   UPPER WORKS-above main deck.
USCG-United States Coast Guard.   USPS-United States Power Squadrons.
USEFUL LOAD-the vessels dead weight tonnage.

V BOTTOM-hull form with bottom V section, page 17.
VANE-a mast head wind vane.
VANG, BOOM-purchase to flatten sail with boom, 23-75, 118-121.
VANGS-gaff steadying line leading from gaff peak, page 269.
VAST-order to cease or stop.
VEER-wind direction change;slack sheets and allow to run off.
VEER and HAUL-to alternately slack up and haul away.
VEIL-thin cloud formation.
VELOCITY of TRANSLATION-speed of a storm center.
VERY SIGNAL-red, white & green star signals fired by a pistol, page 225.
VIOL-larger messenger often used in breaking out anchor by capstan.
VIOL BLOCK-similar to snatch block but minus a hinge.
VISIBLE-capable of being seen with clear atmosphere on a dark night.

W WAIST-portion of upper deck between f'c'sle and quarter deck.
WAISTERS-elder seaman or green hands used in an old fighting ship.
WAKE-disturbed water foamy path behind a moving vessel, pages 140-141.
WALES-strengthening timbers running fore & aft in a vessels sides.
WALE SHORES-timbers holding vessel upright in drydock.
WALL-a knot on the end of a rope.   WALL SIDED-vessel with vertical sides.
WARDROOM-commissioned officers quarters in a warship.
WARE-same as WEAR or to WEAR SHIP, pages 101, 111.
WARP-move vessel by hauling in on lines going to dock or anchor.
WARPING CHOCK-on dock used for hauling or warping along a vessel.
WASH-waves made by a boat moving thru the water.
WASHBOARD(washstrake)-thin planking above railing on a small boat to increase the height of the side, especially for heeling.
WATCH-working shifts aboard ship.   WATCH, ANCHOR-small port watch.
WATCH AND WATCH-shifts in which watches alternate every four hours.
WATCH CAP-canvas covering a funnel not being used;wool sailors cap.
WATCH HO!WATCH-warning cry of sailor heaving a deep-sea lead.
WATCH TACKLE-one made of a single and double block.
WATER BORN(water borne)-not touching bottom.
WATER BREAKER-small drinking water cask.
WATERLINE-painted on vessels side to indicate proper trim, 254-257.
WATERLOGGED-swamped but afloat.
WATER MONKEY-clay jar used to keep drinking water cool.
WATERS EDGE-inshore waters such as next to a beach.
WATERWAY-navigable channel;gutter drain on deck leading to scuppers.
WAY-movement thru water;HEADWAY-going forward;STERNWAY-a boat going backwards;a vessel is underway when drifting.
WAYS-framework in shipyard on which a vessel is built.

WEAR -on square rigger it meant changing tack by changing the wind over the stern to advance to windward instead of coming about, page 101.Fore and after sailing downwind changes tack by changing the wind over the bow instead of over the stern to prevent an accidental jibe, also called wearing, page 111.The lateener wears ship by changing tack with wind over stern, page 277.
WEATHER-windward side, shroud, bow, etc. of vessel, pages 98, 113.
WEATHER, TO-safely pass to windward of object without changing tack.
WEATHER BOUND-sailboat staying in port due to storm or wind direction.
WEATHER EYE OPEN-be on the alert.
WEATHER GAGE (or gauge)-the vessel which is to windward of another.
WEATHER HELM-heeling sailboat wanting to come head to wind, pgs. 132-135.
WEATHERLY SHIP-one making little leeway working to windward.
WEATHERLY ROLL-ship rolling going to windward.
WEATHER SHORE-wind coming off the shore.
WEATHER TIDE-current and wind going opposing directions.
WEDGE-used to steady a mast in many older classes, page 26.
WEIGH, TO-raise anchor.
WELL-order meaning sufficient;cockpit for legs, 33;cb & db wells, pgs. 18,19.
WELL DECK-portion of main deck having poop and raised f'c'sle.
WELL FOUND-well equipped vessel with all gear in good condition.
WESTING-position of sun between noon and sunset.
WESTERLIES-prevailing winds in temperate zone coming from NW & SW.
WET BULB THERMOMETER-device to measure humidity.
WHALE BACK (turtle back)-sailboat with high crown so person always walks on a horizontal part of the deck when boat is heeling.
WHALEBOAT-double ended navy lifeboat and utility boat 24-30' long.
WHEEL-steering wheel used instead of tiller or lever, pgs. 67, 69, 108, 110.
WHERRY-light rowboat belonging to the navy.
WHIP-rope rove   block;whipping a ropes ends to stop them
from fraying, page 200.   WHIP upon WHIP-one added to another.

It was difficult to find adequate glossaries of sailing terms in the initial preparation of our book from 1950-1956 ... the reason for so many terms in our glossary.

The picture has changed considerably in recent years due to worldwide sailing interest beginning with, "Lever's Young Sea Officer's Sheet Anchor", pg. 184, which is an exact reprint of an 1819 sailing text for professionals.

We had the pleasure to meet Karl Freudenstein of Bonn, Germany, pg. 82, in 1974, after he wrote to us, questioning derivation of port and starboard. We were soon to find he and his wife Ingrid linguists mastering a combination of six languages, their hobby translating sailing terms when not traveling on official business.

Karl recommended the Country Life Book of, "Nautical Terms Under Sail", the world of square riggers, iron men, and wooden ships, distributed by Hamlyn Pub. Group, London, NY, Sydney, and Toronto ... ISBN 0 600 36586 7.

WHISKER POLE-spar used to hold out clew of jib while running, pg. 121.
WHISKERS-crosstrees at bow to spread bowsprit shrouds, page 73.
WHISTLE BUOY-one having a whistle actuated by water movement, page 249.
WHITE CAP (white horses)-breaking crest of a wave, page 137.
WHITE SQUALL-sudden furious storm.   WHOLE GALE-page 137.
WIDE BERTH-to give room.
WINCH-mechanical device to increase hauling power, page 108.
WIND BOUND-adverse winds trapping sailboat in port or channel.
WIND FUNNEL-narrowing hill or canyon condition that compresses and
accelerates the speed of the wind, page 211.
WINDLASS-winch for hauling in cable.
WINDJAMMER-square rigged sailing vessel;a windy person.

■WIND FORCE SCALE (BEAUFORT SCALE)-page 137.

WIND RODE-anchored boat swings to wind rather than to the current.
WINDSAIL-canvas air scoop funneling air into a vessel.
WINDWARD-toward the wind, weather side of a boat, pages 98, 99, 123.
WING and WING-running before wind with sails on opposite sides, pages
WITHE, WYTHE-metal band on end of mast or boom, with eye or ring thru
which another mast or boom or rigging is made fast.
WISHBONE-ketch, page 266.   WISHBONE ANCHOR-page 158.
WITH THE SUN-clockwise or right handed.
WOOLD-to wind rope around a spar.
WORK (working to windward, on the wind)-sailing closehauled-pages 100-101.
WORKING GEAR-general term for gear.
WORKING SAILS-used for ordinary weather & conditions, page 9.
WORK UP-advance to windward, pages 100, 101.

WORMING-filling in the lay of a rope with small stuff to make a smoother
surface for parcelling and serving.
WRECK BUOY (English)-red and white horizontally striped buoy marking a
wreck. A similar type buoy doesn't exist in the U.S. buoyage system.
WRING-strain, bend or twist mast out of shape by setting rigging too tight.
WRING-BOLTS-bolts which secure planks to the timbers.
WRING-STAVES-strong planks used with wring-bolts.

X XEBEC-lateener often three masted with long overhanging bow & stern, 279.

y YACHT-vessel designed for pleasure or state, this can include the presidents
yacht or the neighbors dink (rowboat is not included).
YANKEE-large triangular headsail, also called raffee, pg. 131.
YARD-spar from which square sails, lateen sails and lugger sails are bent.
YARDARM-outer tapered extremity of a yard.
YARDARM to YARDARM-square riggers alongside with yardarms touching.
YARD SLINGS-chain suspension of square rig yard.
YARN-fibers twisted into strands for rope, page 184.
YARNS-tall tales.   YARE-prepared, prompt, eager, lively.
YAWL-two masted sailboat, after mast stepped abaft rudder post,66-71, 265.
YAW, TO-sailboat having hard time holding steady course as when a rough
sea is on either quarter or the stern, page 152.
YELLOW FLAG-signifies ship is in quarantine.
YEOMAN-sailor in charge of a store room.
YOKE-athwartship plate attached to rudder head to control rudder.
YOKE LINES-rope leading from either end of rudder yoke to turn rudder.
YOUNG FLOOD-beginning of flood or incoming tide or current.

Z ZAROOK (zaruk)-lateener little changed since the original 12th century
Venetian design.
ZULU-Scotch lug-rigged fishing vessel.

AUTHORS NOTE: Key USYRU Racing Rules are shown, a few due to space are left out. Purpose is to provide visual presentation of the rules plus pictorial understanding of intent, as well as varied rules involved in a situation out of context with rule numbering. Such familiarization will reduce study time and help locate surrounding rules involved in a protest.

When displayed on a committee boat—
RED flag-"Leave all marks to port".
GREEN flag-"Leave all marks to stbd".

All marks are to be
<u>passed to port</u> on both
courses shown above.

BLUE flag or shape-Finishing Signal-"When displayed by committee boat means "The committee boat is on station at the finish line".

Sailing the Course, 51-1(a) A yacht shall START and FINISH only as prescribed in the starting and finishing definitions.
51.2 A yacht shall sail the course so as to round or pass each MARK on the required side in correct sequence, and so that a string representing her wake from the time she STARTS until she FINISHES would, when drawn taut, lie on the required side of each MARK.

4.4(a) Unless otherwise prescribed...signals for starting a race shall be made at five-minute intervals exactly, and shall be either—

Thistle

System 1–WARNING Signal–Class flag broken out or distinctive signal displayed.
PREPARATORY-International Code flag "P" broken out or distinctive signal displayed.
STARTING Signal-Both warning and preparatory signals are lowered.

System 2–
WARNING Signal–WHITE shape
PREPARATORY Signal-BLUE shape
STARTING Signal–RED shape

In System 2 each signal shall be lowered one minute before the next is hoisted.

R 2

4-International Flag Code Signals

| Lima | Mike | November | Papa | Sierra | X-ray |

L-When displayed ashore, "A notice to competitors has been posted on the notice board".
When displayed afloat, "Come within hail", or "Follow me".

M-Mark Signal-When displayed on a buoy, vessel, or other object means-"Round or pass the object displaying this signal instead of the MARK which it replaces".

N-Abandonment Signal:-"All races are ABANDONED".

N over X-Abandonment and Re-sail Signal:- All races are ABANDONED and more will shortly be re-sailed".

N over First Substitute:-"All races are CANCELLED".

X-Individual Recall:-Broken out immediately after the starting signal is made, accompanied by one long sound signal, means:- "One or more yachts have started prematurely or have infringed the Round the Ends Starting Rule 51.1(c)".

P-Preparatory Signal:-"The class designated by the warning signal will START in five minutes exactly".

First Substitute-GENERAL RECALL signal means:-
"The class is recalled for a new start as provided in the sailing instructions".

Unless the sailing instructions prescribe some other signal, the warning signal will be made one minute after this signal is lowered.

S-SHORTEN COURSE Signal means:-

(a)at or near the starting line, "Sail the shortened course prescribed in the sailing instructions".

(b)at or near the finishing line "FINISH the race either:
   (i) at the prescribed finishing line at the end of the round still to be completed by the leading yacht or
   (ii) in any other manner prescribed in the sailing instructions under rule 3.2(a) (vii)".

Y-Life Jacket Signal Means... "shall be worn while RACING by all helmsmen and crews, unless specifically excepted in the sailing instructions"... A wet suit is not adequate personal buoyancy.

44—Yachts Returning to Start

wind

1.(a) After the starting signal is made, a premature starter returning to START, or a yacht working into position from the course side of the starting line or its extensions, shall keep clear of all yachts which are STARTING or have STARTED correctly, until she is wholly on the pre-start side of the starting line or its extensions.

44-2. A premature starter . . . until it is obvious that she is returning to START, shall be accorded the rights under the rules of Part IV of a yacht which has STARTED.

51-1.(b) (also applies) . . a yacht which either crosses prematurely . . .

BOOM

starting line

a b c d e f

yachts that are barging

closehauled course

42-4. (Anti-Barging Rule). When approaching starting line to START, a LEEWARD YACHT shall be under no obligation to give any WINDWARD YACHT room to pass to leeward of a starting MARK surrounded by navigable water; but, after the starting signal, a LEEWARD YACHT shall not deprive a WINDWARD YACHT of room at such MARK by-

sailing either above the course to the first MARK or above CLOSE-HAULED.

Definition-A yacht is CLOSE-HAULED when sailing by the wind as close as she can lie with advantage in working to windward.

Section B-Opposite Tack Rule

port tack — a

stbd tack — b

wind

36. A PORT-TACK yacht shall keep clear of a STARBOARD-TACK yacht.

port tack — e

stbd tack — f

port tack — c

stbd tack — d

Section C-Same Tack Rules.

37-1. A WINDWARD YACHT shall keep clear of a LEEWARD YACHT.

stbd tack — e

stbd tack — f

The following pages give illustrated excerpts of the United States Yacht Racing Union Racing Rules. These have been reprinted in part by permission of the USYRU and illustrated by the author.

Copies of the complete official racing rules may be obtained from USYRU headquarters, P.O. Box 209, Newport, Rhode Island 02840.

These regulations are very complex —know them thoroughly before racing. Otherwise a person may be disqualified, ending with expensive damage claims.

wind

windward

b

windward

c

leeward

a

windward

leeware

d

Def. -the LEEWARD side of a yacht is that on which she is, or, if LUFFING head to wind, was carrying her mainsail. The other is the WINDWARD yacht.

leeward

e

windward

f

Def. -When neither of two yachts on the same tack is CLEAR ASTERN the one on the LEEWARD side of the other is the LEEWARD YACHT.

The other is the WINDWARD YACHT

Def. - LUFFING — Altering course towards the wind until head to wind.

Def. -BEARING AWAY -Altering cour away from the wind until a yacht begins to jibe.

39. A yacht which is on a free leg of the course shall not sail below her PROPER COURSE...

when she is clearly within three of her overall lengths of either a LEEWARD YACHT or a yacht CLEAR ASTER which is steering a course to pass to LEEWARD.

a

b

'foul

R 6

no overlap

a

TWO overall lengths

b / wind

38-3. For the purpose of this rule: an OVERLAP does not exist unless the yachts are clearly within two overall lengths of the longer yacht; and an OVERLAP which exists between two yachts when when the leading yacht STARTS,

clear ahead

or when one or both of them completes a TACK or JIBE, shall be regarded as a new OVERLAP beginning at that time.

c

Def.- A yacht is CLEAR ASTERN of another when her hull and equipment are abaft an imaginary line projected abeam from the aftermost point of the other's hull and equipment...

d

clear astern

The other yacht is CLEAR AHEAD.

no overlap

The yachts OVERLAP if neither is CLEAR ASTERN; or if, although one is CLEAR ASTERN, an intervening yacht OVERLAPS both of them.

The terms CLEAR ASTERN, CLEAR AHEAD and OVERLAP apply to yachts on opposite TACKS only when they are subject to rule 42-Rounding, Passing Marks & Obstructions.

HAILING-34.1. Except when LUFFING under rule 38.1, a right-of-way yacht which does not hail ... when making an alteration .. which may not be forseen ... by the other yacht may be disqualified as well as the yacht required to keep clear when a collision resulting in serious damage occurs.

a

b

R 7

38-6. A yacht shall not LUFF unless she has the right to LUFF all yachts which would be affected by her LUFF, in which case they shall all respond even when an intervening yacht or yachts would not otherwise have the right to LUFF.

38-5. A WINDWARD YACHT shall not cause a LUFF to be curtailed because of her proximity to the LEEWARD YACHT-

unless an OBSTRUCTION, a third yacht or other object restricts her ability to respond.

no overlap exists

overlap exits

Definition . . . the yachts OVERLAP if neither is CLEAR ASTERN, or if, although one is CLEAR ASTERN, an intervening yacht OVERLAPS both of them . . . .

Same Tack, Fundamental Rule

37-3. A yacht which establishes an OVERLAP . . . shall allow the WINDWARD YACHT ample room . . to keep clear, and during the existence of that OVERLAP the LEEWARD YACHT shall not sail above her PROPER COURSE (also 38-1 & 40).

luffing

h (2.)

g

windward

h

(1.) leeward

g

R 8

wind

Right - of - Way Yacht
LUFFING after STARTING

38-1. After she has STARTED and cleared the starting line, a yacht CLEAR AHEAD or a LEEWARD YACHT may LUFF as she pleases, except that:

38-2. a LEEWARD YACHT shall not sail above her PROPER COURSE while an OVERLAP exists if . . .

overlap started

at any time during its existence the helmsman of the WINDWARD YACHT (when sighting abeam from his normal station and sailing no higher than the LEE-WARD YACHT) has been abreast or forward of the mainmast of the LEEWARD YACHT.

38-4. When there is doubt, the LEEWARD YACHT may assume that she has the right to LUFF unless the helmsman of the WINDWARD YACHT has hailed "Mast Abeam", or words to that effect.

overlap completed

The LEEWARD YACHT shall be governed by such hail, and when she deems it improper, her only remedy is to protest.

38-5. Curtailing a Luff — a WINDWARD YACHT shall not cause a LUFF to be curtailed because of her proximity to . . . . . unless an OBSTRUCTION, a third yacht or other object restricts her ability to respond.

wind

Definition — An OBSTRUCTION is any object, including a vessel under way, large enough to require a yacht if not less than one overall length away from it to make a substantial alteration of course to pass on one side or the other, or any object which can be passed on one side only, including a buoy when the yacht in question cannot safely pass between it and the shoal or object which it marks.

Rule 64—Aground or Foul of an Obstruction

A yacht after grounding or fouling another vessel or other object . . . in getting clear, use her own anchors, boats, ropes, spars, and other gear . . . but may receive outside assistance only from the crew of the vessel fouled. A yacht shall recover all her own gear used in getting clear before continuing in the race.

a
this yacht keeps clear

b
tacking

c
jibing

d
this yacht keeps clear

41-4. When two yachts are both TACKING or both JIBING at the same time, the one on the other's PORT side shall keep clear.

Section D-Changing Tack Rules

Definition-a yacht is TACKING from the moment she is beyond head to wind until she has BORNE AWAY, when beating to windward, to a CLOSE-HAULED course; if not beating to windward, to the course on which her mainsail has filled.

A yacht begins to JIBE at the moment when, with the wind aft, the foot of her mainsail crosses her centerline and completes the JIBE when the mainsail has filled on the other TACK.

41-1. A yacht which is either TACKING or JIBING shall keep clear of a yacht ON A TACK.

41-2. A yacht shall neither TACK nor JIBE into a position which...unless she does so far enough from yacht ON A TACK to enable this yacht to keep clear without having to begin to alter her course until after the TACK or JIBE has been completed.

41-3. A yacht which TACKS or JIBES has the onus of satisfying.. she completed..with rule 41-2.

43-1 to 3, further clarify the rule at obstructions.

wind

tacking

jibing

b

c

a

d

e

f

g

h

j

k

R 11

Except when race area is officially patrolled by the CG or CGA, yachts racing have no special rights over yachts not racing. Standard rules page 232, apply meanwhile.

Since 1960 we have recommended a special RACING PENNANT be flown from bow of sailboat the moment five minute signal is given for that class (above) until the yacht has finished or dropped out of the race.

If practiced, especially in areas having considerable pleasure boat traffic, sailboat and powerboat owners may give racing sailboats more advantage of existing situation. We see no reason why this racing pennant also acting as a dinghy telltale, can do anything but help racing sailors. Why doesn't USYRU promote this idea?

35. Limitations on Altering Course

When one yacht is required to keep clear of another, the right-of-way yacht shall not so alter course so as to prevent the other yacht from keeping clear, or so as to obstruct her while she is keeping clear, except: (a) to the extent permitted by rule 38.1 .. and (b)... assuming a proper course.

Definitions - LUFFING - Altering course towards the wind until head to wind.

BEARING AWAY - Altering course away for the wind until a yacht begins to jibe.

R 12

Close-Hauled, Hailing for Room to Tack at Obstructions.

43-1. Hailing. When two CLOSE-HAULED yachts are on the same TACK and safe pilotage requires ... to make a substantial alteration .. to clear an OBSTRUCTION... but cannot TACK .. she shall hail .. for room to TACK ...

wind

"Sea Room"

(1)

(2)

(3)

f   g

43-2. The hailed yacht .. shall either: –
(a) TACK, in which case, the hailing yacht shall begin to TACK either: –
(i) before the hailed yacht has completed her TACK,
(ii) when she cannot then TACK without colliding with the hailed yacht....

(b) reply "You TACK", or words to that effect, when in her opinion she can keep clear without TACKING or after postponing her TACK. In this case: –

(i) the hailing yacht shall immediately TACK and
(ii) the hailed yacht shall keep clear.
(iii) the onus ... shall lie on the hailed yacht which replied "You TACK".

43-3 (a). When ... an OBSTRUCTION ... is also a MARK, the hailing yacht shall not be entitled for room to TACK and clear the hailed yacht and the hailed yacht shall immediately so inform the hailed yacht.

(b) If, thereafter, the hailing yacht again hails for room to TACK ... she shall after receiving room ... retire immediately or exonerate herself by accepting an alternative penalty ... in the instructions.

(c) When, after having refused to respond to a hail under rule 43.3(a), the hailed yacht fails to fetch, she shall retire immediately, or exonerate herself by accepting an alternative penalty ... in the instructions.

52.2(a) When a yacht touches a MARK surrounded by navigable water, she may exonerate herself by completing one entire rounding of the MARK, leaving it on the required side and thereafter re-rounding it or repassing it without touching it, as required to sail the course in accordance with rule 51.2, ...

42.1.Room at Marks and Obstructions when Overlapped. When yachts are about to round or pass a MARK, other than a starting MARK surrounded by navigable water, on the same required side or an OBSTRUCTION on the same side: —

(a) An outside yacht shall give each yacht OVERLAPPING her on the inside, room to round or pass ...

(b) When an inside yacht of two or more OVERLAPPED yachts either on opposite TACKS ... will have to JIBE ... to assume a PROPER COURSE to the next MARK, she shall JIBE at the first reasonable opportunity.

(c) When two yachts on opposite TACKS are on a BEAT or when one of them will have to TACK .. rule 42.1(a)(i) shall not apply (being) subject to rules 36 ... and 41.

(d) An outside LEEWARD YACHT with luffing rights may take an inside yacht to windward of a MARK ... (see opposite page)

MARK (def) ... every ordinary part of a MARK ranks as part of it, including a flag, flagpole, boom or hoisted boat, but excluding ground tackle and any object either accidentally or temporarily attached to the MARK.

14

disqualification

o.k.

Definition – a MARK is any object specified in the sailing instructions which a yacht must round or pass on a required side.

51-2. A yacht shall sail the course so as to round or pass each MARK on the required side in correct sequence, & so that a string representing her wake from the time she STARTS until she FINISHES would, when drawn taut, lie on the required side of each MARK.

51-3. A MARK has a required side for a yacht as long as she is on a leg which it begins, bounds, or ends. A starting MARK begins to have a required side for a yacht when she STARTS. A finishing MARK ceases to have a required side for a yacht as soon as she FINISHES.

51.4. A yacht which rounds or passes a MARK on the wrong side may exonerate herself by making her course conform to the requirements of rule 51.2 (which is listed above).

42-1 (d). An outside LEEWARD YACHT with luffing rights may take an inside yacht to windward of a MARK ... provided she hails ... and ... she also passes to windward of it.

51-5. It is not necessary for a yacht to cross finishing line completely. After FINISHING she may clear it either direction.

42-1 (d)

either course o.k.

Finishing Signal – BLUE flag or shape.

P. S. How about thanking the race committee for their help?

R 15

Day Sailer

 Skimmer, Moth

 Butterfly

 Cottontail

 Javelin

 Five-O-Five

 Y Flyer
or Yankee

 Jet 14

 Cal Series

 Holiday Series

 Flying Scott

 Arrow

 Columbia Series

 Islander Series

 Luder 16

 Renegade 27

 Loa 17

 Pearson Series

Kettenburg Series

 Vaurien

 Twin Keel
Imperial

 Twin Keel
Alacrity

 Polar Bear
'Tail to Wind'

 Mobjack

Pilot

 Tartan 27

Commander

 Morgan Series

 Mustang

Kestrel

Rawson Series

Hinkley Series

Lapworth 36

 Nipper

Catfish

 Westphal

 Starfish (sailboard)

 Starfish (dinghy)

 Sea Scouter

 Widgeon

 Constellation

 Flying Saucer

 Pintail

 Scorpion

 Osprey, Gannet

Vineyard Haven

 Redhead

Town Class

 Tempest (cabin)

 Vivacity

 Whistler

 Buckeye

Outlaw

 Lehman Interclub

 Teal

 Quad Trainer

Pacific Class

Corsair

Flying Kitten

Wanderer

 Tech Dinghy

 Narrasketuck

Elvestrom Junior

 Indian

New Terms

The sailing language developed from slang, with numerous terms going back many centuries. The sounds or slang terms that were successful became the basis of our sailing language listed in our glossary.

As sailing technology advanced, our language changed from the older international language, to a national, then a specialized, localized sailing language with new terms required to define new products and new techniques... especially for popular, competitive one-design classes.

Let us try to keep the new developing sailing language simple and accurate for communication with other sailors instead of developing individualized slang terms that often confuse the issue.

Orderly and thoughtful development of your sailing language will make it of more use to new sailors as well as those with considerable experience. The following terms are those emerging during the past 15 years which are often easier to show than describe with words.

● the MAINSAIL
aspect ratio - 8, 9
boom thrust adjuster - 119
deck sweeper boom - 29, 119
draft, drive area - 9, 10
foot reef, Cunningham reef, Hooligan reef - 11, 117
gaskets - 63, 86, 87
gooseneck 23, 27, 35, 46, 59, 89
Hyfield lever - 26, 27, 33
leachline - 116, 117, 118, 119
luff downhaul, Cunningham
. cringle, hook, or hole —
  26, 33, 43, 47
prevang - 63, 120-121

roach line – (leachline)
rod (horse) with ring or rollerslide - 38
slugs, stops — 87
tack pennant - 63, 67, 232
Twistfoot main has 'shelf' or full radius foot - 43
tube halyard lock - 29
vang (kicking strap, Br.) -
7, 23-45, 63, 116-121, 143, 149
traveler, track with car —
27, 43, 47, 116, 117
wind funnel - 13, 34, 104, 119.
window - 7, 25, 26, 29, 31-45
zipper foot & luff - 26, 116

●the JIB
Barber hauler - 34-37, 43, 47, 118, 119
bridle, jibstay - 79
fairlead - 7, 12, 31-35, 43, 47
furling line, lanyard - 13, 39
jib telltale yarn - 7, 12, 13, 118, 119
windowshade reefing jib, roller reefing jib - 13, 27, 39, 47
reaching hook - 33
reaching track - 79
cloth downhaul, adjustable luff jib, variluff, stretchy luff jib - 13, 33, 35, 45
Swedish hook, snap hook with 'panic' button - 92, 96
Swedish jib, genoa jib - 125
tack downhaul —used on a stretch luff jib (above)
tunnel, jib luff - 13
wind funnel, slot effect between sails - 34, 104-105, 119

●the SPINNAKER
dip pole jibe or lazy guy rig - 130
fixed guy - 128
guy downpull, curley-cew, pigtail - obsolete terms
mizzen staysail, also called mizzen spinnaker - 69
running guy - 37, 39, 45, 128
running guy downhaul or downpull - 37
reaching strut - 125
reels, clothesline - 43
retriever - 39

spinnaker well or tub — 39, 41
tang holder for sp. sheet, guy, halyard assy. - 35
trapeze operation is not detailed due to lack of space in book
trapeze ring - 47
tunnel, launching tube - 39
turtle, spinnaker bag with metal ring - 126
twinger - 37, 81, 128, 130
tri-radial spinnaker - 125

●the MAST
arc bend - 33, 35, 41, 43, 91
Bendy (flexible) mast, floppy rig, flexible rig, automatic mainsail flattener, 'wet noodle' rig — 33, 39, 43, 91, 117-121
breadboard - older Lightning Hyfield lever - 27
jumper tension adjust - 27
limited swing spreaders - 33, 39, 43
mast jack - 26
mast partner - 23-4, 27, 43
mast puller - 33, 43
mast wedges - 27
movable mast step - 29 (the 5.5 uses a similar method mounted on rollers, wheels)
rake - 116-121
self-swiveling mast - 24-5, 28-9, 47
shroud release - 27, 121
sidestay (shroud) - 24
stubby mast (outrigger) - 49
tang, bow (Lightning) - 35
tang fittings - 68, 69

Your author above had endless problems when buying our first sailboat in 1950. The first mate watching my continuous comedy of errors provided the answer— "Why don't you draw the book on sailing you tried to find in libraries and bookstores?" We had eleven books at the time, but none of them made any sense as they tried to communicate a technical sport in words alone.

"Sailing Illustrated" is based on the principle that a picture is more valuable than a thousand confusing words. The most difficult part of sailing is its technical language, which must be understood to learn boat operation. The universal language, art, was the only way to bridge the semantics word gap which grows each year.

We advise a newcomer to study a little of this information each day, then discuss it with another sail enthusiast, the way our book was designed. After a little analysis you will find patterns developing with most of the ideas simple, yet with endless variations on different boats.

Majority of readers seem to buy sailboats under 22'. If you buy a 14' dinghy, still spend considerable time studying our information on larger sailboats as you may suddenly be invited on a wide variety of larger boats by skippers always looking for new, good, congenial crew members.

We took a survey in one of our evening classes, to find how many books on sailing the students had. Those in our sail class averaged 5 to 6, those in our racing class had 10 to 11 books, continually comparing the ideas with one against the findings in another. It was interesting to find good sailing books don't compete, but help each other.

A sailors definition of experience is the mistakes that he's made that he remembers, so expect to make your own contributions. The most important idea to remember .. sailing is fun!!!!

Happy Sailing, Patrick M. Royce

boating safety? 246-7

●STEERING
barndoor rudder - 5
high aspect rudder- 27
keel rudder - 20
keel trim tab- 'Intrepid'
  used small keel trim tab
  to reduce weather helm
  while steering with aft
  spade rudder
rudder lock - 23,28,29,33
spade rudder - 20,74
tradewing steering - 131
wind vane gear - 131

●BOARDS and KEELS
bilgeboards, twin bilgeboards,
  twin boards- 44, 45
bilgeboard adjust- 45
bilge keels - 21
bulb keels - 21,41,43
fin keel-20, it doesn't have a
  bulb on bottom of keel
jibing board - 26 (Int'l 14)
keel window- 43
retractable keel - 51-53
saddle - 26, 38, 39, 119
stubby keels - 21

●HULL terms
"Ama" float - 49,81
Barney post - mid cockpit
  post for mainsheet cleat

bitt, mooring bitt-59,190-191
breadboard-old Lightning
bridge deck-79
catamaran-17,46-47,78-79
console-older Stars
crossbar, strut-38,47,79
Displacement, def. -20
hiking bar-49
hiking post, "ladies aid"-26
hiking straps-23-5,28-37,43
"Iako" arm-49
inspection port-38,39,43
monkey bar-44
outrigger-17,49
pedestal-41
raised deck-62
scow-44-45
self bailer-33,43,47
smoke head-67,75
strut, crossbar-38,49,79
thwart-23,24,26,39
trailboard-70, 75
transom flap drain-38
trimaran-17, 81
tunnel, scow-45

●EQUIPMENT
flopper stoppers - 63, 162
Mexican Hats - 63,162
Para-Anchor- 63,155-6,161

We bought our first sailboat at Staten Island in 1950. It was christened the "Lady Hilda". The boat not only didn't like us, it wanted to drown us. The first mate suggested I keep a record of my mistakes so as not to repeat them, which kept growing... it was never dull. How were we to realize we would eventually share our endless frustrations with you in a book called "Sailing Illustrated".

Contents

SAIL, HULL BASICS
sail types 3
gaff rig 5
marconi rig 7
kinds of sailboats 9
the mainsail 11
staysail, jib 13
other sails 15
weight stability 16
leverage stability . . . 17
dagger, lee boards . . . 18
centerboards 19
keel variables 21

SAILBOAT DETAILS
Naples Sabot 23
Penguin/Laser . . . 24 — 25
Int'l 14 . . . . 26 — 27
Kite/Finn . . . . . 28 — 29
Lido 14 31
Thistle/Snipe . . . . 32 — 33
Lightning . . . . . . 34 — 37
Flying Dutchman . . 38 — 39
Int'l 110 41
Star . . . . 42 — 43
M20 Scow . . . . . 44 — 45
Pacific Cat . . . . . 46 — 47
Malibu Outrigger 49
Catalina/Balboa . . . 50 — 53
balance/tb mast . . 54 — 57
cockpit controls . . 58 — 59
"Pink Cloud" . . . . 62 — 63
level racing . . . . 64 — 65
"Finisterre" . . . . 66 — 69
older yawl . . . . . . 70 — 71
structure terms . . 72 — 73
Newporter . . . . . . 74 — 75
your choice . . . . . 76 — 77
"Patty Cat II" . . . . 78 — 79
trimaran 81

FUNDAMENTALS
bearings 83
model sailboat 85

SAIL HANDLING
sail storage 87
bending a main 89
flexible mast 91
bending a jib 93
leave mooring 95
sail sequence 97

SAILING METHODS
courses and tacks . . . 99
windward terms 101
windward theory . . . 103
sail theory 105
drive forces 107
coming about 109
jibing, wearing 111
rigging tension . . . 113
aluminum mast 114
hull trim 115
airfoil controls 117
upwind adjustments . . 119
sail twist 121
downwind methods . . 123

SPINNAKERS
kinds 125
operation 127
jibing 129-130

BALANCE
trade wind rigs 131
steering balance . . . 133
hull/sail trim 135

HEAVY WIND
WIND FORCE SCALE . 137
storm warnings 139
hull speed factors . . 141
planing methods . . . 143
the upset 145

reefing #1 147
reefing #2 149
heave to 151
the broach 153
beat or run? 155

ANCHORING, DOCKING
surface anchors 157
bottom anchors 159
anchoring 161
anchoring methods . . 163
crowded moorings . . 165
permanent mooring . .167
docking 169
approach lee dock . . . 171
leave lee dock 173
docking variables . . . 175

ENGINE OPERATION
single screw action . . 177
inboard operation . . .179
outboard operation . . 181

ROPE
rope basics 185
rope size, kinds 187
joining rope 189
hitches 191
bowline, square 192
coiling 193
heaving line,
    waist lifeline . 194
braided eyesplice 195-199
whipping 200
eye splice 201
short splice 202
tugboat tow 203

WEATHER, TIDE, CURRENT
cloud formations . . . 205
thunderstorm 207
advancing fronts 209
funnels, sea breeze . . 211

barometer 213
tide variables 215
currents 217
humidity vs fog . . . 219
fog signals 221

EMERGENCY PROCEDURES
aground 223
George Sigler · · · · .225
preservers 227
overboard 229

ARTIFICIAL
    RESPIRATION . 231

REGULATIONS
sail right-of-way . . . 233
power right-of-way . .235
lights 236-239
72 COLREGS 241
large vessels 243
rdf 245
boating safety? 247
buoyage system . . . 249

MISCELLANEOUS
fire fighting 251
flag etiquette 253

SAILBOAT KINDS
the lines 254-257
handicap rating 259
the sloop 261
the cutter · · · · · · .263
yawls 265
ketches 267
schooners 269
older types 272-275
lateeners 276-279
luggers 281
square riggers . .282-287
naval terms 289

GLOSSARY G1-G35
RACING RULES . R1-R15

470 Four Seventy

420 Four Twenty

 Electra

F Folkboat Firefly

 Peanut

Dear Readers: this is YOUR book that is tailored to your needs, your wishes, and your requests. Any ideas you have ... please let us hear from you!   Patrick M. Royce

J Jolly Boat

 Coronado 25

Ω Omega

 Rhodes 33

IC Interclub

 Shark Cat

 Cyclone 13

R Rebel

 Rainbow

 Twin Keel Signet

ST 12'6" Signet

 Shields

 Windsurfer

Dolphin

E Enterprise

S Snowbird, Squall, S Class, Spencer

 Malibu Outrigger

Kings Cruiser

 Cascade

 Victory

 Wildcat

 Swiftsure

 Ghost

Fish

 Lion